Design for Living

Design for Living

Regard, Concern, Service, and Love

Robert Friedmann
Edited by Maxwell Kennel
With a Foreword by Leonard Gross

WIPF & STOCK · Eugene, Oregon

DESIGN FOR LIVING
Regard, Concern, Service, and Love

Copyright © 2017 Mennonite Church USA Archives. All rights reserved. Except for brief quotations in critical publications or reviews, no part of this book may be reproduced in any manner without prior written permission from the publisher. Write: Permissions, Wipf and Stock Publishers, 199 W. 8th Ave., Suite 3, Eugene, OR 97401.

Wipf & Stock
An Imprint of Wipf and Stock Publishers
199 W. 8th Ave., Suite 3
Eugene, OR 97401

www.wipfandstock.com

PAPERBACK ISBN: 978-1-5326-3205-1
HARDCOVER ISBN: 978-1-5326-3207-5
EBOOK ISBN: 978-1-5326-3206-8

Manufactured in the U.S.A. NOVEMBER 28, 2017

To my students

at Western Michigan

College of Education

Kalamazoo, Michigan.

Contents

Foreword by Leonard Gross   ix
Acknowledgements   xiii
Editor's Introduction by Maxwell Kennel   xv

Introduction: The Educated Heart   1

Part 1. Preparation   9

1. What Design for Living is Not   11
2. Positive Preparation   52
3. The Ascent to the Problem   83
4. The Human Situation   98

Part 2. Design for Living   115

5. Regard, Concern, Service, and Love   119

Part 3. Troubles Ahead   155

Conclusion. The Human Situation   157
Postscript: The Freedom of the Will and the Issue of Escapism   169

Select Bibliography   177

Foreword

Robert Friedmann: His Life, His Philosophy

Born in 1891 in Vienna into a liberal, non-practicing Jewish family, Robert Friedmann first studied at the Technische Hochschule, earning a civil engineering diploma in 1914. He served as an officer in the Austrian army from 1914 to 1918 and witnessed the war first-hand. Postwar disillusionment deeply affected Friedmann, and he entered the University of Vienna in 1920, majoring in history and philosophy. Oswald Spengler, Leo Tolstoy, Nikolai Berdayev and Leonhard Ragaz influenced him deeply during his doctoral studies. His 1924 dissertation was called *The Principle of Harmony in Metaphysics* (*Das Harmonieprinzip in der Metaphysik*), and after its defense he taught at various colleges in Vienna from 1925 to 1938.

Friedmann began his scholarly work on Anabaptism in 1923 when he prepared a seminar paper on the contents of three Hutterite codices, which gripped him profoundly, setting the course of both his scholarly pursuits and his faith for the rest of his life. That same year, the *Verein für Reformationsgeschichte* commissioned him to edit a volume of Hutterite epistles. Friedmann's first publications on Anabaptist themes came in 1927, and his scholarly efforts led to a host of publications in Anabaptist studies over the next four decades. In 1934 he was baptized into the Christian faith.

On November 10, 1938, Friedmann was imprisoned in Vienna, along with other Jews, and after twelve days he was freed by friends who counseled him to emigrate immediately. He left Austria, reaching the United States via England in the following year. Through the efforts of Yale professor Roland Bainton and Goshen College dean Harold S. Bender, in 1940 he became an

Honorary Fellow at the Yale Divinity School; and shortly thereafter, Visiting Lecturer and Research Fellow in Anabaptist Studies at Goshen College (a position he held from 1940 to 1943). During this time he formally joined the Eighth Street Mennonite Church in Goshen, Indiana. He was assistant editor of the *Mennonite Encyclopedia* (1947-1959), responsible for Anabaptist-related articles relating to the former Austrian-Hungarian territories, and for those concerning the Hutterian Brethren—himself writing more than two hundred entries. He was a perennial contributor to *Mennonite Quarterly Review*, and his published books include *Mennonite Piety Through the Centuries* and *The Theology of Anabaptism*.

From 1945 until his retirement in June 1961, Friedmann was Professor of History and Philosophy at Western Michigan University in Kalamazoo, Michigan. It was during this time that I learned to know him personally, thanks to his visits to Goshen College where he lectured regularly on Anabaptist themes. He died in Kalamazoo in 1970, and in 1971 a new Western Michigan University seven-story edifice, Friedmann Hall, was named in his honor. Friedmann Hall currently houses classrooms and offices for the Economics and History departments, advising for Arts and Sciences, and is often used for art exhibits.

All of this leads up to the story that Robert Friedmann told me, how a book-length manuscript titled *Design for Living* came into being. In 1954 he taught a course in philosophy dealing with this exact theme. Friedmann was known to prepare meticulously for his presentations, but would then lecture extemporaneously using only a brief outline. So when, several days after the end of the semester, one of his students who had typed everything out stenographically unbeknownst to him, presented it to him, Friedmann was taken by utter surprise. Friedmann then edited and retyped the manuscript, transforming what had been an oral presentation into a text that would read well as a published volume.

Friedmann also told me the following about the nature of *Design for Living*: at a secular university, it would not have been appropriate to reference Anabaptist core values directly—theologically and historically—especially in a philosophy course. Believing that the Anabaptist approach to life held clues to life's meaning, however, he attempted to describe such a synthesis indirectly, via the voices of many philosophers and thinkers throughout history who arrived at some of the same conclusions. *Design for Living*, consequently, was Friedmann's attempt to get to the very center of what a meaningful life is supposed to be about—described philosophically and ethically, rather than solely historically and exclusively on the basis of theology.

Robert Friedmann never formally studied theology, and was, in his training, a philosopher. But as a philosopher, he came to the firm conclusion that, regarding the probing of the meaning of life, philosophy has its built-in limits. It cannot, ultimately, fathom spiritual truth, which does indeed exist as an existential reality, and which transcends our thought processes, only to be found in another dimension: "Love is no longer a philosophical concept to be defined by reason. It is rather the manifestation of a spiritual reality belonging not to the realm of philosophy but to that of faith" (p. 144). He writes that "Stronger than reason is life itself" (p. 63), and "Meaning is always first-hand experience (what the Germans call *Erlebnis*) and not a rational idea" (p. 93). In *Design for Living* he stresses that humankind "belong[s] to two worlds, the world of the natural (with its urges, appetites, etc.) and the world of meaning and value which would best be called the 'spiritual' world" (pp. 93–94).

In *Design for Living*, Friedmann defines the nature of the meaningful life in a manner that is simultaneously, and to a great extent, the sum and substance of the Anabaptist view of discipleship, close community, and the way of love and peace—without using the term discipleship, yet describing the same in philosophical terms, using the term "design." He writes that "'Design' thus is always maximum ethics for the individual, no dictation from outside, but absolutistic and total from the inside" (p. 116). As for the content of discipleship, Friedmann turns to the Sermon on the Mount: "[T]he Sermon on the Mount, purposely exaggerating in its demands, proclaims to achieve just this: giving direction and meaning to life in its totality, representing a maximum ethics; a 'design,' in the purest sense of the word, 'for living'" (p. 97).

Friedmann has a whole chapter on community, a relatively rare commodity in general society, yet essential for fulfilling life's meaning. At the same time, community needs to be balanced by the individual who possesses infinite worth. Friedmann recognizes that both a radical individualism as well as a radical collectivism miss the mark, forgetting that an I/Thou relationship is integral to a true We-Philosophy. He concludes his whole thesis with a detailed description of the substance and spirit of *the design for living*, divided into Regard, Concern, Service, and capped by Love, which is the undergirding Spirit and reality behind everything else encompassing the Design for Living, for both individual and community.

He dares to say, at one point: "Perfect love was achieved possibly only once" (p. 139), and that "Love alone will eventually redeem this world of man. Gandhi, Schweitzer, Kagawa, Quakers, Mennonites, Brethren—they all believed and believe in this self-propagating force of love if rightly offered. It is like the ripples on the surface of water when a stone is thrown in—they spread into ever-widening circles" (p. 142). Friedmann clinches his inquiry, declaring that the Design for Living is "less a philosophy than a faith" (p. 152).

As noted above, Friedmann developed his ideas within *Design for Living* in the year 1954. He noted that at that time, "although love is the core of Jesus' teaching, . . . it has to be rediscovered in every generation, and in times of confusion like ours, its reformulation seems doubly needed" (pp. 120–121). He spoke to the prevalence in the 1950s of popularisms that in no way led to meaning and fulfillment—such as hedonism, self-interest, self-realization, and even minimal ethics (including the limitations of the Golden Rule as an end in and of itself). But such "isms" are not unique to the 1950s. Each one of Friedmann's categories concerning what Design for Living is *not* are as equally valid in this day and age.

Friedmann held *Design for Living* to be one of his central writings, and wanted it published. He told me shortly before his death that this was his best work! He hoped that it would find the light of day as a published tome. He gave me a copy, entrusting it to me with this in mind. And here we owe Maxwell Kennel our deepest gratitude for having taken on the intricate task of editing the work and seeing it into print.

– *Leonard Gross, February 2017*

Acknowledgments

This book would never have been published were it not for the help of Leonard Gross, who took an interest in my work on it in 2015 and provided extensive editorial suggestions and important biographical details during the editing process. For help in moving *Design for Living* from manuscript to publication, I am grateful for the assistance of the Mennonite Church USA Archives staff, particularly Jason Kauffman who assisted me with acquiring the relevant permissions. I am grateful for the work of Brian Palmer and Matthew Wimer at Wipf & Stock, both for their editorial assistance and for their support of the project. I also would like to express my deepest appreciation to both of Robert Friedmann's sons, John† and Martin, for their substantial support and interest in the publication of *Design for Living*. Lastly, and most importantly, I am grateful for the unflagging support of Dr. P. Travis Kroeker of McMaster University, whose guidance and appreciation of existential Anabaptism continue to inspire me in my doctoral studies.

Editor's Introduction

Discovering the Other Friedmann

As we learn in Leonard Gross's preface, Robert Friedmann (1891-1970) is a well-known historian of early Anabaptist sources, widely recognized for his major English-language studies: *Mennonite Piety Through the Centuries* (1949), *Hutterite Studies* (1961), and *The Theology of Anabaptism* (published posthumously in 1973).[1] In addition to these book-length research projects, Friedmann wrote numerous articles on Anabaptist history and contributed extensively to both the *Mennonite Encyclopedia* and the *Mennonitische Lexikon*. He grew up in a Jewish family in Vienna and completed his doctorate at the University of Vienna while working on Hutterite codices—a subject that fascinated him and motivated his lifelong study of Anabaptist history. Fleeing Vienna, Friedmann moved to the United States, first to the Yale Divinity School at the invitation of Roland H. Bainton, and then to Goshen College at the invitation of Harold Bender. Beginning in the mid-1940s, Friedmann began to teach history and philosophy at Western Michigan University in Kalamazoo. He died in 1970, and a memorial issue of the *Mennonite Quarterly Review* appeared in April 1974, which included an appreciation by Walter Klaassen, an interview with Leonard Gross, and an extensive (if incomplete) bibliography of his work.[2]

---

1. See Friedmann, *Mennonite Piety Through the Centuries*; *Hutterite Studies*; *The Theology of Anabaptism*.

2. The bibliography of his writings in the 1974 *Mennonite Quarterly Review* issue fails to mention *Design for Living*, but it does include a reference to another unpublished two-hundred page manuscript entitled *Abenteuer eines Täufers in der Türkei, 1607-1610*. The issue also translates a pseudonymous account of Friedmann's own brief political

EDITOR'S INTRODUCTION

This is the established history of Robert Friedmann's life that has been disseminated in the Mennonite theological world, but this story is not whole. Several interesting facts complement and enrich this narrative, as distributed on the dust-jacket covers of his books and in the secondary texts on his work. In one exceptional appraisal—the 1987 *Mennonite Encyclopedia* entry on Robert Friedmann by Leonard Gross—there is mention of a work that enriches this story in important ways. At the end of the encyclopedia entry, Gross mentions that "[a]n important book-length manuscript that was never published is Friedmann's "Design for Living," which defines the nature of life in a manner that is to a great extent the sum and substance of the Anabaptist view of discipleship, but described in philosophical terms."[3] In addition to this reference, the *Mennonite Encyclopedia* entry on "Philosophy" by J. Lawrence Burkholder also mentions *Design for Living* as one of the few expressions of Mennonite engagement with philosophy.[4] Apart from these two entries, however, the manuscript has barely been cited in the years since Friedmann's death.

During my research on the relationship between Mennonite theology and philosophy,[5] I encountered these two intriguing references and wondered: how could such an interesting manuscript by a major Anabaptist historian sit unpublished (and largely unmentioned) in an archive for so many years? When I acquired a copy from the Mennonite Church Archives in early 2015, I found my answer. After reading the page-length endorsements of the manuscript by Leonard Gross and Clarence Bauman, and contacting Leonard Gross, I learned that the manuscript had a fascinating history. Along with the manuscript for *The Theology of Anabaptism*, Friedmann had also entrusted *Design for Living* to Leonard Gross with the aim of eventual publication. In the end, unfortunately, only *The Theology of Anabaptism* was published, and *Design for Living* was rejected for publication on the grounds that it would not have a significant-enough readership. But upon reading the manuscript I began to believe that this assessment was not the case, not merely because the manuscript could enrich the reception and understanding of Friedmann's work, but because the text communicates something fundamentally valuable, and potentially perennial.

---

imprisonment in Austria before he fled the country in 1939. See Klingelsmith, "A Bibliography of the Anabaptist Mennonite Writings of Robert Friedmann," 255.

3. Gross, "Friedmann, Robert (1891-1970)," para. 5.
4. Burkholder, "Philosophy," para. 9.
5. Kennel, "Mennonite Metaphysics?", 403–421.

In *Design for Living* we encounter another Friedmann, one who—in addition to the inspiration he found in the history and lived experience of the Hutterites—also found his way to Anabaptist principles through the study of philosophy, particularly existentialism. *Design for Living* represents nothing less than a sustained inquiry into the human condition; not from religious, Christian, secular, or Humanist perspectives alone, but drawing on the fullness of each (and defying the categories of each in its synthesis). Citing what some call the "classic" works of philosophy, theology, and literature, Friedmann takes the reader on a journey toward what he calls "the educated heart." Beginning by clearing the ground with a critique of the ethical and psychological sentiments of his day, Friedmann then draws upon sources from Ovid and Confucius to Nietzsche and Dostoevsky, and he initiates the reader into a "Design for Living." Truly ahead of its time (perhaps even prophetic), *Design for Living* not only deals with the aforementioned existential questions, but critiques the racism, sexism, and ableism of the 1950s, anticipating many changes in theology, philosophy, and cultural studies that we now take for granted, but which must have been revolutionary in 1954. Let the reader take notice *not* when the text sounds dated, but when the text feels far closer to the present day than it does to the 1950s.

Design for Living confronts the reader with another Friedmann: someone who was not only an Anabaptist historian but also a philosopher and literary commentator, someone who was not only a theologian of existential Anabaptism but also an individual deeply affected by the Russian personalists and existentialists, like Berdayev and Tolstoy, and someone who was not only a member of Eighth Street Mennonite Church in Goshen but a professor at a public institution, and someone whose breadth of interest reflected the openness of the Quaker meetings that he attended with his wife in his later life. *Design for Living* is presented here in edited form with the goal of giving not only the Mennonite reader, but curious readers of any background, a more complete picture of Friedmann as a person and a scholar.

In the manuscript Friedmann's writing is both elegant and abrupt, and his method of critique is both fair and unapologetic. My editorial process began with the task of creating a version of the text that matched the typescript found in the MCUSA Archives. Following the completion of a faithful copy I then produced an edited version that corrected the few extant typos and smoothed some of Friedmann's more Germanic sentences.

EDITOR'S INTRODUCTION

While the majority of my editing was relatively non-invasive, I did insist upon altering Friedmann's use of gendered language (very often changing 'mankind' to 'humankind'), given that Friedmann himself also uses non-gender-specific language throughout the text, and especially given that he makes arguments that resonate with the spirit of feminist critique, obviously considering his use of 'mankind' to refer to humanity in general. Occasionally I have retained the use of terms like "mankind" and "brotherhood" where the context appeared to be descriptive and historical, rather than prescriptive. In making these changes my goal was to prevent the interrupting effect that constant reference to "mankind" may have on contemporary readers, so as to ensure that this text could not again be relegated to an archive. I have not, however, "sanitized" or "updated" the text in such a way that would veil Friedmann's views on marriage or psychology (to cite just two examples) that might cause some readers discomfort. Apart from these editorial changes, my only other interventions were the removal of two extensive composite quotations from Buber and Nietzsche in the interest of retaining the flow of the text.

I have added some references throughout the text (marked by "–Ed") and provided a select bibliography. However, I have not been able to provide a citation for every case of direct quotation, given both my limited access to Friedmann's sources (most of which are now housed in the Friedmann-Sakakibara library in Tokyo),[6] and the fact that he does not consistently provide the title of the work from which he is quoting. The editorial footnotes are meant to supplement the few references that Friedmann himself included in his typescript, and at times they only specify the work that I suspect he is quoting from and not the page number. In the case of quotations from the Bible, I have generally retained Friedmann's use of the King James Version. In some cases of Biblical quotation, as well as many quotations from Tolstoy and Ghandi, the reader ought to treat the use of quotation marks lightly, as many of these quotations appear to be Friedmann's paraphrase. In general, my goal has been to regularize and modernize the structure of Friedmann's sentences, but not to change the substance or content of his work,[7] meaning that I have not endeavored to provide a critical edition of *Design for Living* but instead a popular edition

---

6. Von Schlachta, *From the Tyrol to North America*, 222-223.
7. See Kelemen, *Textual Editing and Criticism*, 24.

that can be widely read, and also one that would contribute to the scholarly understanding of Friedmann's work.[8]

Robert Friedmann's contribution in his first book, *Mennonite Piety Throughout the Centuries*, was in part to argue that the Anabaptist focus on outward *Nachfolge* (discipleship) was superior to the inner preoccupations of Pietism. Mennonite historical theologian Thomas Finger suggests that Friedmann linked together Harold S. Bender's Anabaptist Vision with social ethics, implicitly connecting the transcendent theological claims of Bender with the existential and lived discipleship of Anabaptism (Bender was important for Friedmann, both personally and theologically, with Friedmann going so far as to call Bender an "existential event"[9]). Although his reading of Pietism and his historical justification of existential Anabaptism are both deeply contested, I suggest that through *Design for Living* Friedmann can come to be appreciated anew for his philosophical depth and breadth.[10] Friedmann's book *A Theology of Anabaptism* also received very critical reviews, one by Vern Ratzlaff in *Direction: A Mennonite Brethren Forum* and one by C. Norman Kraus in the memorial issue of the *Mennonite Quarterly Review*. Both reviewers accuse Friedmann of straying from his sources, and both fault him for projecting his categories onto the historical materials that he drew upon.[11] Although these interpretive moves do not make for good historical writing (especially by contemporary standards), they may still have theological value. For example, P. Travis Kroeker has held up Friedmann's existential Anabaptism as reflecting a greater tradition of inquiry from Plato to Augustine, and as evident in the dramatic unfolding of certain great works of literature.[12] This understanding of theology as existential—whether evident in Plato's *techne*, Augustine's *caritas*, Dostoevsky's asceticism, or Menno Simon's *agon* of rebirth—for Kroeker, the existential nature of theology troubles simple divisions between church and world.

---

8. One such contribution may be to confirm the findings of Levi Miller, who argues both that *Mennonite Piety Through the Centuries* uses "Tolstoyan categories," and that *Theology of Anabaptism* is "a Tolstoyan reading of Anabaptist theology." Miller's essay also mentions *Design for Living*, calling it "a philosophical mix of moral betterment and secular discipleship." Miller, "Leo Tolstoy and the Mennonites," 176.

9. Finger, *A Contemporary Anabaptist Theology*, 48-50.

10. These critiques include Roth, "Pietism and the Anabaptist Soul" and von Schlachta, "Anabaptists and Pietists: Influences, Contacts, and Relations."

11. Ratzlaff, Review of *The Theology of Anabaptism*; Kraus, Review of *The Theology of Anabaptism*.

12. Kroeker, "Anabaptists and Existential Theology," 69-88.

This notion of an Anabaptist existential theology as encompassing a broad experience of church and world resonates even more deeply when considered alongside *Design for Living* and its secular (or postsecular) source base and concern. Even more so, the secularity of existential Anabaptism resonates with the life of Robert Friedmann, who himself was not always a clearly defined confessional Mennonite, but also a self-described "Jew who sides with Christ" (circa 1930), and someone who considered himself to be situated between religious socialists and Anabaptists (circa 1952).[13]

Beyond these questions of Anabaptism—which risk remaining in the provincial realm of Mennonite theological and historical reflection—*Design for Living* presents the reader with a unique mixture of ethical and spiritual reflection that cuts very close to the bone of everyday experience. Although Friedmann freely abstracts and distances himself from lived experience at many points in the text, he always returns to it, leaving the reader with insight into both their everyday interactions with others and the workings of the self. Unbinding ethics from its theoretical moorings, and releasing the question of the good life from both Christian and secular shackles, Friedmann's *Design for Living* is nothing less than a call to be instructed by the "world," understood in the broadest sense of the term, between and beyond both secular and Christian visions. These two streams merge in Friedmann without the kind of paralyzing contradictions that many expect from such a confluence. Friedmann seems to suggest that the Christian and the secular individual could indeed become friends and engage in dialogue with one another in the common pursuits of regard, concern, service, and love. As a contribution to both the theology of the Mennonites and the literature on the ascents and descents of the human spirit, *Design for Living* is incomparable, especially given its wide-ranging sources and massive scope. In no other Mennonite thinker of Friedmann's generation do we see such a broad range of interests and sources in the areas of philosophy and literature, and for this reason and the reasons outlined above, *Design for Living* is a late but essential contribution.

Maxwell Kennel, July 2017

---

13. Von Schlachta, "Robert Friedmann—Searching for the Meaning of Faith for the World," iv, vi.

Introduction

The Educated Heart

"A new heart I will give you, and a new spirit I will put within you; and I will remove from your body the heart of stone and give you a heart of flesh."

—EZEKIEL 36:26

Strictly speaking, this book deals with one topic only: the description and discussion of what might best be called "the educated heart." Since it will take an entire book to elucidate this idea, one should not expect a definition or sufficient description in this first paragraph. The subject of this book has to do with the business of living. There are many sciences to learn from but there is none that can help us in the most important concern of all our human existence, namely the building up of a life that would meet its challenges and intricacies in their fullness. Too important is life, and too great are its stakes, to allow us just to ride on the waves of chance wherever they may take us. The proper design for living and the endeavor toward a meaningful conduct of our existence cannot be dismissed lightheartedly as a secondary matter, at least not by people who are serious. Life is not child's play, and it demands more than practical skill or cleverness. In a sense, the "educated heart" is just the answer to this central search after a design for living. In other words, it leads to an ever-present and most real concern for the things that matter most in human existence. It will need a good deal of earnest thinking and a wide detour through the thickets of philosophy, psychology, and religion, to make obvious the importance of such a basic concern.

INTRODUCTION

Education is a big word today, and it has a noble connotation. It is almost a keyword of today's civilization, and many efforts and means are directed toward it. Unfortunately a good deal of effort is of an intellectual nature, dealing with the accumulation of knowledge. It is true that modern educators are interested, too, in the education of a well-rounded person, a category which includes sports, the graces of the body, manual skills, and other extracurricular activities. But this "progressive" program grievously neglects the most vital element of the human personality: its moral character, or figuratively speaking, "the heart." Now, should and could this heart be educated? Is there not enough common sense everywhere around us, not enough general decency that by merely living together human beings get all they need in this regard? Or to say it otherwise: while there are many well trained people to guide in academic knowledge or in extracurricular activities, there are hardly any leaders available who could help us in this most central concern of all: the proper design for living, or as we called it before, the concern for the things that matter most. We do have certain moral standards, mores, etiquettes, and conventional patterns which regulate our social life. Whatever goes beyond these standards, however, is considered a private affair in which each individual is left completely on their own. This absence of directives is often praised as the height of personal freedom, allowing everyone to find their own solution. And if they do not find it, or if life becomes hard to bear or even a complete failure, then we just call it the individual's own responsibility. And here the case would rest.

I think that actually much more is involved, and the simple answer above is in reality no answer but the acknowledgment of knowing nothing better. Here then begins the search for a design for living that goes beyond the conventional standards of everyday routine. Such an Odyssey is, of course, not undertaken to judge fellow people but only to find a more meaningful existence, a life of value and worthwhileness, which can stand up to the often-terrible predicaments and the tests and trials through which people must pass. Who can teach us such wisdom and lend us a guiding hand in the confusion of practicality and value? Many books have been written in this field, practical and theoretical ones, books on ethics and the art of living, books on wisdom and the way to "peace of mind (or soul)"—in fact, books on any moral issue whatsoever. Obviously there should be no lack of information on this topic. Likewise, modern psychology supplies us with a new language refined enough to satisfy even the most sophisticated minds. And yet, the general confusion persists, and with it our predicaments. For it is a long and intricate process by which one's "heart" may or may not be educated, and ever-renewed attempts should be made to help in this direction.

This is no book on "ethics," for it has no theoretical concern at its core, as befits a study in ethics. Yet it will deal with ethical situations. It is no book on wisdom, either, for its intentions are merely practical. I would say that it is a book fitting into the new trend of thought called "existential"; that is, it is interested in the ways by which values can become concrete and real in the human person. Perhaps we could best call the book an existential philosophy of life. The "educated heart" is just a well-suited term for this concern: how to make life truly meaningful and worth its tremendous prize. The *quest for meaning*—is it not a subject worthy of the most serious endeavor and self-search?

Our way will not be a psychological one—although psychology will be considered, too, along the way—but rather one "beyond psychology," for which no ready name is at hand. "Spiritual" would perhaps come nearest to what is intended here, if this word is properly understood and defined. "Things that matter most" can be met existentially but on such a spiritual level, and an educated heart is just this delicate organ which is sensitive to its requirements and receptive to its exigencies. The impersonal objectivity and relativity of the scientist will have little place in an undertaking of this kind. Decisions stand at the very outset of life's adventure, and of such decisions we will have much to say. Modern ethics usually tries to evade decisions in an attempt to be urbane and noncommittal, for such is the attitude of so-called educated persons. Everything else would be looked at as somewhat provincial.

And yet, someday every one of us will arrive at a point where all civilized relativism comes to naught and where we find ourselves at a loss as to how to proceed further. Nervous breakdowns are then often the answer—or rather no answer, as they lead into a blind alley. Life has never been merely a big play, although at times it has been looked upon this way. One cannot shut one's eyes to the fact that conflicts exist everywhere, even under the most favorable conditions. There are conflicts between the sexes, conflicts in the community and in international life, and above all there are bewildering conflicts in the mind itself. Everywhere we are confronted with a need for decisions that exclude easy subterfuges and escapes.

INTRODUCTION

A good case study in this regard is supplied in the life story of Count Leo Tolstoy, the great Russian author.[1] He was wealthy and gifted, widely acknowledged, an aristocrat admitted to the highest society. Happily married, he had a large and healthy family, he was a great writer, he had a robust physique which never tired—could there be anything more to make a life perfect and a man happy? Only one small item was somewhat hazy to him: the meaning of all this bountiful life, and the dark threat of death. Could he forget about it? Conflicts did not delay, and with them tragedy and suffering, ending in a flight from home and a painful break with the companion of half a century of married life. Perhaps Tolstoy was oversensitive. It is true that he was a "thin-skinned" person (as his wife used to call him), and this made life difficult for him. But is not such sensitivity an excellent indicator of an "educated heart," with its awareness of the uniqueness and responsibilities of life? Even though his life was by and large a failure (heroic though it was), we might nevertheless learn much from it. He was no saint and often lacked consistency in his actions. But perhaps it is just for this reason that his life provides us with such a perfect lesson in the art of right living, or rather the art of finding the right design for living. We do not propose that it was a life to be emulated, but we may learn both problems and possible answers from such an example. In the search for permanent values, it was a deeply genuine and concrete life. If it was a failure, it was one of a man down to earth who longed to realize in his existence something which cannot be called something other than spiritual. Only on this spiritual level can be found the answer to meaning and design, and to the question of what, after all, matters most. Yet, the design for living is at an elusive level, and failure to comply with its principles is part of the human tragedy.

All responsible life begins (or at least should begin) with a decision. Often enough it is not a conscious and deliberate act, but nonetheless it is a decision concerning the kind of life that one wants to live and work for, and if need be, to suffer for. One could call this an "existential decision" since it implies a judgment concerning value and design. We have but this one life to be used for a possible design and to be filled with meaning and purpose; there is little excuse for dallying around with it. Of course, changes are always possible as long as life goes on, for decisions can be revised and the directions of life can be altered. If such changes lead to higher planes, we call it conversion. Design for living, as it is understood here, is never a rigid frame or pattern into which life is pressed. Many possibilities are always

---

1. See Friedmann, *Leo Tolstoi*.—Ed.

open if only we take the business of living seriously enough to visualize the nature and the consequences of our decisions.

Just by way of illustration of what is meant here, let us look around and study some of these possibilities for or against which we make a decision. They will make us recognize what actually could be at stake, and at the same time they will also show what we mean when speaking of the things "that matter most." I propose to consider here, in brief, four such typical designs—understanding of course, that such a discussion has but a preliminary nature without prejudicing any final stand. The four "designs" then are: (1) The Christian way, the term standing here for the ideal of love and brotherliness; (2) The Stoic way, which in a general sense means the preference for calmness of the mind and peace of the soul, in short, dispassionate detachment; and (3) The Nietzschean way, the affirmation of life in its effervescent richness and multifariousness. However, it might, and most likely will, result in a sheer lust for power—if restraining principles are absent. And finally (4) the conventional pattern of modern middle-class life. Its ideals might be described by the slogan: "earn as much as you can and enjoy it as intensely as you can." Whether it be called "pursuit of happiness" or "gospel of wealth," it is a way seemingly more tempting than any of the aforementioned ones. Whether or not it actually offers things that matter most may remain undiscussed at this point. Of course, many more such possibilities exist, and perhaps there is not a single formulated one that would satisfy the fullest yearning of a particular person. But these four named ones are good examples and may serve, in a general fashion, to make intelligible what we mean when speaking of a design for living. Each of these ways has its special value and its special appeal. But such is modern life that all too often we stop at this point and dare not make further distinctions lest we become narrow and too much committed to one particular way.

It is, however, not the philosophy of the present study that all values are relative and equally good, depending on the person who uses them. We do not solve problems by "riding on the fence." Actually even the "liberal" evasion of any decision is, basically, also a sort of decision, although it lacks a real design behind it. The much-praised idea of the free development of a well-rounded personality with its unpredictable potentialities is certainly enticing at times, but its complete lack of directives cannot help but lead to confusion and bewilderment. No, decisions belong to life and cannot be shirked. It certainly makes a great difference whether we decide for the

Christian or, say, for the Nietzschean way, existentially to be sure, and not only as a theoretical predilection. Many pay lip service to the Christian ideal and flock to the pulpits. But it is a hazy picture that they claim or wish to follow, and they rarely go so far as to think through all the implications of the ideal in their absoluteness and challenge. Of course, we admire an Albert Schweitzer, a Toyohiko Kagawa, or to name a noble American: John Woolman, the thirteenth century Quaker; and books dealing with such men find wide acclaim. But here the story usually ends. Existentially we make our home nowhere, being inclined rather to follow the conventional pattern; or as the saying goes, to keep up with the Joneses. Yet that means forfeiting a design, or the chance of making life genuinely meaningful.

To be sure, no simple answer regarding the ranking of designs or the proper choice between them can be given here off-hand. To be dogmatic would be of no use. And to be critical would require a groundwork not yet available. In fact that is, in part, just what we are out to search for—principles of a spiritual nature which govern and constitute life. It could be easily argued, however, that the decisions we are talking about concerning the real life-pattern and the giving of meaning to one's existence are of the most personal nature and therefore beyond the scope of general discussion. It almost appears as if there is no real way toward an effective education of the heart. Preachers and teachers may try, but how is it possible that anybody advises or guides to what is well-nigh the most private and personal concern of a person?

And yet, there seems to be good sense in an attempt like the present, if only the approach remains dynamic enough. Let us make this search a sort of adventure in thought, with the arguments flexible and the mind open for the unexpected. Figuratively speaking, let me invite the reader to a trip into yet-uncharted land, or even better to a certain mountain climb (with a descent afterwards, to be sure). From the summit, high above the lowland in which we are wont to live, we might get a view permitting us, so to speak, to arrive at distinctions as yet foreign to our thinking. Such a climb will prove most necessary in case we genuinely want to separate that which matters most (and therefore is truly meaningful) from all the rest which but fools us and cheats us into false and illusory patterns of life.

It is certainly correct to say that in the last analysis it is but the heart that makes the final decision and tells us which way we should go. It is the heart which sets the goal high, rather than low, and which makes us long to extricate ourselves from the confusion and bewilderment of modern living.

But to this end it must be an educated heart. And here is where we may begin, namely with a study of how to educate the heart. It is the theme of this book—an exciting one, though not an easy one.

Life is given unto us, so to speak, for one purpose only: the realization or the actualization of genuine values. That means that we face everywhere what we have learned to call "the existential situation." It means the need for decisions, and at the same time the human predicament of how to translate into concrete acts what is otherwise known to us as abstract values. That is no small program, and it will require a good deal of serious thinking together. But perhaps the goal is worth the effort.

Part 1

Preparation

Schweitzer, Kagawa, Gandhi, Tolstoy, Woolman—a noble company of men from whom we might well learn how to educate the heart. However, it can hardly be expected that their ways will be generally accepted without serious criticism. What these men represent, the critics will say, is certainly fine and worthy of our admiration. Nevertheless, their principles can never be made into a general pattern of behavior for everybody. They represent extreme attitudes, only rarely attainable, and there are certainly other, more down-to-earth ways of shaping one's life along moral lines which offer easier realizations. Why climb mountains if there are beautiful vistas also on hills around us? Moreover, is not every radicalism somehow provocative? Are we not also compelled to acknowledge that ours is not, strictly speaking, an age of Christian ideals, as science and technology have taught us different pursuits full of happiness and satisfaction?

It is the purpose of this chapter to enter into a critical study of these other ways toward life's design, and to find out whether they will lead to this end or not. No general agreement is expected because, fundamentally, these questions are not decided by way of arguments but by way of an inner attitude or style of life. P. Sorokin's three types of "sensate," "ideate," and "ideational" might usefully be quoted here as such attitudes or styles.[2] They speak different languages, hence do not understand each other easily. It is further a question of seriousness and concern. The easier the answer, most likely the less serious was the question. After all, not everybody is aware that there is a question at stake—life is taken as it occurs, at least as

[2]. Sorokin, *Social and Cultural Dynamics.*—Ed.

long as it is fairly bearable, and the quest for design is rashly answered: live as everybody lives, or live by having a good time, be decent, and all will be right. And the highest ambition might be couched in the formulas, "be yourself," or "realize your full personality," and then you will have achieved the maximum of what you can ask for in life. Unfortunately, life is a rather complicated affair and is not so easily satisfied once you look deeper into its problems. And if our first statement is only partly true, namely that we have to educate our heart toward greater sensitivity regarding meaningfulness and general human concerns, then how can we be so rashly satisfied with stereotypical answers? The education of one's heart is a long and searching process, though rewarding in the end; and it seems to be worthwhile to embark on this long intellectual adventure to understand better what somebody once called "the grim business of life."

Chapter 1

What Design for Living is Not

The Case of Hedonism

The easiest and most popular of all answers to the question of what we seek in life is Hedonism, the theory that pleasure is the end and purpose of life, or its highest good and value. It is a theory of old tradition and remarkable persistency. The Greeks have taught it (for instance Epicurus) as well as modern Englishmen (who devised the name Utilitarianism for it). Although it is not really difficult to show its inherent fallacies, people will yet continue to stick to it in spite of all, for it has a ready appeal to common sense. To give a good illustration of recent times, we might point to a round-table discussion in 1948 concerning the meaning of "pursuit of happiness," man's third inalienable right stated in our Declaration of Independence. The majority was openly leaning toward this ideal of life's enjoyment. One correspondent of *Life* magazine expressed it quite graphically:

> . . . a way of life in which everyday needs are *automatically gratified*: the pantry is full, the closets have ample clothing, the radio, the washing machine, the car, and other comforts are complete. Into this existence I would introduce the pleasure of good companionship . . . I would include music, good books, and those things generally classified as cultural refinements . . . And my final requirement would be that other's and I might enjoy our particular forms of happiness in such a manner that our desires would in no way conflict.[1]

---

1. *Life*. July, 1948.

One might readily admit that this writer actually expressed the ideal of a good many people, and one can almost hear the question in the background: "After all, what is wrong with that?"

It all depends on the basic attitude that we accept. The ideal of the writer is obviously plain hedonism disguised by the reference to "cultural refinements." What is actually striking is the ideal of "automatic gratification" of life's desire, something which a friend of mine once wittily called "pursuit of happiness through gadgets." Does that not smack pretty much of a fool's paradise, with its vain dream of happiness, of doubtful substance? But this is not the place to argue for or against a particular formulation which was quoted mainly for the sake of illustration. That our scientific and naturalistic age, the "sensate" culture, as Sorokin calls it, is particularly predisposed toward hedonistic viewpoints is without question and needs no further comment. It is up to us, however, to inquire more in detail about what this position means and implies, and by what arguments it may be refuted, or at least be demonstrated as unfit for any higher and nobler interpretation of life.

The hedonistic idea appears in many forms and formulations. We meet it as detached withdrawal from the affairs of this world in the famous gardens of Epicurus where friends practiced a restrained enjoyment of the amenities of life. We find it again as desperate skepticism regarding the values of life in the writings of the wise Preacher of the Old Testament which say in so many words that pleasure is nothing but vanity. We find it once more in the robust love of life and lust with Omar Khayyam who does not tire to sing its praise in his famous *Rubayat*. And then again we meet Hedonism as the dominant mood during the days of the great transition from Medieval to Modern thought, the Renaissance. The somber concept of "sin," as emphasized by the Christian doctrine, was thrown out together with all its implications. A different philosophy was now espoused: morality is drudgery, and sin is what we now call the enjoyment of life in its fullness. And so it goes on. Jeremy Bentham at the turn of the eighteenth century invented even a "felicific calculus" as the yardstick in life.[2] All pleasure, he claims, is basically the same; thus we may figure out how to gain a maximum of happiness (which he identified with pleasure or absence of pain). Pleasure, however, is gained mainly by the pursuit of one's own self-interest. John Stuart Mill later modified this rather simple philosophy in doing away with the basic equality of all pleasurable experience. That

---

2. Bentham, *An Introduction to the Principles of Morals and Legislation.*—Ed.

this undermined the entire position of Hedonism will be discussed later on in this chapter. For all practical purposes Utilitarianism was the moral philosophy of nineteenth century liberalism, both in Europe and America.

In our own day, Hedonism has found a new and particularly strong support by Sigmund Freud and his psychoanalysis. When the very depth of our mind is uncovered and the unconsciousness analyzed, then, it is claimed that the psychologist finds nothing there but the "pleasure principle" (in German *Lustprinzip*).[3] The instinctual energies of man derive exclusively (or at least predominantly) from the *libido*, the urge to gain some sort of pleasure, bodily if possible, or (if transformed) mentally. That such "scientific" proof has given strong support to hedonistic tendencies—vindicating them so to speak—can easily be seen. After all, it is asked, what else could one seek in life but just this, the gratification in one way or another of the pleasure principle? That there is a flaw in this theory, as might be surmised, will be shown presently. It is almost the same flaw which defeats the position of John Stuart Mill.

Pleasure, it should be emphasized here, is not the same as general well-being or, still more, the high satisfaction which derives from a work well done. Pleasure as a guiding principle is understood rather as something valued and sought for in itself, and should not be confounded with something that accrues to us indirectly, as an unintended byproduct. Hedonism therefore does not allow such generalizations as, for instance, that a selfless act and a dedicated life are basically guided by the principle of pleasure. It only beclouds the issue and hardly helps toward its understanding.

Hedonism, we might say, is rooted in a specific style of life. *First* and above all it emphasizes the self-centered and uncommitted individual whose seeking of pleasure it justifies. That the duties and responsibilities beyond the realm of the ego are waived aside is only natural for this attitude. The story of early laissez-faire capitalism with its unbelievable slums and squalor of proletarian life speaks too loud a language not to be heard. *Second*: Hedonism is anti-metaphysical in every regard (hence also unsympathetic to religion), accepts a skeptical position, and—since pleasure is such an elusive good—is fundamentally bitter and pessimistic, doubting whether there is any validity in so-called higher values. Hedonism is definitely "naturalistic," considering humans as biological beings only. *Third*: (and here we face an existential point of great importance) Hedonism has no answer to the calamities and afflictions of life. How could it be otherwise? We are

---

3. Freud, *Beyond the Pleasure Principle*.—Ed.

taught only to figure out how and where to find a maximum of personal pleasure with little regard for the neighbor's troubles. (Should he not take care of himself?) But when things go wrong and the calculus fails, which way out may man then seek? Neurosis, suicide, crime? These are certainly no inviting answers, but they give us a hint that something must be faulty in the very presuppositions of this philosophy of life.

Is it then actually necessary to refute Hedonism at great length? Its insufficiency to serve as life's design is so obvious that no serious seeker would stop here. Nevertheless, we have to learn the first lesson first if we ever hope to advance in that great process of educating the heart, and Hedonism is a strong obstacle along this way. It seldom asks the question of life's design, and concepts such as meaning, value, higher purpose, and the like are little appreciated by the skeptical practitioner. Still, the hedonistic argument is persistent and we must not shirk it. Before entering into this pro and con however, let us make absolutely clear one point which might so easily spoil our entire position. Even though we decidedly decline the principle of Hedonism and its view of life, we likewise decline any sour look at life. Nothing is more creative than a mood of genuine serenity, nothing more positive than genuine joy and, perhaps, a hearty laugh. Life would not be human without it. Of course, such joy is no program or design, but the result or grand finale of a life of earnest endeavors. It was in Beethoven's great legacy, the Ninth Symphony, that he eventually introduced the tremendous chorus, "Ode to Joy," the final conclusion of how he had learned to conquer the afflictions of his life. Needless to say, this joy is no profane pleasure, but a sublime experience. On the other hand, whosoever seeks nothing but the light side of life, something which Nietzsche so strikingly called *Das Kleine Glück* (the little happiness), misses altogether the real joy of life, the great happiness.

The first and most popular argument against Hedonism is its so-called "paradox." If you seek pleasure for its own sake, you will never find it and will always be fooled. If, however, you do not pursue it but seek higher values of a non-egotistic nature, then pleasure will fall into your lap, as a by-product to be sure, when you thought the least about it. This is, of course, a very old argument, and a very simple one. Nevertheless, we have to open our eyes to see it. Perhaps it was for that reason that Epicurus taught restraint more than anything else.

A second well-known argument, still in need of being thought through, is the "balance sheet of life." One cannot overlook the fact that pain and suffering are rampant in our existence, and that periods of genuine happiness are the great exceptions. From Goethe, whose life was certainly one of the most harmonious ever experienced, the word is recorded that "taken all in all, life has been want (*Entbehrung*), and the time of true happiness was not more than perhaps a couple of weeks." If we look all around the globe and observe the conditions as they really exist, we will see a great deal of suffering, privation, and pain, and perhaps also a small shimmer of happiness in spite of misery and want. To this the "reformer" will answer, "just for that reason let us improve conditions so that everybody might have his good time, if not always, so at least to a great extent." Unfortunately, the balance sheet will still remain the same. We might be reminded here that Gautama Buddha, the sweet prince of India who gave to the world his great teaching of peace of mind, has uncontestably demonstrated to us the great truth that life is by its very nature suffering. The well-known story of his three outings from his palace may illustrate this point. His kingly father wanted to prevent his son from knowing the ugliness of reality and built a little paradise for the prince. That worked alright, so the story goes, until the prince broke the "golden prison" and went out to see for himself what the world was like. And then he saw with his own eyes the three basic ills of mankind of which no one is spared: sickness, old age, and death. No reformer can abolish these. But hedonists might shut their eyes and drink another cup of wine. It is just a matter of the educated heart. The great Indian prince had it to the highest degree, and so too, the sublime preacher on the Mount who went to those who were in need of the physician.[4]

If suffering and pain are basic in this human existence, then we must find an answer to conquer them, if not materially (which is impossible) then on a non-material basis. As a matter of course this does not exclude the devotion of a good deal of our energies also to material improvements, that is, to social and technical reforms. But he who devotes his life to such a goal has already transcended the principle here discussed, and serves a purpose yet unexplainable to the hedonist.

The story of the Buddha is perhaps the strongest argument against Hedonism at our disposal. It permits a further elaboration which will reveal another paradox of life that is not always visualized. It says that suffering, hard as it burdens our mind, has its positive side too. With this I mean no justification of evil and suffering, and no "theodicy" of any kind. But a comparison of the life of the proverbial playboy with that of an individual

---

4. Mark 2:17—Ed.

who has to go through hardship, privation, and suffering, will teach us a lesson. To be sure, it might happen that someone lacks the capacity to learn from such experience, and then bitterness and even hatred might come forth from these calamities. But in general, one matures under the impact of difficulties and in conquering them enriches his life. On the other hand, the day of the playboy who flinches under all unpleasant experiences and seeks but his good time, is empty, boring, and dull, and corresponds in no way to the external glamour usually connected with such a life.

There are further arguments of similar immediacy which will prove again that happiness understood as pleasure (the absence of pain and the gratification of desires and appetites) is an impossible goal and devoid of value. They have something to do with the theories of John Stuart Mill on the one side, and with Sigmund Freud on the other. Essentially they are of the same nature and concern the question of the hierarchy of values. We remember that Mill could not accept the only consistent position of Hedonism, namely that pleasure is always one and the same even though the causes might be different (whether a good meal or the music of Beethoven). Mill quite correctly distinguished between lower and higher pleasures, but in so doing he actually introduced a new principle totally foreign to Hedonism. If values can be graded, then it is not pleasure but the new standard of ranking that actually matters and makes for the supreme good. Nobody can doubt that such a scale exists, but the pleasure principle then loses all its former validity and stringency.

The same holds true with the mechanisms of the libido as described by psychoanalysis. Freud, an inveterate naturalist, could not deny human endeavors in the fields of art, thought, morality, and religion. It was, at first, not easy to deal with them from the viewpoint of a simple biologism. Then the term "sublimation" was introduced to link the sexual libido and humanity's higher endeavors. Its function, however, is totally mysterious. What, we may ask, makes the individual sublimate urges into higher planes since nothing else is acknowledged besides these urges, which, of course, belong to the realm of biological and instinctual energies? The unconscious, the claim goes, is completely ignorant of any higher planes. How then can something which is lower want to rise higher unless this "higher" was already here, prior to such sublimations. Again a new principle comes to light, a principle of differentiation completely foreign to the working of the principle of pleasure. Or to say it otherwise, the fact of sublimation refutes this principle in its absoluteness, and with it, its naturalistic presuppositions.

Eventually we should also consider once more the most disquieting fact of all—namely that Hedonism is, by implication, self-centered, egotistic, and completely negligent of the neighbor and their conditions. In other words, Hedonism (though fond of friendship and good company) is basically asocial, denying, at least theoretically, that human beings are bound together in fellowship and under mutual obligation to each other. English Utilitarians occasionally admitted a feeling of sympathy for other people (as Bentham did and even more so John Stuart Mill), but elsewhere in hedonistic teachings even that is questioned, as for instance in the claim made by Freud that it is more natural for the individual to have an aversion to his neighbor than the opposite. That arguments like these contribute to unrestrained competition in the economic world (equating riches with happiness) is easy to see. Acts of selflessness and dedication remain unexplained by this school or are misinterpreted in one way or another.

Reality, however, speaks another language. Above all, it is common experience that shared joy is greater than the "pleasure" of the lonely one. Certainly, says the Hedonist, that is why we like company, as long as it does not commit us to any obligation, to be sure. But greater still is the joy of responsibility. If we can take care of some duty and task beyond our narrow self-interest, then life receives a new meaning and depth, and values are enjoyed which were heretofore unimagined. A person without responsibilities is actually the poorest of all. Forces of solidarity and concern cannot be argued away by a philosophy of withdrawal and splendid isolation. No one must shut their eyes if their neighbor is in need of help—even if they live in faraway countries (for example, I might point to the long list of voluntary relief actions in foreign countries). We might still go one step further. Can we truly be happy if people around us die from hunger or lack of care, or who are otherwise in need of a helping hand? Do we approve of the golden prison which the father of Prince Gautama had so carefully prepared to protect his son from the view of human misery, or do we rather sympathize with the later Buddha who left this "island of happiness and ignorance" in order to share the woes of his fellow people? Surely every one of us will at times retreat into his own self and forget the world and the ills in it. But we do so not out of principle (which would mean callousness), and thus our argument still stands.

PART 1: PREPARATION

Perhaps the strongest point against Hedonism is the experience that people actually do more things that imply privation and sacrifice than is generally assumed. The mother who spends the night at the bed of a sick child, the doctor and nurse who give attention and care to patients (and in most cases this is not done primarily for the sake of making money), the teachers who selflessly devote energy, time and concern to their pupils, the social worker to whom the interests of his wards come first . . . are they all just sublimating their private pleasure principle? What a strained interpretation! It could easily be shown that the non-egotistic attitude is more frequent than its opposite. Who has not heard of Dr. Reed and his fight against yellow fever in the Caribbean area, or of Robert Koch who fought sleeping sickness in Africa? The number of men and women of good will and self-sacrifice is actually legion, even though they do not always stand in the limelight of publicity. They are not seeking pleasure or the gratification of desire, for their secret is rather that for a time they forget themselves and open their hearts to the subdued cry of a suffering other. And that is the road—the kingly road, I would say—which leads toward the education of the heart.

The pursuit of happiness is an inalienable right, indeed, which cannot be denied. But all depends upon the correct interpretation of the term "happiness." Did the authors of the Declaration of Independence mean to say that it is an inalienable right "to have one's pleasure, or good time," or did they rather intend to say that man has a right "to his supreme freedom of choice"? To use this famous document as an alibi for Hedonism is certainly a distortion of its inherent philosophy. It becomes quite clear what Jefferson, and before him George Mason,[5] actually had in mind when they changed Locke's third fundamental right "to property" into that of the "pursuit of happiness." It means the right of following the path of one's own choosing. That one person might choose the path of pleasure and the other the path of duty or service is clear. But here we will leave the subject.

It is true that the "sensate" skeptic cannot see any other motivation in people than pleasure (namely the gratification of desires and appetites), for he lives under the naturalistic bias that humans are nothing but animals. He has a deep-seated doubt concerning the genuineness of any "higher" impulse, and deep in his heart he despairs of noble motivations in humanity. "Life," said Thomas Hobbes, "is solitary, poor, nasty, brutish and short."[6]

---

5. Jones, *The Pursuit of Happiness*, 9, 12.
6. Hobbes, *Leviathan*. Ch. XIII.

That a life based on such a philosophy issues forth into trouble, needing all kinds of stimuli, becomes all too apparent in our present day civilization with its thirst for mechanical entertainment and cocktail parties. Pleasure, we should be reminded, is evasive and evanescent, and pleasure seekers are never quite sure whether they will actually be able to gratify their insatiable wants. The pursuit of pleasure provides no safe bulwark against the sorrow and the misfortunes of life. But when they occur, they are looked at as obstacles rather than as challenges to be conquered or transformed. Humanity goes on to trust science and technology and medicine as the means which eventually guarantee perfect happiness. But to us, such trust is an illusion and the term "happiness" a misnomer. The state of mind thus achieved would better be called smugness, contentment, or complacency, and these are ideals of those who lack a strong and noble heart. They lead into blind alleys, neurosis, or war, or under certain circumstances, even into crime. Suicide, too, is not an infrequent escape if attainment of pleasure fails.

What then, the reader might ask, is the alternative? The answer to this is the very contents of our book, and cannot at least be presented at this point in a nutshell. But in order to hint at what we have in mind, let us conclude this first meditation of "what design for living is not" by putting side by side a few quotations pertaining to our subject.

When Albert Schweitzer was asked whether or not he was happy in his jungle hospital at Lambaréné, French Equatorial Africa, he had only this to answer: "Yes, when I am working and getting somewhere. As a private individual I have really ceased to exist and I do not know personal happiness anymore."[7] The outstanding Russian philosopher Nicolai Berdayev makes the following confession in his *The Russian Idea*: "There is a basic contradiction between freedom and happiness. Freedom is always linked with suffering."[8] And the third word comes, surprisingly or not, from Nietzsche, who concluded his *Thus Spake Zarathustra* with the often-quoted dictum: "Do I strive for happiness? I strive for my work."[9] It only remains to be considered which kind of work we are striving for.

---

7. Schweitzer, *Africa Notebook*.—Ed.
8. Berdayev, *The Russian Idea*, Ch. 8.—Ed.
9. Nietzsche, *Thus Spoke Zarathustra*, 191.—Ed.

PART 1: PREPARATION

The Case of Enlightened Self-Interest

In spite of all the arguments presented, the realist will most likely still be far from being won over. The realist believes in common sense and is by no means at a loss in naming the real springs of human action. If you take off all idealistic masks, the realist will tell us, you find humanity as it truly is, an ego motivated primarily by some sort of self-interest. If you look at life without the rosy glasses of an idealist, you will find that below the surface the "law of the jungle" still dominates as the law of life. Of course, humanity no longer lives in that earlier stage where war of everyone raged against everyone, as Hobbes once claimed. Human beings have learned to live together more or less peacefully, having learned to restrain somewhat their primal urges in the pursuit of their ends. In view of this restraint, Adam Smith in the eighteenth century called this kind of self-interest "enlightened," for to him it was the exclusive motivation of all our activities in the field of economy. It is nature's law, so to speak, that everyone follows first and above all their own interests, while talking of selfless action (for which, by the way, Adam Smith had much understanding). This indicates a sort of self-delusion, at least where material interests are at stake. "Economic man," so we learn, is an egotist and will always be so by necessity. And are we not, more or less all such economic men?[10]

This then is the counter-proposal. If it is correct, then what could ethical teaching achieve? Should we be satisfied with Adam Smith's position, his distinction between the economic and the private sphere, the one dominated by self-interest, the other by well-meaning sympathy? This is a most serious issue since a predominance of egotistic tendencies in the human mind can hardly be denied. Realists (including many psychologists) are thoroughly convinced on this viewpoint, leading to complete skepticism regarding value-realization. Strangely enough, a strain of that kind runs through much of Anglo-Saxon thought: from Hobbes, through Adam Smith and Malthus, to Darwin and Spencer, we find time and again this type of philosophy. Struggle for life is the law, we are told, and only the strongest or fittest will survive. In economics this means laissez-faire and free competition; in Spencerian sociology it means the abandonment of the indigent and weak and the unwillingness to cooperate. Unfortunately also modern depth-psychology proved not immune to this view—a hopeless attitude, by the way, for the therapist. It is true that most neurotic ailments

---

10. Smith, *The Wealth of Nations*.—Ed.

have their roots in such an egocentric, self-interested retreat from any form of cooperative tendencies. Yet, how can such ailment ever be conquered if the theory does not transcend the preconditions?

Rugged individualism is also part of the American tradition. The daring but lonely pioneer conquered this country and later developed a unique business civilization which made the country strong and self-reliant. Competition is also praised here as the law of life, and the strong are not much moved by the predicament of the weak (which, of course, does not exclude philanthropy on the sideline). "It is too bad" is just as popular a saying among average people as "I do not care." It indicates often enough a certain lack of sensitivity, and since the current theories even support such a state of mind, few ever become aware of it.

Let us approach this problem from two sides: from the outside first, and then from inside. Is it actually true, we ask, that "the law of the jungle" is the only one, or at least the leading one, which directs life? In 1893, Thomas H. Huxley, the most fervent popularizer of Darwin's ideas, gave a public lecture under the title, "Evolution and Ethics," in which he persuasively elaborated the idea that the struggle for life is basically a wholesome, ethical principle which leads to the (natural) selection of superior individuals, and thus serves humankind to its own best interest.[11] The prosperous English middle class of the late Victorian age enthusiastically responded, recognizing in this theory a moral vindication of its reluctance toward social reforms. Such reforms, they claimed, would only aid the weak in their incapacity for initiative and work. Huxley and Spencer were then the generally accepted authorities of the age, and no counter-argument was visualized. Rudyard Kipling, for his part, glorified the same idea with his poetical pen. How he did praise England's "selfless" interest in India, willing to shoulder "the white man's burden" in order to help "the little brown brother." And the jungle. Was it so bad after all? Who does not know the lovely story of Moglie, the boy of the jungle?

This type of thinking, of course, did not remain unopposed; it was above all the Russian Prince Peter Kropotkin who fought it with the entire apparatus of science. With great erudition in both the natural and social sciences, he collected material to defeat Darwin's basic contention. In 1902, his *Mutual Aid among Animals and Men, A Factor of Evolution*, was

---

11. It might be worth mentioning that this lecture was reprinted again in 1947 together with a likeminded lecture by Thomas's grandson Julian Huxley, called *Evolutionary Ethics*, offered at the fiftieth anniversary of "Evolution and Ethics." The volume bears the characteristic title, *Touchstones of Ethics 1893-1943*.

published and soon attracted wide attention, even up to our own day. He admitted that the struggle for life exists, but there exists likewise a mutual aid or cooperation, everywhere, among plants, animals, primitive societies and throughout the march of history. Without such cooperation and mutuality no living being could expect to exist for any span of time. It is not our intention to enter here into the biological details of this thesis which modern Ecology and even medicine have amply vindicated. Taken from a strictly human angle, no doubt can be raised as to the fact that cooperation is as old as struggle in the development of humankind. Modern cultural anthropology knows much about the behavior of primitive societies, and Hobbes's thesis of "war of everyone against everyone" has been evinced nowhere. In fact, primitive societies had more collective institutions than our contemporary civilization. "Social Darwinism" has long since been recognized as a false generalization and a poor justification for unwillingness to accept responsibilities beyond one's own circle.

The human mind and with it the springs of action are, to be sure, an intricate structure of conflicting tendencies. The same Anglo-Saxons who so ardently theorized about self-interest also emphasized the idea that sympathy is the chief principle of personal morality. Count Shaftesbury (circa 1700), and later the skeptical David Hume, deserve mention here, and even Adam Smith in his *Theory of Moral Sentiment* (1759) advocated such principles. Likewise most of the common sense moralists of the eighteenth century agreed with this idea. Sympathy, a warm feeling of interest in one's neighbor and concern for their well-being are apparently more genuine in the human mind than the much more advertised self-interest which prevented social reforms for so long. Only by sympathy will our hearts be unlocked and enabled to rise to another level of awareness where terms such as "I do not care" and "It is too bad" are no longer accepted without a flush of shame.

It is beyond doubt that not only sociological facts but also psychological introspection supply arguments against the universality of "enlightened" self-interest as the main motivating power of humanity. Sympathy, good will toward others, charity in its double connotation—they are no "idealistic" illusions, no hypocrisy, but everyday experiences. We would not be human without such an urge to be good or, to say it otherwise, without social sensitivity. And it is indicative of these facts that at the height of Darwinist philosophy and unrestrained laissez-faire practices, the Salvation Army was founded in England (between 1865 and 1880) and Toynbee

Hall established, the first university settlement among the workers of Whitechapel, London's East End (1885). Needless to say, what we seek in this book goes way beyond such programs. But they help demonstrate that self-interest, even if "enlightened," is a poor principle for the conduct of life, and a person given to it has forfeited indeed a great chance. One cannot fool oneself by denying that there is a genuine longing for meaning and design in the human heart despite all predominance of self-love and self-centeredness. But such longing cannot be satisfied unless we show a certain care, concern, and even love for our fellow people. As a strong witness to this, let us quote once again Nietzsche, the great anti-idealist, otherwise known only for his apology for the strong man. "One ceases to love oneself in the right manner," he writes in a letter to his friend Peter Gast on July 18, 1880, "if one ceases to train oneself in the love of others. For that reason I would very much advise against the latter [namely the stopping to love others—*Friedmann's interpellation*]. I say it from my own experience."[12]

The Case of Conventional Morals

The call for morality, or for some sort of moral conduct, seems to be well established by now. Pleasure and self-interest are obviously insufficient principles and do not provide that satisfactory life toward which one endeavors once one's heart has been unlocked. Philosophers might quarrel about the highest good, or *summum bonum* in ethics, and they might be at odds regarding a refined definition of right and wrong, but we all will agree at least that there are values to be realized, that it is meaningful and also legitimate to speak of moral conduct or behavior, of some sort of striving toward a nobler concept of life which makes this human existence hospitable and worth living. This, we agree, is no illusion, no deception, no lie, all naturalistic arguments notwithstanding.

Yet here we might stop. Why should we use high sounding words, why write about ideals attainable only by unusual exertion? Have we not grown up in a society which accepts certain moral standards as a matter of fact, unchallenged and with greatest ease? Are these standards not sufficient? We take them for granted usually (as we learn them from earliest childhood), but of course they are more of the nature of etiquettes and mores than of morality in the strict sense of the word. Nevertheless, they are the standards by which society operates. The principle of such conventional

12. Middleton, *Selected Letters*, 172.—Ed.

morals is rather simple: behave as everyone behaves, accept the taboos of society, and follow the mores which are time-honored.

Convention is a great power in this world, as, for instance, public opinion—or in another way, women's fashions—prove. Although its requirements are not really of a moral nature, it runs under this label, calling good or bad what corresponds to it or contradicts it. Its rules of behavior are accepted without much critical thought, and are based on the idea that "everybody lives this way," or nobody wants to do otherwise. The principle of personal responsibility is foreign to it. Conventional living is a strong temptation, indeed, for the average person, and a blinding one. The distinction between conventionality and genuine moral endeavor often vanishes, and textbooks on etiquette become too often the arbiter and councillor, not only concerning right manners but also concerning right judgments and moral valuations. To the searching eye it appears truly strange to observe someone run away from their best and most reliable friend, their conscience, and let societal prejudices rule and regiment everything.

Conventionality fools people and prevents that opening of the heart toward greater sensitivity in all things moral. The best way, perhaps, to demonstrate this point will be a study of some novels, plays, and short stories considered to represent a mirror of life and its moral problematics as the authors see them. One of the best examples is perhaps the well-known figure of Babbitt, the symbol of smug acceptance of the ethical and social standards of ordinary business and middle class respectability. With superior artistry Sinclair Lewis has depicted all the emptiness and conventionality of this type which, to a certain extent, lives in every one of us. Now that we see such a portrayal we smile, good-naturedly or sourly or haughtily, as it happens, and become dimly aware of all the conventional lies which dominate our lives so much without our becoming conscious of them. You slap your friend on the back and call him by his first name, but do you actually care for him and his worries and problems? As long as everything goes well, we are "good fellows," but will we be good fellows also in times of trouble? A Medieval play called *Everyman* (revised by Hugo von Hofmannsthal) gives the pathetic answer. A rich young man, happy and healthy, enjoys life with his paramour and many friends like him. They meet around a banquet table to praise the joy of life, when all of a sudden Death appears on the scene, calling Everyman away from his friends to his eternal rewards. Of course, no one is willing to stay with him in this hour of need, they all depart and do not know him any longer. The only comfort he experiences on his hard last stretch comes from a symbolic figure, his former good works.

The play has been shown on many stages, strongly appealing to the audiences, though it is no doubt moralistic in tendency and as such not quite up to the style of today. But its genuinely human problem finds a resonance in the background of our hearts which makes us understand that conventional morals are of little avail when life becomes difficult. A short story by Leo Tolstoy brings this experience still nearer to our mind. *The Death of Ivan Ilyitch* is one of Tolstoy's profoundest and most stirring short stories. Strictly speaking, nothing happens in it at all, except that Ivan Ilyitch, the typical Mr. Average of the upper middle class, suddenly discovers that the end of his life has come. He has lived as everybody lived, not good, not bad, and he has fulfilled all the conventional expectations of his circles. He was quite satisfied with his life, was even proud of his status, being a worthy member of his town. And now, for the first time he faces no conflict in society (he has learned to overcome real conflict with a smile) except the balance sheet before the full stop of this life. What has this life actually been, actually achieved, beyond smiles, illusions, titles, and a dignified civic position? These last hours of life are a real awakening, a seeing-through for Ivan Ilyitch. Like scales these illusions fall from Ivan's eyes, and he sees that this was not life's meaning, that he has thoughtlessly fooled himself about life's design. Obviously, it has been a life of lies. And he sees how all the people around him lie, his own wife, the physician, his colleagues, everyone except a simple valet, a peasant boy to whom all this conventional life is foreign and who is happy in the service of Ilyitch.

Literature is rich in this type of story. There was hardly a greater critic of conventional morality than Hendrik Ibsen. Whether we read *An Enemy of the People*, *Pillars of Society*, *The Wild Duck*, *A Doll's House*, or any other of his unforgettable plays, they all contain, by and large, the same subject: the deep conflict between morality and conventionality. Whenever an individual, out of a call of his conscience, tries to break the rules of society (conventional morals), the individual experiences dismal failure and often tragedy. Conscience and conventionality contradict rather than supplement each other. Whosoever takes conventionality for a moral standard, without giving much thought to the why and how, is bound to fall into a snare at one point or another. Only a sensitive heart will prevent us from making such a mistake, but the price is not small and the effort is not to be minimized.

In spite of all our criticism it has to be admitted that there is something good, too, in the mores and etiquettes of society. It is the minimum level of human moral endeavor, which everyone can accept without much strain. Conventionality represents not "the good" of which man is capable but only the *moderately good*. Viewed from an angle of the greatest human potentialities, this way cannot be justified as final, even for the timid and weak ones. No real satisfaction can be expected where a last effort is absent. Meaning or design is lacking in a life which follows a pattern only because others expect the individual to do so. Yet, this should be emphasized too: mere opposition to such a pattern would not suffice either, and simple revolt against such conformity (as toward the end of Sinclair's *Babbitt*) is of little avail. The anti-conventional radical, the "bohemian," the crank, the odd person, has little to brag about in spite of all his contempt for conventionality. His attitude is merely negative, as he is trying to be different and to oppose, but for this reason alone he has not yet attained any higher and more responsible level. And he has not used his freedom of decision to serve a higher principle. To say "no" to conventionality is, in itself, still a far cry from any design for living.

Minimum Ethics

Decency

In the last section we learned that it is not enough to follow only the rule of thumb, conventional mores. Now we want to consider the significance and value of the answer which might be offered next: decency. A great many people will claim that decency, rightly understood, is the sum total of all moral behavior and encompasses all that can reasonably be asked for. Decency, no doubt, belongs to the moral foundation of society, guaranteeing the well-being of its members in their mutual relationships. Unquestionably, decency as a conscious effort goes far beyond those conventional mores which are performed almost mechanically and with little meaning or significance attached to them. Decency, to the contrary, is a principle not taken for granted like mores, or accepted by mere imitation. It has to be taught to each rising generation and its acquisition means definitely a step in self-education, self-control, and social awareness. Decency has something to do with the behavior of a gentleman. It implies in the man the virtues of honesty, gentleness, propriety, righteousness, and also a certain charity—within limits, to be sure. Such decency is not only the ideal of the Anglo-Saxon gentleman, but also of his Chinese counterpart, the Confucian gentleman. In fact this is one of the few occasions where East and West can understand each other and may speak a similar language. Decent behavior comprises many things: a certain correctness and fairness in the economic field, a certain dignity and orderliness in private life, a certain attention to the duties of society, including cooperation in public affairs when needed. It implies also a certain well-meaning disposition toward younger people who try a new start, and of course a certain reliability concerning promises and arrangements. "Fair play" is a good English term, and "Square deal," somewhat its American counterpart, expresses typical traits of such middle-class decency. There is nothing revolutionary in it, and nothing radical or hard which would go beyond a person's strength. Nevertheless, decency has to be learned and assimilated into one's nature so that we may achieve that amount of self-control which is expected in a society of free people. It belongs to the idea of decency that we learn to resist the many temptations in the economic field, or to regulate one's relation to the other sex, or to make the proper use of one's leisure time, and so forth. Occasionally, material sacrifices also might be required which go beyond the enlightened self-interest of the person. The smoothness of modern life is to a great extent due to this kind of general education to decency. It makes one feel good and trustworthy, and gives the satisfaction of living up to the expectations of our fellow citizens.

Thus decency represents a well-circumscribed set of values, reaching beyond egotism, pleasure, and the conventional mores of the group. Decency belongs legitimately in the realm of right behavior, and it is intimately connected with true values. In fact, it is not difficult to discover in it secularized traits of the great Christian tradition of Western civilization. The virtues of the Ancients, on the other hand, were certainly quite different from those just described.

To arrive at a fair judgment of this principle within the context of our main problem, some new considerations are needed, which at the same time might help advance our understanding a great deal. They have to do with the distinction between *minimum ethics* and *maximum ethics*. As already stated, we have to admit that within the realm of moral endeavor, levels of value exist. Each level has its own rights, but is qualitatively different from the next one, if viewed from the angle of purpose and meaning of life. Decency belongs, as far as can be seen, definitely to the minimum requirements of a value-directed life. It is something to be demanded and expected from everyone who belongs to the so-called good or decent society. We might even go so far as to say that decency constitutes the essence of such minimum ethics. Figuratively speaking, it is the lobby of the edifice of value-directed life.

That more may be required, and greater efforts and greater victories, can hardly be denied. If we recognize that our highest goal is the realization of "things that matter most," no one will contend that decency complies with such a requirement. Decency is good, but it certainly does not matter most. It deals with those issues which have to be solved in order to make a peaceful and orderly life within society possible. It does not, however, imply radical aims or maximal intentions. Viewed against the background of the pleasure principle, the enlightened self-interest or the conventional and stereotyped mores, it can easily be seen that decency fulfills a great and fundamental task, namely the unlocking of the heart, the awakening of social consciousness and the restraint of certain natural urges. And that is no small achievement. But beyond that decency will hardly go. There is nothing exciting in the demands of decency, no "ought" or higher duty toward which one would have to devote one's life.

And of course, decency remains within the limits of a certain type of society. The "publicans and sinners," that is the social outcasts and underprivileged, remain unreached by this principle and its representatives. Righteousness all too easily turns into self-righteousness. An almost pharisaic self-consciousness of middle class respectability makes people inclined to look down on all those who have failed to reach this status. Human dignity is always tempted to change into some sort of staidness and self-assertion which soon becomes more a pose than a genuine expression of a moral principle. Do we not occasionally catch ourselves patting our own backs for being such fine people? One can understand why the Pharisees and scribes frowned upon Jesus who went to the people outside the fold of their good society.

Decency, as a collective term for a set of approved civic virtues, has its values and its limitations. Any moral radicalism, any reaching beyond the accepted norms, any self-sacrifice or self-denial, is foreign to it. The depth of the human heart is never fathomed by its code nor is any claim ever made of that kind. The idea of a "design for living" with its struggle and victories has nothing to do with such minimum ethics. In our search for such a design, we might learn much from it as we will also learn from similar teachings presently to be discussed. But we must not stop at this station and linger on our way. Where higher values can be attained we cannot satisfy ourselves with lesser goods. It is an old wisdom that no prize is ever won without effort.

The Decalogue

Decency is not the only form of minimum ethics. The Decalogue, God's Ten Commandments (Exod 20:1–17; Deut 5:6–21) as well as the so-called Golden Rule represent two other possibilities on the same plane, predominantly Biblical morality made secular and accepted without further questioning by our civilization as general principles of human behavior. Let us then take up one item after the other to see what these principles imply and in what regard they do or do not satisfy our vision of a meaningful life-conduct.

The Decalogue in its historic setting must be considered as a tremendous event in the rise of humankind to higher levels of morality. Research in ancient records proves this claim beyond doubt. Here for the first time, as far as we know, a people, a tribe, was taught to restrain itself and to behave in a way which was unheard of in those far away periods. No Egyptian, no Babylonian, or Hittite law, ever asked so much from its constituency. A nomadic tribe without home and power was to lead humankind in a direction taken for granted today, but absolutely new in its time. Indeed, only divine power was strong enough to establish such strict requirements among not a few but so many. Thou shalt not kill, steal, bear false witness, and covet—in short thou shall take thy neighbor as a whole person, as a child of God, with equal rights as thyself. Today we recognize that a higher society is possible only on such foundations. Here begins a type of civilization heretofore unknown, even though the greater part of these commandments had most likely been observed before, though only sporadically. If we look at classical Greece or Rome (where these commandments were practically unknown), we find a most orderly civilization not unaware of certain necessary taboos. Yet, in its totality the Decalogue was never accepted among the pagans of antiquity, and it was only through the medium of the Christian church that the teachings of these divine injunctions became a general possession of humankind. Their effect upon the Western world during the long centuries of medieval ascent is no less impressive than that upon the Children of Israel two millennia earlier. If this impact is not quite so obvious to us today, then it is only because we have become so accustomed to these basic standards that we no longer question them. The Ten Commandments have become part and parcel of our civilization and its inherent form of education. We take them for granted as the minimum requirement of human decency and morality.

Here then are norms and standards to be lived by, and here are "oughts" to be obeyed under any circumstances. Should we not rejoice in possessing such a set of rules, and be satisfied, as were the Children of Israel prior to the advent of their great prophets? Much has been said for and against these ten injunctions (of which at least the first three are of a strictly religious character, and not immediately concerned with human conduct) which need not be repeated here. The merits of their promulgation, first to a particular tribe and later to the whole world, are undisputed. Here is a beacon of light, so to speak, which shines for all, a standard beyond casual wisdom, and unspoiled by non-moral interest or considerations. Here we learn how to act under any and all conditions, disregarding all personal arguments or exceptions. The general nature of the Ten Commandments is beyond dispute; they apply identically to everyone everywhere. They were the new canon of behavior, the new minimum requirement for everyone. It might not have been easy at first to obey all these laws, which were so contrary to the impulses of human nature. To be sure, the utility of some of these commandments for an orderly society (for instance the commandment not to steal or not to kill) could be easily seen. Likewise the commandment to honor one's parents was accepted as the most natural thing. But how could it be made understandable that one should not even covet, down in one's heart, that which the neighbor calls their own? This certainly went beyond the minimum requirements and called (and still calls) for self-conquest, and a very definite change of mind. But it guaranteed a society with less friction and with a mutual trust and good feeling. While the aforementioned injunctions worked for external security within the tribe or society, the Tenth Commandment worked so extraordinarily also for the inner security of everyone within the group.

Again, as mentioned above, we approach these moral rules and prescripts from the viewpoint of our basic search for a design for living. It becomes quite obvious that the Ten Commandments cannot be considered sufficient for this goal. With perhaps the exception of the last Commandment they represent formulated minimum ethics whose intention is primarily educational. They do not represent the fulfillment of a higher calling and were never intended as such. Moreover, most of these commandments are of a negative nature (thou shalt not . . .) that is restrictive, and therefore are not really suitable for the positive and creative guidance of life.

The Decalogue has always found much attention among the philosophers of morals, and has been praised or criticized according to their particular standpoint. To us a critical evaluation is of interest only insofar as it touches upon the realities of life proper while all purely theoretical speculation might be left undiscussed at this point. The first thing which we note is the fact that we face here a moral "law," a prescribed and demanded order, to which the individual has to adhere meticulously, if not out of personal urge then out of an external obedience to it. Laws are necessary and good, making society both safe and stable. But a morality that is based on law only obviously cannot be the last word in matters of value realization. It is a necessary step in lifting humankind to the higher level where more intrinsic relations between people develop. But law as such and its fulfillment do not provide lasting satisfaction or, as we would prefer to say, a meaningful life. This limitation is implied in the nature of law, moral and otherwise. It directs people to become righteous, but it does not and cannot awaken in them a personal conscience with its free acceptance of responsibility and creative response to any human situation. As was said before: the morality of law is educational rather than terminal. It is clearly superseded by an ethics of personal dedication, be it secular as with Greek Stoicism, or religious as with the New Testament. The ethics of law is the great contribution of the Old Testament, or to be more specific, of the Pentateuch, the five books of Mosaic Law. The prophets later on were reaching far beyond, even though they left the Law itself untouched in its validity. Their principle was the conscience, or to say it with Ezekiel, "the heart of flesh." Not the external commandment, but the inner call to righteousness was their message. The New Testament finally introduced what one author so aptly called, "the Ethics of grace" which teaches that we cannot fulfill the great aims of human life without the support of powers from on high. Ethics of grace is, of course, always a maximum ethics. But whatever is taught, the ethics of law precedes all other ethical principles because it lays the foundations for them, both educationally and also systematically. It is with the Law that we ought to begin our ascent in the realm of morality. "I tell you truly, until heaven and earth pass away not an iota, not a comma, will pass from the Law until it is all in force" (Matt 5:18, MNT, trans. Moffat).

Or: "All therefore whatsoever they bid you observe, that observe and do, but do not ye after their work" (Matt 23:3).

The idea of an "ethics of law" poses a most central problem of moral philosophy. Some thinkers favor this type of ethics above all because of the strictness and universality of the law without respect for persons, while others decline it as an insufficient principle of guidance and value foundation. They say that the type of person presupposed by this ethics has not yet reached full human stature and maturity. Or else one must and will find the principle of decision in one's heart and not in any outside commandment, be it even of the highest authority. Thus, argument stands against argument: the principle of law on the one side, and the principle of conscience and purpose on the other side. How should we decide? In this dilemma we might be greatly helped by certain ideas which have their origin in Kant's "practical" (that is moral) philosophy. Kant's great distinction in matters of ethics is between the autonomous and the heteronomous principle of conduct; that is, between the law within the moral personality and the law without. The autonomous moral principle appears as an inner call (what Kant called "Categorical Imperative"), the heteronomous moral principle appears as a commandment imposed by some outside authority which requests obedience. Under certain circumstances, as with the children of Israel in the wilderness of Mount Sinai, or with youngsters under the authority of the paternal home, such heteronomy is good and beneficial. In other cases, as for instance in dictatorial countries, such heteronomy becomes catastrophic. In all cases it discounts the full freedom of decision which alone makes a person morally mature.

In the mind, autonomy and heteronomy always stand in tension. Now one gladly obeys a commandment given on high authority, and in so doing one feels secure and safe. At another time one consults and follows one's conscience, the small voice, and may even revolt against the former commandment if one feels so prompted (to be sure, freedom of conscience never means arbitrariness). Somehow, this inner tension must be solved. It does not matter how valuable the heteronomous commandments are, the fact remains that they do not derive from a free decision of the person. All moral value, however, rests in the last analysis nowhere else but in this personality. Otherwise there would be no freedom of decision, no dignity and worth of the individual, and no meaning in the endeavor toward value realization. It must be the person who sets the law, the "ought," hence the term "autonomy of morals." And the agency of this self-setting of laws is nothing else than the conscience. All adherence to even the best law coming from an outside source (in our case the Old Testament) means an abandonment of the most precious human good, freedom. It is this freedom that creates dignity and meaning, while heteronomy works opposite to all of this.

The prescriptions or prohibitions of the Decalogue have validity only if we take them into our own being so that they may become part of our moral personality and expression of free acceptance. By this, the Decalogue has fulfilled its function, and a new level of creative responsibility is reached. It little matters then whether we interpret the human conscience in rational fashion as Kant does, or in spiritual fashion as every Christian is inclined to do. In effect, they both mean the same—the inner conquest of the law.

The Golden Rule

This is the third possible interpretation of ethics which least offend the common sense of people of good will. Decency was our first answer to minimum ethics, and we found it deficient in making our heart truly sensitive and awakened. The Decalogue, in its moral aspect, was the next suggestion concerning a rule of practical morality available to everyone. Outstanding as it is, and educational in function, it yet cannot be accepted as the last word. It requires some self-control in order to be true, and some restraint (and does so in contrast to the earlier discussed principles of hedonism and enlightened self-interest), but inasmuch as these commandments have become the common taboos of our civilization, not too great an effort is required in keeping them. However, any good achieved is always in strict ratio to the price we are willing to pay for it. This proved the character of minimum ethics also in our second case.

Our third case is not less popular and by common consent, accepted, even though it is not always practiced. It is the Golden Rule, whose finest formulation we find in the Gospel according to Matthew 7:12: All that you want that people do unto you, do also to them. There exists also a negative form of this rule: Whatever you do not want that people do to you, that do not do to them. Occasionally it is called the "Silver Rule." Since this negative form, however, is so obviously insufficient as a rule of conduct (looking almost as a disguised expression of enlightened self-interest), we will not consider it any further at this point. The positive formulation, however, deserves our earnest attention. Jesus calls it the epitome of "the law and the prophets." In its conciseness and appeal to popular grasp, it is certainly unsurpassed in the wide realm of morals, and its fitness for all sorts of applications is easily seen.

What should then be our stand with regard to this question? Does the Golden Rule replace decency and the Decalogue, or does it just supplement both by adding a still more general principle and a new viewpoint? That the Golden Rule belongs to minimum ethics only cannot easily be questioned after so much preparatory discussion. It is a handy rule, condensing all other rules into one, and giving them a new turn. But as an ultimate principle of conduct it appears hardly sufficient. Taken in isolation (as is usually done) it is primarily a "rule of thumb" for the small decisions of everyday, asking too little and setting too near a goal as to satisfy more serious moral intentions. The Golden Rule does not ask for concern or love or the like, but rather expresses the simple acknowledgment that we live in a world where mutuality is a necessary precondition of all human relations.

This might become clearer if we study briefly the interpretation given by Confucius, the great Chinese sage, to whom this rule assumes an outstanding significance in his moral teachings. Here the Golden Rule means mutuality or reciprocity, the very quality of gentlemanlike behavior. Yet it is important to keep in mind that such quality does not in itself imply true universality. In the teachings of Confucius, this rule is distinctly limited to the circle of the good, since "evil" persons are judged unworthy of mutual consideration and sympathy. "Repay kindness with kindness, and repay evil with justice."[13] The difference from the spirit of the Sermon on the Mount is unmistakable. In Confucius's teaching of moderation and propriety, the Golden rule receives the connotation of politeness and mutual trust as is befitting among people. This is at the same time its charm and its limitation. In general, however, we may say that our rule, if interpreted thus as reciprocity and mutuality, attains the character of a new principle and a significant addition to the two principles discussed earlier, namely: decency and the Decalogue. With this statement our survey of minimum ethics is completed.

That we meet the Golden Rule in the Sermon on the Mount might at first surprise us. Did not Jesus say just a short time before in the same sermon, "For if you love them which love you what reward have ye? Do not even the publicans do the same?" (Matt 5:46), words which sound almost like a condemnation of the Golden Rule. The contradiction is obvious. But

---

13. Confucius, *Analecta*, XIV, 36. Compare also the main formulation in XV, 23.

we do well to keep in mind that the Golden Rule assumes a completely different meaning when isolated from its context and made into an independent principle of morality. It is certainly not meant as such in that great set of moral instructions that we call the Sermon on the Mount (Matt 5–7). After having presented the requirements of the most outspoken maximum ethics imaginable, Jesus adds also this brief verse, derived from the rabbinical tradition, to remind his disciples that this simple rule of thumb, too, belongs to the preconditions of higher achievement. Nowhere else in the entire New Testament do we find any further mention of this injunction. One could perhaps formulate the relation succinctly in this way: love implies also the Golden Rule, but the Golden Rule does not imply love. The Golden Rule has nothing in it to make it a satisfying design for living. Its requirements are simple, and no great effort of the heart is expected. In brief, this rule will always be welcomed as a preliminary guidepost on the pilgrimage toward higher goals, but in itself it has nothing final or superior in it.

To demonstrate the universality of the Golden Rule and with it its finality, it has become customary in recent years to collect sayings from many sources, religious and philosophical, which more or less express the same idea, namely that the sum total of all morality is to be found in the principle of mutuality. "What you want that others do to you, that do to others." Its great merit, the claim goes, is its formalistic character. It does not in itself suggest any particular contents, any "what," and wisely restricts itself to the "how," in which area greater agreement can be reached. And thus we read side by side a word by Confucius, a paragraph from the old Indian Code of Manu (200 BC), a quotation from Rabbi Hillel, the near contemporary of Jesus, the above quoted passage from the Sermon on the Mount, part of a Surah from the Koran, and last but not least, even the "Categorical Imperative" of Kant. Looked at from a strictly formal angle, the similarity of these dicta cannot be denied. That a totally different interpretation is intended in each case is likewise beyond doubt. If one wishes to boil down the essence on all practical wisdom into one formula, then any one of these dicta might be acceptable as an answer. But I doubt whether this will be of great help in any search for that which actually matters most in moral endeavor. A mere formalism in ethics is by necessity empty. It is not until the form is filled with meaning, contents, purpose, idea, that this formula becomes alive and concrete. However, as soon as we change from vague generalities to concrete ethical formulations we cannot help discovering that the similarities, first so striking, quickly disappear. To place side by side Confucius, Jesus, and Kant with the claim that they taught more or less the same ideas indicates a great lack of finer distinction in the field of spiritual values. To give only one example: what Kant intended with his famous Imperative was (in spite of its apparent formalism) the idea of duty as supreme moral value. Nothing was farther from Kant's mind than to try the coining of another formulation of the Golden Rule. And in like manner, it has been pointed out earlier in this chapter that Confucius definitely declined the universal application of this rule, very much in contrast to the intentions of Jesus.

As far as can be seen, the Golden Rule is the finest abstract of practical wisdom, providing well for the peaceful living together of the members of society. It is obvious that any cooperation requires mutual regard, trust, and reciprocity as well as gentleness and politeness. In view of these conditions, we could perhaps best interpret the Golden Rule as "decency in mutuality." It is highly necessary to learn and to practice such decency in mutuality. But it is likewise necessary to realize the limitations of this principle. These limitations become particularly obvious when we think of the ever present evil tendencies in the human mind. The Golden Rule as such does not provide motivation or impulse to combat these tendencies and to overcome them in some way. Although the Rule is most useful for the common decisions of the day, true advancement of society cannot be attained this way. It is true that modern people are inclined to value highly this rule for its succinct formulation and easy application. But to consider it as the final word in matters of morality, as is often done, must be regarded as a misjudgment.

A life governed by the Golden Rule only would be smooth but also sterile. What we are longing for is richness in life and action, an inducement toward the unfolding of the full personality, and the endeavor toward a worthwhile purpose in life. Of course, a life of that kind is not simple; it appears as an inner struggle between conflicting tendencies, and it demands the giving of the entire personality to the anticipated goal. The result of such an approach is then a joyous consciousness of accomplishment, incomparable to the small satisfaction which accrues from a fulfilled minimum requirement. It is therefore impossible for us to stop at this formulation as it has been impossible to stop at the earlier discussed cases. A noble aim and a great endeavor will never halt at an early compromise. True meaning and design are possible only within the framework of a maximum ethics.

Amoralism?

We are not yet ready for the ascent toward our goal, for the prejudices and easy answers which obstruct a wider vision toward the more noble strivings in life have not yet been fully removed. Human nature is generally of such kind that it will choose a line of least resistance if that is at all possible, and loathe exertion beyond it. That is at least the nature of the person who has not experienced the transformation worked out by a spiritual urge and the unrest prompted by a sensitive heart. Thus we go on studying the different tendencies which prevent any higher advancement and yet give people the good feeling of doing "all right."

In order to clarify our problem still further, we might do well to consider in some detail the terms "moral," "immoral," and "amoral," which roughly circumscribe three basic attitudes in life. A "moral" person is one who strives for high values and their realization in life. A moral person does more than might reasonably be expected from a person in general, and overcomes the "line of least resistance" by being drawn to this higher goal. Since all our further discussions will deal with this type, we need not go further at this place in our description.

Likewise it does not seem too difficult to describe the "immoral" person who represents the exception rather than the rule. The immoral person not only does less than is expected from any individual but attempts to destroy what the moral person builds and to counteract the other's intentions. The immoral person arrogates exceptions from the social order in which this person lives and does not care for this order. Immorality is basically a negative attitude, a denial of values, and an indulgence into the dark and destructive urges of the human soul which prevent the individual from even seeing the potentialities of the positive side of life. The immoralist (such as the criminal, the gangster, the impostor, in general the person of ill-will) denies the existence of values other than those which can gratify his own urges. To be sure, nobody can live this way all the time, and there exists no pure representative of "radical evil" (to use a term of Kant's). Everybody, including the worst evildoer, has spells of kindness and moderation. In general, however, the immoralist is the victim of his own overriding ego. Disregarding any need for restraint and regard, immoralists consider themselves to be above any rule or law. Personal needs, wants, and desires are the exclusive standard, and any step taken to satisfy these wants and desires is justified to the immoralist.

The term "immoral" carries still another connotation. Any person could be called immoral who accepts a set of values different from those commonly agreed to. In this understanding one likes to speak of "transvaluation of values." This applies, for instance, to the strong man, the dictator, the superman of some sort, who proclaims his own moral yardstick and scoffs at the traditional ones. Under this description falls also what modern philosophy likes to call "the demonic," the so-called creative evil (if there is such an evil), which is, unfortunately, often admired and avidly studied. A great part of our popular literature, such as murder and mystery stories, have this type of evil as their leading motif. Immorality is then called a thriller, and evil "the human all too human." To be sure, a chaotic and destructive element—an element which causes pain and suffering—is never completely absent in the human mind, and if not properly checked and restrained may easily run wild. Today, these phenomena are discussed and studied without moral judgment in a sort of scientific neutrality, as if such neutrality could persist where the basic values of life are at stake. But confusion and beclouding are nowhere as easy as in the intricate field of moral judgment. When Hitler's evil genius was rampant in Germany, scribes were busy justifying all his mad actions, calling black "white" and evil "good." They simply "transvalued" the values of two thousand years of human civilization, both Christian and classic. Many otherwise well-meaning individuals fell victim to this moral confusion, and committed acts considered impossible before, and they were not even fully aware of the darkness which they promoted in this way. The devil, we should learn, is a master of disguise.

But let us stop here. There is a certain agreement among people of good will regarding the nature of immoralism, and our analysis need not go further. The temptations in this direction are too obvious as to be misunderstood, presupposing some vigilance. Few people will be indifferent in this field once they are informed and instructed.

A far greater danger for the well-disposed person, it seems to me, is met on a third road, that of "amoralism" or moral indifference. This road is not frequently mentioned in books on ethics or practical wisdom, due to its neutral character, and may easily escape the attention of people of good will. In fact, such neutrality looks, in general, perfectly harmless, and at times we all follow this line. That it is a very real obstacle and impediment to moral endeavor becomes understood only after the human heart has become sensitive and awakened.

Amoral behavior stands, so to speak, on the borderline between moralism and immoralism. Most people belong to this group. They are neither good nor bad, but essentially indifferent to moral issues. They obey the rules and conventions of society, yet without giving much thought to their meaning. In a general fashion they are well-disposed and willing to be good citizens whatever the trends may be. Consciously they do not provoke evil, but their bluntness in things moral permits evil to continue to exist and to grow. That we do not oppose the increasing spread of horror stories and the like on the radio and in movies belongs in this category of moral indifferentism. The bad effect of this type of entertainment is well known to every educator. The "amoral" person is more a spectator and bystander in life who enjoys watching the struggle between the moral and the immoral, alternately cheering the one or the other side and dodging any judgment. Being asked, this person will say that they are of course in favor of the good, but at the same time they think that in a scientific age no one knows what actually could be called good. By and large the "amoral" person will attach little meaning to such discussions, and their interest in moral affairs is rather distant and without much consequence. Selflessness and self-denial through service are hardly appreciated and there is even an inclination to poke fun at people of such leanings. Who has not heard, for instance, remarks of that kind about Gandhi and his peculiarities? In general there prevails a coolness toward the great masters of life whose behavior is beyond the comprehension of the amoral man. Of course, kindness and occasional acts of neighborliness are by no means unknown to this emotional climate, but they are not its style and way.

Thus far our picture, though not attractive, looks harmless and not too serious. After all, the promotion of the highest moral values cannot be expected to be the business of everyone. And yet, it is the amoral majority rather than the immoral minority which appears as the biggest obstacle on the path of moral ascent. It is their inertia that kills every great effort and enterprise. They do not grasp the quality of such effort, and thus contribute in some way to make it ineffective. Amoral indifference must be removed first before the human heart may find its chance to become educated. Not infrequently aesthetic sophistication takes the place of moral concern. Not the good but the artistic is considered to matter most, and of course to such a view life would not be what it is without its dark and allegedly immoral features. We might regard it quite as a general law that the "aesthetic" and the "ethical" dominate the human heart in inverse ratio. The sophisticated connoisseur has almost a condescending smile for those who take their moral task too seriously.

A subject of great moral urgency, relevant in the present discussion, is the human awareness of social responsibility. It might be regarded as an indicator of one's sensitivity to the needs of the neighbor. Such an awareness is, no doubt, not too familiar to many. "Am I my brother's keeper?" they might ask. On an average day, walk through the streets of our big cities and you will see many indications that the average person does not feel this way. I even venture to say that at times we all are thick-skinned, or outright callous, which means we are indifferent to human needs around us. It is our amoralism. Great teachers of life are needed in each generation to show us how to pierce through this crust of our heart. Few people have ever given serious thought to the suffering of the many; usually stereotypical answers are repeated. If we read the classical laissez-faire economists (such as Malthus or Ricardo) or the defenders of Social Darwinism (like Spencer and his followers), we find such callousness on nearly every page. In an earlier chapter we discussed similar observations under the heading of self-interest. At this point it should be added that the egotist is not necessarily a "bad" person (though we would not consider the egotist good either). In fact, he almost prides himself on being neutral, that is amoral, in his practical doings, and this it is that he likes to call his "realism."

Such pushing aside of great human concerns is definitely harmful to the human person. If we dodge and look away from what is needed, the strain of humanity in us will wither away. And that means missing one's great opportunity for development and maturation. Every one of us has periods of slackness of the mind, to be sure, and stands in need of a certain push to be awakened to one's true nature and responsibility. But be vigilant for excuses and false self-vindications.

Amoral people are not much motivated by a desire to realize moral values. Their type of mind might best be described by the term "thoughtlessness." The sin of the amoral person is the sin of omission, of which more will have to be said in the course of this book. Thoughtlessness, omission, indifference, lack of active sympathy: these prevent real ascent along the moral road. As long as we remain imprisoned in the narrow world of our ego there is no chance for any higher development and discovery of our better self. For such a better self exists only in a sphere where the fellow person is taken into our own being and their concerns are made part of our own concerns. Only that person will find themselves who loses their self and gives their self. Yet, in order to be able to do so, one first has to become a real person.

Is Self-Realization the Answer?[14]

Our discussion of the topic of "what design for living is not" has thus far centered on some common sense answers which offered themselves most immediately when the question of morals and the right way of living came up. We cannot conclude this discussion, however, without a few considerations about a more sophisticated answer which appeals particularly to the refined mind and which seems to suggest an almost ideal design for living. That is the principle of "self-realization," a thought of special appeal to Anglo-Saxon and American ethical idealism. It is usually understood to represent the climax of moral endeavor and to be superior to any other principle of ethics. With such a claim, unfortunately, I cannot agree. Self-realization, when taken in isolation (that is, without further supplementation and qualification), does not appear to hold what it promises and might even lead away from its intended goal. To demonstrate this contention will not be quite simple, due to the intricacy of the problem, and it will become necessary to enter into a more elaborate analysis of it. Such a discussion, however, might prove in the end to be worth its effort and may even yield a real step toward the creative approach of our basic concern.

Let us start by making one very important distinction of terms, lest we get confused in the course of our arguments. Self-realization, the full unfolding of the true self of a person, can easily be interpreted as the postulate of honesty to oneself. "Be fully and wholly yourself" might mean the requirement of genuineness and truthfulness in all our actions and endeavors. It is quite obvious that nobody would ever question the legitimacy and the intrinsic nature of such a principle. It is unthinkable to begin an earnest enterprise or to claim any moral qualification without such genuineness and truthfulness to one's own being. In fact, it is the precondition to any higher aim. It is evident that as long as we imitate someone else or pose for something which we are not or have not in ourselves, there is no chance for any earnest value-realization. This is nearly a truism, though important enough to be stressed. It points not to a final motive of conduct but to an assumed (although not easily realized) precondition at the start. It means an honesty to oneself, and a breaking of conventional clichés and self-deceits. For that reason it belongs to the first lesson of human self-education.

---

14. Although I have opted to include it, Friedmann writes on a separate page, "This chapter may be omitted."—Ed.

We might be reminded here of Peer Gynt, Ibsen's immortal figure, who was never himself but was always running away from his self, being one day this and other day something different, changing according to mood and situation. It was his lesson (which he had to learn the hard way) to "be himself" and nothing else. If self-realization means this, and this alone, then we certainly endorse it wholeheartedly. But I repeat that in this understanding it is only the first lesson to be learned, not a final ideal of moral endeavor and not at all a "design." For this higher purpose it lacks any concrete standard and any principle of guidance that would reach beyond the subjectivity of the self. We shall meet the principle of honesty to oneself more than once in the course of this study, mainly in the chapter on Self-Education. But naturally, it by no means exhausts our idea of morality. On the other hand, what most ethical theories really mean by self-realization goes far beyond this self-evident postulate, and implies more and higher issues of moral endeavor. For that reason we cannot stop at this early agreement.

It appears as if self-realization as an ethical ideal is the Anglo-Saxon counterpart to the German moral principle of "autonomy," as developed primarily by Kant and his followers. In either case, emphasis lies in the acting personality, the free agent who sets the values to be obeyed and opposes any outside influence in this regard. Find the principle of your conduct in yourself and nowhere else, for only then have you as a person moral worth and dignity. And only then are you really free. "Begin from within" is a call to be heeded.

The difference, however, between the German "autonomy" principle and that of "self-realization" seems to be as follows: the Kantian principle that the self must find the law of conduct in its own mind or reason implies a super-personal or general law that is valid for everyone, though to be discovered in oneself only and freely agreed to (the Categorical Imperative). The coincidence of personal decision and general law is explained by the rational nature of humanity and morality. Self-realization, on the other hand, does not carry with it any such rational and obligating principle, in fact by its very definition it declines any general and transpersonal principle of guidance. It is much more subjective and self-centered and for that reason was appropriately called a "romantic" idea (Bertrand Russell). It says essentially this: all that can reasonably be expected from an individual is the free and full development and unfolding of their given (peculiar) personality or character. The more fully this unfolding is achieved, the nearer a person reaches, humanly speaking, to personal perfection. Nothing more, yet also nothing better, can be expected from a person in their striving, as it provides for the highest satisfaction of the self.

In brief, self-realization seems to mean not autonomy but *self-sufficiency*. No other principle and no general obligation (such as duty, justice, generosity, or the like) must interfere with this realization of the personal self which is the supreme good. Thus interpreted, it vaguely suggests that a person will find all that is needed for a satisfactory realization of values in their own natural conditions, gifts, and faculties. Obviously it asks something different than just honesty to oneself. It indicates that the highest possible achievement of life lies in the most complete unfolding of our self, of our personality or perhaps (I dare say) of our ego. There is no doubt that in an age of outspoken individualism this principle assumes a tempting quality. "Be a full personality." "Be yourself and nothing else." Does that not sound almost like the very answer to our question for life's design?

In order to arrive at a proper judgment in this regard, it seems advisable to find out in some detail what the proponents of this theory actually have in mind, and to look critically at its strong and weak points. So we find, for instance, in Baldwin's *Philosophical Dictionary* the following information: "The supreme end of conduct is self-fulfillment, the realization of the richest possibilities of one's self."[15] Nothing is said with regard to the nature of the self which strives for fulfillment. The picture of the Renaissance man, the *homo universalis*, comes into our mind; for instance, a Leonardo da Vinci in his many-sidedness, or the picture of a Goethe whose life shows such a multi-faced richness. Are they perhaps the prototypes of this ideal of self-realization? I did not find any answer to this. Another contemporary author (Radoslav A. Tsanoff), who devotes much attention to this idea, elaborates on it in about the following fashion. The harmonious realization of all our capacities is the very center of what is called "perfectionist ethics." "Good conduct is the progressive self-expression of man in his fullest significance." "Only by integrating all moral activities man fulfills his very personality." "Moral worth is revealed as realization in the fullest *naturalistic* sense, the sap and savor of man's soul. It is the active harmony of all the capacities of the self, in brief, it is the function of character." "There is no paramount virtue as there is no single principle, neither happiness nor survival nor duty but an all around complex harmony."[16]

15. Baldwin, *Dictionary of Philosophy and Psychology*.—Ed.
16. Tsanoff, *Ethics*.—Ed.

The character of ideal self-realization will become still more revealed when we turn to an outstanding protagonist of our principle as a source of reference. As such I suggest to study some of the ideas of Ralph Waldo Emerson. From him many ethical idealists have derived (and most likely still derive) inspiration, as he combines in a happy synthesis many a well-liked trait: rationalism and mysticism, naturalism and practical idealism, and above all a strict, almost aristocratic individualism. Perhaps the best expression of our principle of self-realization may be found in Emerson's much read essay on "Self-Reliance" of 1841. Do not seek anything outside yourself, he teaches here, but find your very foundation in yourself alone. It is Emerson's dominant motive and, in itself, definitely a healthy one. It is only by its further development that its meaning and character become revealed and at the same time more questionable. We should remember that Emerson was an outspoken "monist" and that his ethical interest was focused not on a possible tension between good and evil, but on the problem of how the self might find its expression in a more or less perfect fashion. To him there is no evil, darkness, or sin. For to him, as to all monistic optimists, there exists the certainty of a final general harmony, if people only develop all their best personal qualities. Self-sufficiency is still the great watchword of radical individualism. Be your own microcosmos! Since we all participate in the one Over-Soul, things will be all right in the end. For we realize in ourselves lastly, though without being aware of it, just this all embracing Over-Soul.

How does such self-expression look in practice and what is expected from the individual who is about to realize all its noble faculties? Here we read: "Be a non-conformist. If I am the Devil's child I will live then from the Devil," under the condition, to be sure, that I will be self-relying. The ulterior thought, of course, is that no Devil exists, hence no danger exists either in this injunction to be a "nonconformist" at any price. Then Emerson develops the ramifications of his principle. "Your goodness must have some edge to it, else it is none," which is true, we must admit, if goodness were interpreted only as softness and sweetness.

> The doctrine of hatred must be preached as the counteraction of the doctrine of love when that gules and whines. I shun father and mother when my genius calls me. Do not tell me of my obligation to put all poor men in good situations. *Are they my poor?* I tell thee, thou foolish philanthropist, that I grudge the dollar, the dime, the cent, I give to such men as do not belong to me and to whom I do not belong. There is a class of persons to whom by all

WHAT DESIGN FOR LIVING IS NOT

> spiritual affinity I am bought and sold. [Here he means the "intellectual elite."](Friedmann's interpellation.—Ed.) I do not wish to expiate but to live. My life is for itself and not for a spectacle.[17]

This was primarily an attack against the mediocrity of conventional patterns inside and outside organized Christianity. But what is his counterproposal? It is almost Nietzschean in its exaggerated individualism.

> Power is in nature the essential measure of right. Nature suffers nothing to remain in her kingdom which cannot help itself. The self-sufficing and therefore self-relying soul . . . Let us enter into the state of war and wake Thor and Woden, courage and constancy in our Saxon breast. First of all I must be myself . . . We have lost some vigor and wild virtue. For every Stoic was a Stoic, but in Christendom, where is the Christian? Nothing can bring you peace but yourself. Obey your principle and you are always right. In nature is unity and no dualism.[18]

And so on. The main emphasis is the concentration upon our own self. No other concern really matters, as the rhetorical question, "Are they my poor?" so characteristically reveals.

The essay of Emerson is perhaps an exaggeration of the ideas of self-realization, but it certainly is nearer to life than the treatises of the academic philosophers who have mellowed down those ideas and have made them more urbane. In any case, the meaning of our principle should have become clear by now, and it is our next task to look critically at the question of whether self-realization is the answer to our search or, at least, might contribute to it in some intrinsic way.

On the positive side I see definitely two important contributions of this ideal of self-realization. The first point we have to agree with is the emphasis upon the idea of personality, which also in our philosophy appears as the very center of all activities connected with valuation. To stress the need for reaching a stage of personal development and maturity where we become ourselves in the widest possible sense is a major concern to us. Only if we become fully and wholly human will we be able to fulfill our life's greatest possibilities and chances. In this we thoroughly agree with the representatives of self-realization. And we agree with them also in a second point which, however, appears more as an undercurrent in this theory than as a strongly expressed argument. That is the opposition to any false

17. Emerson, "Self-Reliance," 22.—Ed.
18. Ibid.—Ed.

"altruism" or self-denial if taken as a virtue in and for itself. This subject will be discussed in greater detail in the chapter on "We-Philosophy," but it might be good to state already at this point that any true design for living must go beyond the alternative "egotism-altruism." True giving, true dedication, and true commitment presupposes always the fully developed personality, or self, as the active center. "We must forget the self, but never lose it"—this epigram definitely carries a great truth. Nowhere in this book will we stand for a false and unhealthy self-denial, as it can never lead to a meaningful and richer life. If the idea of self-realization would mean only this, namely the moral right of the self to self-affirmation and fullest development in order to perform true service or to do true justice or whatever transpersonal acts intended, I would not argue any further. This belongs just as much to the preconditions of any creative life as the principle of honesty discussed earlier in this chapter.

Unfortunately, these points do not exhaust the inherent ideas of our principle, and it is left to us to show the shortcomings and the insufficiency of the traditional understanding of self-realization, all in order to clear the way for our further ascent. It should be said, however, right at this point, that although we decline the ideal of self-realization proper for reasons presently to be discussed, we nevertheless recognize its great moral value, if properly supplemented and placed in a wider context.

The first difficulty with this theory seems to lie in the fact that it oscillates between a manifest high idealism and an underlying, though usually disguised, egocentrism. The idealism, to be sure, is of an irrational nature which throws together indiscriminately Plato and Jesus and Hegel as examples of "self-realizers" (Jesus for his words, "Be ye perfect as your Father in Heaven is perfect").[19] In any case the reference to these names as examples or representatives of this theory would indicate its "idealistic" orientation, and truly enough some of the English representatives of the theory (such as Bosanquet or Bradley) are usually counted among the Neo-Hegelians. At the same time, the outspoken monism of practically all philosophers of self-realization betrays their genuine (I would say almost existential) naturalism. The mere choosing of the term "self-realization," emphasizing not a general or transpersonal value but the centrality of the self and its development, contradicts the earlier idealistic pretensions. Whosoever puts the self in the highest place will end in some sort of enlightened self-interest. And since most thinkers were not willing to formulate their principle as bluntly

---

19. Matt 5:48—Ed.

as Emerson had done, they could not help showing a double-sidedness which somehow beclouded their existential position. It is this double-sidedness which accounts for a good deal of the vagueness and elusiveness of this theory.

Another reason for its inherent vagueness is the indefinite use of the term "self." We know from philosophy and psychology that this concept has many different meanings. Thus, for instance, William James distinguishes—in the famous chapter about the "Self" in his *Psychology*—three different layers of the "empirical ego," as he calls it: the material self, the social self, and the spiritual self.[20] Which one of these have we then to realize according to our theory? Apparently such distinctions do not fit into the theory, and we have to look for some other descriptions. Generally, the "self" is understood to mean the same as "character," the totality of our individual traits and gifts as they are born with us and are now in need of unfolding to their fullest actuality. The comparison with the unfolding of a flower from its tender bud suggests itself. Naturally, any guiding principle not contained in the self must then be declined just as one could not tell the flower in what particular way it has to unfold. But, so we ask, what then is the moral quality of such an unfolding, for which terms such as growth or maturation would be much more appropriate than self-realization? That becoming or finding oneself through growth does not indicate that a last moral ideal is obvious. Self-education is certainly an important element in all moral endeavors (as we will see again in the next chapter), but otherwise the process of undirected unfolding and maturation is a natural one and has no specific moral excellence. And here the naturalistic bias becomes quite clear. To the monist the ethical problem is comparatively simple: be or become yourself, be honest to yourself, say yes to what you are—that is about all that can be said. Conflicts, struggle, the tension between good and evil are here more or less without meaning. Likewise foreign to such a position is anything not strictly "naturally" given to the self, such as any guiding principle like service or love, justice or duty, which transcends the person and assumes the character of an "ought." This limitation of the self becomes even more striking as we go searching for what the outstanding thinkers actually meant when speaking of self-realization. When Emerson writes, "I shun father and mother when my genius calls me," then he has a special interpretation of the self in mind: the creative potentialities of the self commonly called its "genius." "Be yourself" would then actually

20. James, *The Principles of Psychology*.—Ed.

mean: follow your genius no matter where it might lead you. Although this interpretation contains a certain rightful claim (who would want to restrict a true genius?), yet it is a most dangerous principle taken in its generality. Have we not seen and still see with a shudder how the dictators and master minds of destruction follow their "genius" and nothing else? It would not work if we restricted the term genius to good people only, as the distinction of good and evil is foreign to such romantic interpretation.

A similar danger in the philosophy of self-realization seems to lie in its potential idolization of the self or, as we could also say, in the cult of the self. It is a most popular attitude and has been depicted many times by our great writers. It means that the self has the first claim (Emerson's "I shun father and mother") and that no social involvement or obligation should keep the self from fulfilling its higher obligation toward itself. Classical examples are, for instance, Nora in Ibsen's *A Doll's House*, who leaves home and family and children only to become truly "herself," or Anna Karenina in Tolstoy's famous novel who likewise leaves home and family and children to realize herself in her new and soon tragic relationship to another man. And so we find many figures, above all in the dramas of Ibsen. Brand, for instance, wants to be absolutely true to himself, and thus destroys home and family and finally himself. Self-realization, thus understood, opposes any moral "fetters," any general principle which would restrict the fullest personal development toward a goal which the individual alone would decide. A society, however, in which this kind of self-realization is practiced is actually a society of "single ones" who live in noble isolation and unconcern. Needless to say, such life hardly deserves the epithet "moral."

Self-realization has, doubtlessly, some attractiveness in aesthetic and literary circles. This Emerson would readily admit: there does exist some affinity among like-minded friends, "the intellectual elite," and among then there will be cultivated the generosity of mutual esteem. That such selective or qualified mutuality is insufficient for a life-principle is only too obvious. Aesthetic playfulness and, frequently connected with it, brutal selfishness are then the final outcome of the ideal of self-realization whereby the self is made the absolute and unrestricted standard. One cannot expect moral conduct and with it a life of meaning and satisfaction where obligating and transpersonal principles are so outspokenly neglected.

Whenever self-realization is proclaimed as a final and independent ideal, isolated and without further qualifying guidance, the result will always be tragic rather than happy, a fallacy rather than an answer. Besides the points just discussed, we see still one or two more arguments which should make clear where our ideal falls short and where, if properly implemented, it might be helpful. These arguments show a remarkable parallel to some of those suggested in our earlier chapter on Hedonism. For instance, we spoke then of the well-known paradox in Hedonism: if you seek pleasure, you will not find it, but if you pursue any non-personal aim, pleasure will come to you unexpectedly as a by-product, so to speak. The same holds true with regard to self-realization. Whosoever pursues the realization of the self only and nothing else will never find and never realize their own best self. Only in forgetting ourselves—in giving or dedicating and committing ourselves to something transpersonal, without any thought of what the self might profit by such doings—will we find ourselves and realize the best in us. Self-realization can never be the major goal of our (moral) activities, but will come as a by-product only.

There are some good reasons why it must be this way. Above all, it is clear that the self as such, without definite relationship to something outside of it, has no positive content. Likewise, we might say that "perfection" (usually connected with our ideal) means nothing, ethically speaking, if no concrete ends of this perfection are named. The self receives its contents only by opening itself to the wider world of humanity and never by self-cultivation. It is by giving that we receive, and it is by loving that we grow and become truly ourselves. If we do otherwise, the results will be only too obvious. Neither in nature nor in the world of the spirit does a vacuum exist. Indifference to real goodness opens the gates for the intrusion of some sort of evil, small or big, according to the type of person involved. "If I am the Devil's child," Emerson admits, "I will live then from the Devil." Of course he does not believe in the reality of evil, but by contrast there could also be no reality of good either. To live from the Devil means thinking little of the moral obligations of life, and in the long run our life (as well as that of human society at large) would painfully disintegrate or in some way suffer.

But now we hear very distinctly the most relevant counter-argument of our entire discussion: self-realization does not mean just the cult of the isolated self but rather the realization of one's highest, finest, and noblest self, that self which takes the humankind as a whole into its own being as a dominant concern. That is, genuine selflessness is just a manifestation of true self-realization, and therefore the latter remains yet the supreme ideal. Naturally, every line in this book will implicitly applaud such a statement. The giving and self-forgetting is certainly basic for an educated heart and with it for the proper design for living. Therefore we have to explain why we are nevertheless disinclined to use the term "self-realization" for this higher type of conduct. In a general way the argument will run somewhat like that which defeated John Stuart Mill's new interpretation of Hedonism. We remember that he, in contrast to Bentham, wisely introduced qualities of pleasure, higher and lower, thus making a simple hedonistic calculus impossible. But in so doing he introduced a scale of values totally foreign to the principle of pleasure itself. Higher pleasure is a pleasure plus something and it is exactly this plus which matters. Likewise here: higher, nobler, gentler self-realization, the self-giving to some purpose greater than the self may find in itself, introduces a new element, foreign to the principle of self-realization proper. The scale or hierarchy of values introduced here is derived from areas other than those born with the "natural" self.

With this conclusion we have reached the borderline between monistic naturalism and a world view which distinguishes higher and lower values, good and evil, or to speak with Emerson's friend Thoreau, "the Divine and the Diabolic."[21] To such a philosophic position it appears misleading to call the ethical principle of self-giving "self-realization," even though the latter will be achieved, too, as a by-product. The emphasis in the one and the other case makes all the difference. The introduction of any new ethical principle, such as duty, justice, service, generosity, etc., means automatically a complete change of the life-pattern pursued. Any such principle is not by itself implied in the idea of self-realization as such, for the new principles (and with them the new scale of values) are general and transpersonal. Under such a shift of emphasis the philosophy of values changes, too, and the concept of "self-realization" becomes more or less meaningless; or, as we would prefer to say, it becomes auxiliary only, and in need of major supplementation.

Some defenders of self-realization might persuasively answer that life should be left as flexible as possible and should in no case be put into the straitjacket of any imperative (that is, of course, a major argument against Kant). Humanity is good by nature, they would say, and the fullest self-realization means the becoming more consciously good and social-minded. Why should one make rules and through them prevent or distort the creative unfolding of the self? Part of the answer to this has already been given, and quite a few arguments will still be presented in a later chapter on "natural goodness." But this much should be said here in any case: without

---

21. Thoreau, *On Civil Disobedience*, 7.—Ed.

conscious guidance or without a clear beacon of light that will direct our doings and our growth, the self is on unsafe ground. Some people are good-hearted and some are not, some are considerate while others are thoughtless. It would be a poor ethical theory which would leave everything to the haphazard of natural gifts and inclinations. We might be "God's children," but we might also be "the Devil's children." Certainly any rational ethics with rather inflexible demands (like that of Kant) seems to us unacceptable, all the more so as we do not seek a philosophical theory but the wisdom of life which is rooted in an existential living and striving toward highest goals. The design for living which we are seeking must never be understood as a straitjacket of "oughts" but only as a guiding principle and orientation; all the rest, of course, lies with personal decisions. Thus the argument of flexibility does not really count in the present discussion. The "Human Situation" will find us always in tension between an accepted design and its realization, and it is far from our mind to simplify the ethical problem by any rigid prescription.

With these remarks we have almost reached the end of our discussion, and now have only to sum up our major conclusions. The principle of self-realization is not false in itself but insufficient, that is in need of other, supplementary principles. Such supplementation, however, changes the meaning and emphasis of our principle completely, taking away from the term "self-realization" all its sap and savor. The Self in and by itself is not yet a moral principle, but only its "existential locus." If left by itself, self-realization will easily deteriorate into something tragic, into a nihilistic or otherwise-negative attitude which thwarts the achievement of meaning and deeper satisfaction in life. The principle to be supplemented might be interpreted in many different ways. One author (Melvin Rader) claims that justice (the value of community) must jibe with self-realization (the value of the individual) making both interdependent. Another author (William Stern) emphasizes the idea of taking another's concern into our own being (called "Introception"), and this we shall discuss at some length in the chapter on "We-Philosophy." And so, different goals are introduced, not as strictly binding imperatives but as beacon lights for the individual who gropes their way toward self-education and a meaningful design for living. We shall come back to the idea of self-realization more than once, for it is a useful principle. But taken in isolation it is not an answer and is fundamentally a false design for living.

Chapter 2

Positive Preparation

Self-Education

Thus far we have reached more of a negative than a positive understanding of our theme, namely what design for living (if there is any) is not. This first part was meant as a rather radical and sweeping preparation of our own way, and if the reader should feel somewhat uncomfortable by its verdict, let the reader be warned of all future procedure. In things spiritual there can be no compromise. It is true that the dominant climate of opinion is not too favorable to our journey into more subtle regions, and disbelief and doubt are widely expressed today just in those ideas which represent the very foundations of this treatise of ours. The deeper searching mind, however, will soon recognize them as self-evident. To these foundations belongs above all the understanding that there are levels of existence and of value, ranking from rough and tough self-interest, up to the more refined qualities of nobleness and sensitivity of the educated heart which is conscious of its responsibilities. These higher levels are of course reachable for everyone who is of genuinely good intention, but we have to warn again that no one may expect shortcuts and easy roads. Mountaintops are never easily reached, and many might prefer to stay down in the valley. This is not a theoretical treatise on right or wrong, but a study in the intricate ways by which spiritual things become concrete and personal, so that the individual might be advised in their search and life's endeavor.

POSITIVE PREPARATION

Without a burning urge in the heart, without a genuine longing (a "thirst for righteousness" as the Bible calls it[1]), without yearning for true roots in this existence—no ascent is possible. The summit of the mountain might be in clouds and invisible, but we have to be sure that there is such a summit. Once, a practical man asked me: why such great exertion, why this great effort for so vague and unfamiliar a goal? Why should we not rather make our little home cozy and comfortable, be a good guy and let everybody follow their way where their nose will lead him? Yes, why not? Is not life most pleasant if we live as everybody does, take good care of Number One, and trust in good luck or some sort of pre-established harmony? Unfortunately life is just not this way; at least not for those who have a concern and a more sensitive conscience. There are tragic conflicts and it is by no means so certain that Number One is happy to be "number one." The art of living in this world, together with our fellow people, is a great art, comparable to mountain climbing. Dangers lurk on every corner or cliff, but the higher you reach, the more worthwhile the climb becomes. The horizon is wider, life is richer, you see farther (in space or in the depth of the human heart), every effort at high levels means—if successful—a triumph, an enrichment, a change of the total existence. If you want a true meaning of life, a design which enriches your entire being and leads to the realization of genuine values, then do not dodge the effort. But you can do so only if you are in the right mood or condition, for without the proper training and preparation you will never succeed in your ascent, and your perspective will be bound by the narrow limits of society, or worse, by your unchallenged ego. No enlightened self-interest, no pleasure principle, nothing with an Ego in the center (written with capital E) will lead to an understanding of life true to its name. "Climbing" means here changing the level of your outlook, growing, maturing, becoming genuinely human in the richest sense, grasping tragedy and victory, and above all seeing in your fellow person as a part of your own self.

Self-realization? Perhaps, but only if we rightly grasped the meaning of the higher self. But without a long preparation in the field of self-searching and self-education, no such grasp is possible. Self-realization is a somewhat-cheap formula because it leaves us totally in the dark concerning the self and its optimal potentialities. Once that is understood, we might then accept such formula, but more likely we will not talk any more of the realization of the self after we have found that our fellow people are a part

---

1. Matt 5:6.—Ed.

of our own self. Yet let this subject rest for a short while; the "egotism-altruism" alternative will find its discussion and refutation in the next chapter. At the moment we turn our attention to the subject of finding oneself by self-education.

The old dictum "Know Thyself" is rightly famous and might well serve as a starting point in a study of this nature. But how shall we proceed? Conventional psychology would hardly help us at this place. We remember that few people really know their "true" self which is usually buried in deceit and conceit, in conventional stereotypes, and in a certain dread to face the real picture. We use well-sounding phrases and like to pose in certain favorite patterns, often enough determined by what we assume others like to see in us or think of us. Obviously this cannot be called self-knowledge as it has the nature of an escape rather than of an inquiry. The hidden weaknesses of our personal existence make us seek ways out, and we like to postpone any serious search into our self until, let us say, the proverbial New Year's Eve. Then we admit our subterfuges and resolve a radical change and a real improvement. Who is not familiar with this type of New Year's resolution? Unfortunately, as time drags on we postpone their realization again and nothing is achieved. Thus we go on failing in this most personal business, unless the urge to genuine self-improvement is stronger than our natural inclinations toward self-deceit and leniency. And yet, before we ever can plan to realize values and to make life richer and more according to design, we have to become masters of our own self, or, to use the phrase of H. E. Fosdick, we have to become "real persons." Only a "real person" knows what an educated heart actually is.

Such self-education, to be sure, is a tricky affair and by no means simple. Still, it cannot be shirked. If you want to climb mountains, you have to train your body. If you want to live according to a design, you have to train yourself. Old Benjamin Franklin, being most systematic in everything, was also a master in this field, as everybody knows from his *Autobiography*. Day by day and week by week, he kept his "chart" well checked: what do I want to achieve (in morals) and what have I actually achieved? It is doubtful whether this method will work for everybody; at least it is not the only one. Many books have been written on this topic: "Conquer Yourself," "The Mature Mind," "Ways of Self-Improvement," and the like, and we need not repeat their practical rules. Self-search and self-control, honesty with oneself and a deep self-criticism (piercing to conventional phrases), will be every individual's own job. Success will not come easily since the opposing

POSITIVE PREPARATION

forces in us are strong. It is only after deep and painful crises that we might find the way to our true self. Maybe even then we might fail or fall short of our obligation to ourselves. But there is no ascent to any purposeful living without this personal preparation. In fact, every talk about "design" might sound unintelligible to one who never went through processes of the above-mentioned nature. No realization of higher values is possible without a certain amount of self-control, self-criticism, and self-knowledge. And you know yourself just to the extent that you conquer yourself as you conquer the uncoordinated and often unconscious emotions and urges which but cover up your real self.

Self-education means, fundamentally, readiness to accept responsibility for our acts. That is, no doubt, the very start on the path of higher morality. We like excuses and apologies, such as, "it was not I, it was the little devil behind me who made me do so," or, "I could not help it, the other fellow made my blood boil," and the like. We will always find some reason by which we can preserve our own pride and self-esteem (unfounded though they are), until the next crisis comes or until the next New Year's Eve Resolution is due. But we mature only by accepting responsibility. Observe youngsters around high school age, to see how they grow. Some are young gentlemen and ladies, which means they are conscious of their respective obligations and responsibilities, while others remain what they were before: immature lads and girls with a thousand excuses not to grow up, not to shoulder responsibilities and not to accept the burden of blame if things should go wrong. Our psychiatrists are so busy because there are so many breakdowns—no one can float around forever without solid ground under his feet. And this solid ground, the roots as we called it earlier, is the enriched and controlled self, which knows its intrinsic interrelatedness to all the world around it.

All life has first to begin "from within" (Douglas Steere), meaning that we have to become conscious of our doings and their motivations. What are your resources? What is your real strength which even in days of strain and stress would carry you through? This we have to find out (and it is best done during a quiet hour). Do not turn rashly to your radio, television, magazine, or bridge table, just to forget, but rather stop for a moment and check yourself. Every individual has positively some area of specific strength and value which gives them courage to carry on this business of living undauntedly. To find it would mean to find the direction toward values within your reach. It is your potentiality which requires development or unfolding. Your possible escape is the field of the "amoral," a neutral and indifferent field of interest, not bad at all but likewise helping you to forget that you are a responsible member of your group or society. Of course, self-education and self-control do not exclude relaxation, but beware of deceit. You might be busy in some praiseworthy enterprise and yet knowingly or unknowingly escape the central responsibility of your life.

No author has pictured this devious technique better than Henrik Ibsen in a great number of impressive plays. Take for instance the *Wild Duck* with its theme of *Lebenslüge* (illusion of life), carried on to its tragic conclusion; how Gregor Werle always shirked a last responsibility and how all of this little group lived a life of unreality and deceit. It is a true and most stirring picture. Or take the greatest figure of Ibsen's creative mind, Peer Gynt. He is never, all his life long, himself. He is a restless fellow, full of imagination and charm. But he lives not his own life, but rather beside this "own" life. "Be yourself" is the warning of the Button Moulder in the final scene of the play. And because he has never been himself, true to his real self, he has to be recast, remolded and will have to try again this rather difficult business of living. Or take the play by Eugene O'Neill, *The Great God Brown*, in which some actors wear masks all the time, playing some role, but never their own self. Thus we could scan literature and find this situation over and over again. Man loves to wear masks, loves to run off to far away countries like Peer Gynt, loves to live in an imaginary world, maybe in a *Doll's House*, (Ibsen) because it is easier, more pleasant, and preserves a certain equilibrium, frail though it is. A design for living has no place in it. After all, why should one burden oneself with so heavy a program?

The answer is simple. One should do so because life is no mere play, no fool's paradise, no role to be performed, because basically there is a demand upon you, there is the urge and call to live up to your true potentiality, because there is conflict and suffering in this human existence which has to be solved, and because there is also your fellow person whom you must not forget in all your decisions. But how can one be a giver unless one has something to give out of the treasury of one's riches? Therefore take good care that these riches (to be sure, other than material ones) are developed; nay, first discovered, envisioned, and then firmly rooted in a conscious life of responsibility. That is the way which leads to an educated heart. Once you have found yourself, then escapes into all kinds of amoral activities will no longer mean much to you or satisfy you.

We all live, to a certain extent, in a world of delusion and self-deception, to which fact we should become alert sooner or later. Self-search and self-control should never stop—in fact, it should become a habit of our life. In this regard, the faithful Catholic who takes his regular confessions most seriously has definitely an advantage over his non-Catholic neighbor. His conscience might become more sensitive by such a practice if he has the strength to have absolute sincerity in this matter. Self-search, self-control, and self-discipline—these are the prerequisites of a spiritual life. This is very different from emotionalism, even its exact opposite. Emotions are good, but as everybody knows, they are rather open to deception. Think only of the fine distinction between true love, sweet sentimentality, and wild passion. Here, more than in the realm of intellectual judgment, alertness is needed. We know how passion blinds us (think of Othello!), and we know how much confusion develops between true value and emotional substitutes. What is really morally good and what is only a conventional pattern of what people like to call "good"? It needs great pioneers like Schweitzer, Kagawa, or Gandhi to learn to distinguish the real (and high) value from uncommitted well-meaning which only too often lacks the level where values rest.

And what is true regarding intellectual judgment or emotional reaction is valid also in the field of volitional decisions and acts. They are the hardest of all if genuinely rooted in the true self and made in fully conscious responsibility. That is why we admire a Lincoln as a great president. We all have to learn the difficult task of making decisions; that is to cut the Gordian knot of vacillation and indecision. But by what guide? Shall we follow the easiest line, our "self-interest," or some conventional pattern, or shall we blaze new trails despite offending those who do not like innovations? Does not every decision mean the acceptance of responsibilities? Only after a sincere self-search will such a decision become possible and significant. Once we have learned this praxis of self-control and self-conquest, it becomes easier and more natural the next time. But this is what we have to keep in mind as needed: a profound sincerity to oneself, the piercing of illusion and convention, until we have the awareness that our acts reflect (as far as is humanly possible) our true self. Wait until next New Year's Eve to find out how true you have been to yourself; or better, make such self-checking a standing habit.

I know of a very easy rejoinder to all these well-intended counsels: nobody can pull themselves out of the mire by their own boot straps. That is the actual plight of individuals that they cannot do otherwise, and the more they try the deeper they sink into the mire of their confusion and self-deceit. The strong and straightforward character does not need counsel, and the average person is not served by it, at least not right away. This is all too true and proves the thesis that living is a greater art than most people imagine. That is why we need instructors and examples, the great ones who go ahead of us and show us how to do it. Naturally, it is always a risk. Nietzsche liked to speak of "living dangerously," beyond a certain simple security of the conventional. Going to the jungles of Equatorial Africa was definitely a risk for Schweitzer, but what a rewarding risk! Any responsibility, any such decision is a risk, an adventure, but what would life be without it?

Still, this is not yet the final answer. Psychology has no answer to such central life questions. The psychologist whom you might consult will most likely give some advice but he will not remove the core of the trouble. Personally I believe in continuing growth or even sudden changes of the mind if there is a certain vision of "the other level," the more worthwhile life, and if there is the unrest and urge to a new departure. As St. Augustine wrote in the first paragraph of his *Confessions*, "My heart is restless as long as it does not rest in you."[2] This spiritual drive is the anticipation of the new plane where we hope to find our true roots. "I would not seek thee if I had not found thee," says Pascal in one of his very great paradoxes, and with him many like-minded seekers would say the same.[3] It is the other level which pulls and attracts and which helps us to come out of the mire of old habits and conventionalities. But this other level is not yet an experienced reality but only a faint possibility, a promise worth our deepest endeavor.

Perhaps it would help this endeavor to have experienced that great responsibility of all our doings and neglects. It means our interrelatedness with all other human beings, whose conditions are at least partly co-determined by our own acts, emotions and opinions. "Everybody shares a responsibility in everything"—this challenging dictum of Dostoevsky in his *Brothers Karamazov* reveals, though in an exaggerated way, a great truth. Once we become aware of this basic co-responsibility we awake from our slumber (which, I admit, is very pleasant). No "old fashioned" individualism can ever achieve this result and it has little justification for its own. Read the pages of history or of personal biographies to grasp this truth. There are many who defend the "old fashioned" ruggedness by pointing

---

2. Augustine, *Confessions*, I, 1.—Ed.
3. Pascal, *Pensées*, §553—Ed.

to America's fantastic growth allegedly due to their kind of unconcerned activities. It seems to be a cheap argument forgetting the uncounted victims of this glamour or, as we may better say, "the human cost." Is it not true that America's genuine greatness lies in her Lincolns and Roosevelts, her Lloyd Garrisons, Dr. Reeds and the like, and not in the great robber barons of industry, famous though they are?

We do not propagate a morbid self-castigation and no uncreative *mea culpa* (my guilt) attitude, no inferiority feeling, nor similar attitudes of uninspired self-reproach with its consequential and unavoidable hypocrisy. We stand for a courageous type of living: faring one's liabilities as well as one's assets. We stand not for rigidity but for sensitivity. Pastor Brand (Ibsen) with his "everything or nothing" is just as much at fault in his lack of pliability as Peer Gynt, who has no principles at all, but only dreams. Self-education is education to maturity, emotionally, volitionally, and intellectually. It is a long and often rugged way to this goal, but a necessary one if one wants to discover a design for living, or rather our personal design.

We-Philosophy

This will be perhaps the hardest chapter in our book because it runs so much against the major trend of thought in America and Western Civilization at large. Since the days of the great Renaissance we have been taught to appreciate, even to revere, the independent, self-centered individual. It meant a newly found pride in one's own being and capacity. "Man is the measure of all things," runs the slogan of the humanists, artists, and politicians alike of this era which stands so signally at the beginning of Modern Times. Happiness meant awareness of man's autonomy, the fact that man is a law unto himself, each man different from the other, thrown upon his own responsibility whatever that means. To a certain extent also the teachings of contemporary Reformation fits into this tune of radical individualism, as opposed to any group consciousness of an earlier period: the individual salvation "by faith alone" and the individual election by divine decree worked in effect likewise toward isolation and individualization. The brother or neighbor or fellow person had no proper place in either the philosophy or theology of that great era. And when Renaissance and Reformation had run their course, Rationalism and Enlightenment simply continued this same trend of radical individualism, or "monadism," to use now the term of Leibniz. And monads, so we learn, have no windows: there are numberless I's, but no one is a Thou. Some eighty years later we meet Kant, perhaps the climax of eighteenth century thought. In his ethics he too teaches emphatically the absolute autonomy of the person, carrying in itself the law which could become a maxim for all. It was a great vision, no doubt, as only the strong one is able to be a law unto himself, but it was a vision which worked toward isolation and splendid loneliness. We learn from Kant that not love but duty is the principle that should guide the single one.

From here the path of moral development splits up: in German lands Romanticism follows next with its glorification of the genius in a solitary and lonely abode high above the common person. There might exist friendship between likeminded single ones, but otherwise no road leads to an appreciation of the fellow person and their needs; there is no idea of sharing in joy or pain, no fellowship of humankind seems possible, even desirable. At the end of the nineteenth century we find the lonely figure of Nietzsche and his dream of Zarathustra, the prophet of the superman and his will to power.

The Anglo-Saxon world went quite another way, though no less outspokenly individualistic and I-centered. Contemporary with Kant is Adam Smith, the teacher of laissez-faire, and Jeremy Bentham, originator of the utilitarian school of morals. "Follow your own (enlightened) self-interest; if everyone will do just this the world will soon be all right," apparently by virtue of a tacitly assumed pre-established harmony of interests. Thus general happiness ("the greatest happiness of the greatest number," in Bentham's formula) is insured. Liberalism became soon the unquestioned philosophy of the practical person. And when Darwin and Spencer discovered the principle of the "survival of the fittest," a new and even stronger argument was added to this glorification of the Anglo-Saxon brand of the superman, the adventurous and in most cases ruthless entrepreneur. The results of this philosophy might well be called "success" as long as we do not count the "human cost" involved, and forget the despotism of the industrial magnates on both sides of the Atlantic. Museums and places of research and the like should not deceive us: the new type of individualism (in America proudly called "rugged") was not much different from its Renaissance forerunner, with its Machiavellis and Cesare Borgias. There was no integration of humankind, and no coherent society could emerge; what we see is rather its atomization and disintegration. Big cities arose where people became strangers to each other, loveless and forlorn. The proud but bewildered individual had to find their way in the darkness, hoping for a strange kind of earthly paradise soon to emerge. In his remarkable book, *This I Do Believe*, David Lilienthal confirms this mood, not without a shudder in the recollection. "In the twenties," he writes, "we had a rather definite philosophy, 'Take care of Number One.' Then, obviously, the sum total of the successes of all Number Ones would be prosperity, a golden era. It was plain common sense."[4] Everybody knows only too well what actually followed this golden era of so-called common sense.

Finally let us throw a quick glance across to the banks of the Seine and see how this glorification of the individual has found its expression among the French people (where a Voltairean spirit still prevails). They showed little interest for the German superman and the romantic cult of the genius, but likewise there was not too much enthusiasm for English liberalism with its focus on material success. The dominant mood was rather a cultured estheticism, particularly toward the period called *fin-de-siecle*, with its "art for art's sake" motto, a withdrawal from the great issues and needs of the world to the enjoyment of one's own sense of beauty. And who would take it amiss if an artist insists on being the single one?

For the purpose of the present chapter, let us call this type of behavior "I-Philosophy." Superman, laissez-faire, social Darwinism, and aestheticism are just a few expressions of this basic attitude toward world, society and life at large. It's ideal is the self-conscious but solitary individual, "the Single One" (*der Einzelne*, in German philosophy), responsible to no one but themselves and caring for or being concerned with nothing but their own self-development wherever it leads. The ideal of self-realization, discussed in an earlier chapter, derives its very strength from just this I-Philosophy. "That is ethical," we are informed, "which serves the Self to its highest development." No further guidance or principle is thought necessary as each one has to find his own way. Self-realization might thus be considered the highest justification of the I-Philosophy. Its last word, however, seems to be the Existentialism of Jean-Paul Sartre with its proclamation of the absolute loneliness and isolation of the individual. "Are they my poor?" exclaimed Emerson about a hundred years ago, "Hell is the other people," writes Sartre in *No Exit*, 1947.[5] Is that the road to enrichment of life by and large? Or, if we slightly change our question: does this I-Philosophy in all its many facets actually provide a foundation for a design for living worth its name and satisfying the educated heart in its craving for meaning and value?

4. Lilienthal, *This I Do Believe*, 96.—Ed.
5. Sartre, *No Exit and Three Other Plays*, 45.—Ed.

It is hardly necessary to say that the present study will have little use for this kind of philosophy, whose appropriateness in our search for a design for living is emphatically denied. But in taking this stand the burden is upon us to give the reasons for opposing it and to evince the arguments for the new philosophy which we will propose to substitute for the former.

Our major point is, of course, the neglect of the I-Philosophy of the neighbor, the fellow person, as we have described it, the absence of a social awareness and obligation, any constructive proposition for the building up of a society whose happy member the individual would want to be. For this can hardly be denied: man is a social being, a *zoon politicon*, as Aristotle called him. We may refer here to the concluding paragraph of our chapter on "Self-Interest" where Nietzsche (a very lonely genius, indeed) is our witness. These are his words: "One ceases to love oneself in the right way if one ceases to train oneself in the love of others." As a design for living, the I-Philosophy might be attractive for the adventurer or the Faust-type of person, but pitiable the life to whom the other is at the best a backdrop or foil, and at the worst—Hell. "Hell," Dostoevsky assures us, "is that condition where man no longer can love."[6]

Most likely modern people will ask us point-blank: why should my fellow person be of intrinsic significance to me and my happiness? Would that person not rather spoil it in case of troubles of some sort? Why should we speak of "fellowship" when referring to some unknown person who might be even a nuisance? The Christian tradition, which would have an answer ready (in fact the only possible one), might better be left out at this point as it has lost, unfortunately, much of its conviction for Mr. Average. We shall come back to this tradition at a later point. At the moment, however, I have only two points to present: *One*, let us look at the outcome, the result of such I-Philosophy in its practical application; and *Two*, let us study the actual human experience in the vicissitudes of life, and see whether the claims of this I-Philosophy actually correspond to the realities of life.

As to the first point (the results), some points were already mentioned before, namely the actual disintegration of modern society and the growing loneliness or solitariness of its members. At this place we have to continue this unpleasant catalogue, unfortunately, in spite of the halo which a disappointed public likes to place behind a few shining examples of excellence. A person in isolation has actually no existence, no fulfilled life, and even at the peak of external success (not to speak of those in the shadow), all their

---

6. Dostoevsky, *The Brothers Karamazov*, chapter 41 (paraphrased)—Ed.

splendid loneliness and self-sufficiency ends in despair and moral nihilism. ("Marshall, you have no home, no family, no happiness—nothing but money," we read in a biography of the great Marshall Field of Chicago.) The heavy drinking of our day might be a strong indicator of this situation. T. S. Eliot's *Cocktail Party* (what an appropriate title) must be considered a good portrait of this modern man, "the master," in all his misery. The countless cases of inner disorder of some sort, of need for psychiatric treatment (while the physician would need a physician himself) speak an unmistakable language. Life has become a great bubble. In this day and age nihilism has found its strongest spokesmen among the existentialists of the *rive gauche* who have simply and irrefutably experienced the impasse of human beings without any ties, without God, and without the other (who, basically, belong together). There is no way out, neither for dictators or other grandees, nor for intellectuals or aesthetes who pride themselves on their "autarchy." A person without the dimensions of depth and width—that is, without God and the other—is definitely lacking something in their existence as a human person. But inasmuch as the same individual experiences despair and horror in their isolation, that person thus reveals the very nature of their humanity, though cut off from its life-giving roots. If they would only open the "window" of their hearts, they would easily find their way to the world where meaning and value dwell. For I do not believe that Leibniz was right when he theoretically claimed that "monads" have no windows. Whosoever looks for windows will find windows.

And now to the second point, which concerns the human being's actual experience in life, in spite of Messers, Sartre, Kafka, et. al. It is true that rationally we have no arguments against the theory of the lonely individual who cannot prove the existence of a Thou (a theory called "solipsism" in philosophy). But stronger than reason is life itself. And here, are not proofs abounding? Who would not have experienced at one time or another the fact that no one can extricate oneself from the basic fellowship and co-responsibility with our contemporaries without some punishment, remorse, guilt-feeling, emptiness, frustration, and the like? On the other hand, who would not know the joy of sharing (and were it even sharing of suffering), the happiness of close interrelationship between people (reaching beyond the scope of one's own family which is but part of the ego). Have you ever experienced genuine love, sympathy, compassion, or that strange "feeling-together" for which we have no proper name? Do you know anything about loyalties and commitments, have you ever longed for companionship, a true talk, at night when the hidden compartments of the ego slightly open and allow a glimpse into the deeper and truer self? It might be called a true "meeting" in which loneliness and meaninglessness end. Have you ever served on some board or committee not for the glamor of publicity or the compensation of some inferiority feeling, but for a good purpose bigger than you, which requires self-forgetting and the dedication of your work for higher ends? Do I speak here an understandable language, pointing to a generally known reality? And if that is true and means happiness, how then can the opposite, the I-Philosophy, likewise be true?

There is no doubt that this I-Philosophy does contain a grain of truth, but at the same time it also contains a world of illusion. It presents itself to us as a great detour, a misinterpretation of humanity and the meaning of life. It is our contention that we have to return from this detour, in spite of all familiarity with it, to the main road, the one which is truer to reality and which leads to a foundation for a hopeful and positive design for living.

To this main road then, to the new philosophy of man, we now return. In contradistinction to the I-Philosophy just discussed, I propose to call it We-Philosophy. The name is rather new, but the essence is very old, as old as the Bible, each page of which gives witness to the neighbor (first mentioned in Lev 19:18) and the brother (mainly in the New Testament). Or we may even say it is as old as early human society if we trust anthropologists such as Lévy-Bruhl, who demonstrated so impressively a *participation mystique* among these primitive societies.[7] Nevertheless the idea of We-Philosophy has to be rediscovered for our time, newly formulated and newly argued about. This will be our programme for the rest of this chapter.

The main point here is a picture of human nature according to which we do not become truly human until we recognize our intrinsic and essential interrelatedness to or interwovenness with our fellow people. No *I* can truly "exist" without a *Thou* because this Thou actually constitutes that which makes a human being a real person. As long as we close our "windows" to the person next to us we do not really live. Any design for living by neglecting this basic datum will miss its goal. While the I-Philosophy, grandiose though it is, ends in some negative attitude such as pride, lust for power, hatred, contempt of man, despair, and nihilism, the We-Philosophy we contend is positive in its working, giving strength and self-assurance and in the final outlook redemption. Happiness roots in the awareness of

---

7. Lévy-Bruhl, *How Natives Think.*—Ed.

being needed (to paraphrase a word by A. J. Heschel), or as we also could say, it roots in the chance to respond to a Thou creatively.

More and more, our eyes become opened to this basic verity, not completely unknown heretofore and yet traditionally overlooked or minimized. Here in America it was, above all, John Dewey who first called to the attention of educators the social nature of the human being, to the basic "we" in all correct educational processes and all sound growth. "Shared experience is the greatest of human goods" became a maxim of Dewey's philosophy and subsequently of modern education in general. This is too well-known to need further elaboration. It is obvious that such type of upbringing does not mold strong "single ones," and cooperation during formative years takes away the taste for a (ruthless) "struggle for life" design. In the same line of re-orientation by our academic leaders belongs also the psychology of group-dynamics as begun by Kurt Lewin. It was he who introduced the important term "belongingness" into character description. It is somewhat akin to the older concept of loyalty (once so impressively presented by Josiah Royce). Pitiable the one to whom the feeling of belonging is foreign altogether. Have you ever met those shiftless persons in big cities who belong to nothing and to nowhere? They might be tramps, but you find them in fashionable hotels as well. They know little of the joy of togetherness, sharing, and mutuality. Love to them is just as passing and ephemeral as jobs or duties. No ties, no background, and no roots—who would not know this "flotsam" type, lured by the thrill of negation and adventure but dull for all constructive enterprise. Human beings are psychologically and metaphysically constructed so that they cannot refuse genuine "belonging" without grave punishment to their personal existence.

Strange phenomena of human "solidarity" do happen, proving that such solidarity and regard is stronger than all propagation to the contrary. We read the story of a French housewife during the last war who motherly cared for the young German soldier billeted in her house while her own boy was somewhere out in a trench or foxhole fighting against the Germans. There existed situations of "fraternization" across the enemy lines, let us say at a Christmas Eve, against all rules, just because men are bound to each other and it requires much mental conditioning and high pressure propaganda to make them hate and kill and do the many other things which contradict the educated heart. I know that nearly every soldier in the field experienced one or another story of that kind and they will stand out in his memory as a highpoint of life. *Solidarity* and *belongingness* are two strong supporters of the We-Philosophy here proposed.

Naturally, this we-attitude will not always prevail, and an internal struggle goes on in every human being between the old temptation called self-assertion, egocentrism, will-to power, or any other claim of being master to one self (on the one side) and the sometimes, but dim, awareness that the I is nothing as long as it neglects the Thou (on the other side). Of course, there are always flatterers and "friends" and courtiers of some sort who create the illusion of togetherness. But who would be deceived about their loyalty? Only in giving do we receive. Champions of toughness and self-reliance ("the strong man is strongest if alone," we read in Schiller's *Wilhelm Tell*[8]) will always oppose any deviation from the I-Philosophy until a moment arrives where its specious strength breaks down. The year 1929 was such a moment in America, the consequences of which are too well-known as to need listing here. Facing fifteen million unemployed (together with their relatives, nearly fifty million), an awareness of social responsibility and mutual dependency arose, largely unknown heretofore in America. And President Franklin D. Roosevelt could proclaim general approval in 1938, "During these past six years the people of this Nation have definitely said "yes" to the old Biblical question: Am I my brother's keeper?"[9] This "yes" (alas, it did not persist for too long) arose not primarily out of a motive of self-preservation; it was rather an awakening from a certain egotistic unconcern and the reliance upon a harmony which operates automatically. It failed, and human beings were being thrown, so to speak, upon fellow human beings as always happens in times of emergency. The self-sufficiency of the proud I is basically a myth or an illusion, not a reality.

There is an ever-expanding whole, of which we as individuals are a part: the beloved partner, the family, the group, the country and nation, and humankind. The more we mature, the wider the circle of our participation and concern will become, not only theoretically but existentially. The "we" is greater than the individual and is the root of the strength and joy and growth of this individual. The egocentric person has not much interest in others until their own crisis comes and they find themselves in need of understanding and sharing. Ambition and a competitive spirit are signs of a self-sufficient individualist with a certain nobleness, but kindness and

---

8 Schiller, *Wilhelm Tell*, 24.—Ed.

9. Friedmann notes the source as "Oklahoma City, July 9, 1938."—Ed.

courage in taking sides may be considered the features of the "We-Conscious" person.

Very well then. Let us, at least tentatively, accept this We-Philosophy until stronger motives come up to undergird it. But how, the skeptic might go on to ask, does such "We-Consciousness" operate, how do the I and the Thou come into contact as to make this contact real and existential? Certainly there are the conventional means of communication, the spoken and written word, but have we any way of knowing how genuinely they express what they pretend? Or to say it otherwise: how much do our words reveal, or as the case may be, hide? This is definitely a question that reaches beyond psychology. There does exist a contact between people which transcends common language, a sphere of sharing where understanding emerges, consciously or unconsciously, without words. Have you ever looked into the eyes of a child to understand what I am speaking about here? Such understanding, to be sure, is possible only to a loving, an educated heart. Not otherwise.

A famous little book has been written on this subject which deserves our particular attention, here as it contributes a good deal to this discussion. It is written by Martin Buber, the outstanding Jewish thinker, and its title is *I and Thou*. Strictly speaking it is not a philosophical book, at least not in the traditional sense. And yet, it achieves much in clearing up false concepts and ideas as far as human relations are involved. Buber begins by distinguishing between "I–Thou relations" and "I–It experiences." All traditional subject-object relations are of an impersonal, factual nature. They are I–It experiences, where the I is facing an object or thing. On the other side, all I–Thou relationships have the character of a prime datum, an immediacy of personal experience. The I–Thou relationship exists only as such a prime datum since it is of a non-conceptual nature, call it pure subjectivity or existential relation. It is an *Erlebnis*, to use the German term. "Without *It* man cannot live," Buber asserts, "but he who lives with it alone is no man."[10] Our very existent is rooted in the immediacy of the I-Thou experience, the Thou being anyone around the I, the beloved one, the companion of life, a friend, or any stranger whom we meet in an unconventional situation.

In a later, though no less stimulating, book called *Between Man and Man* (1948),[11] Martin Buber follows up these ideas. He begins with a statement strange and yet elucidating the depth of human relations: there exists,

---

10. Buber, *I and Thou*, 34.—Ed.
11. Buber, *Between Man and Man*, 3.—Ed.

he says, "a silence which is communication," a contact of I and Thou which he calls "a dialogue," though carried on without words, where people understand each other in the immediacy of the "meeting." Anyone who has some appreciation of the power of silence will agree that such "dialogue by silence" is no illusion; to the contrary, it can become a most enriching experience.

Buber is an irrationalist, and his way of thinking might not be open to everyone. Thus we propose to explore further into the wide field of We-Philosophy in order to discover its potentialities and contributions toward our search for a design for living. As far as has become known to me, only two philosophies of this kind seem to fit into this program deserving a discussion in this present context. The one can hardly be called a "philosophy" in the narrow sense, as it originated in the consultation room of a psychiatrist. And yet, it is fundamentally a most sound basis for all further discussions. I mean Fritz Kunkel's "We-Psychology," propounded in many fine and helpful volumes (perhaps the best, one of which is entitled *How Character Develops*, 1940, written together with Roy E. Dickerson). It is a provocative and healthy philosophy quite close to what is said in these pages: we mature inasmuch as we grow out of an earlier egocentrism into that we-feeling which awakes in us responsibility and concern. Very aptly the author distinguishes two layers in the "I," the true "self" which is part of a "we"—the root of all ethics and religion—and the "ego" or sham-I, which is a fooling agent in us, tempting and separating, a "shell" which firmly encases the self and almost prevents the self from achieving its true creativity. Egocentric persons are always rigid and not adaptable, since they live by the preconceived pattern that their ego is the very center of this life. Not until a crisis occurs will this shell be pierced through, at least for short moments, to release the creative strength of the We-conscious self. All our discourse on self-education would find confirmation in this We-psychology of Kunkel.

The other philosophy to be introduced here as a background for our vision of life's design is unfortunately not available in an English translation. It is William Stern's great work on personalism entitled *Person und Sache* (*Person and Thing*),[12] of which the third volume (1924) is devoted exclusively to a philosophy of value under personalistic perspective. Though lesser known and quoted, this book is, in my judgment, a profound elaboration of a We-Philosophy and We-metaphysics. It is not possible or necessary to give a detailed report of this work here but the point which really

---

12. Stern, *Person und Sache*.—Ed.

matters can be summarized in a short paragraph. Like Kunkel, Stern (who was head of the department of psychology at the University of Hamburg until 1935) also speaks not of egoism but of egocentrism as the great wall around the "I" which prevents the working of genuine values. The objective or "non-I" values are always present, waiting, so to speak, either to be accepted and taken into the "I," or being refused, leaving the "I" blind and ignorant of the world of "non-I" values. The absorption of the objective values into the personal unit that William Stern called very appropriately "Introception," which conceptually represents almost the center of value philosophy within the personalistic framework. Introception is that activity of the person which enables it to overcome isolation and solitude. It is an act by which the non-I values are "accepted" and fused with the values of the self. It means the affirmation that, basically, the values of the person and the objective values are one and the same.

Stern names five basic types of such Introception, namely: (1) love (both in its erotic and its spiritual connotation), as the absorption of the value of the other person, the Thou, into our own personal structure; (2) understanding, also called "appreciation by intuition" (*verstehendes Erkennen*), a term first developed by Wilhelm Dilthey for use in all interpretative activities (such as historiography, literary critique, art appreciation, etc.); (3) aesthetic sensibility (empathy); (4) sanctifying Introception, the religious longing toward the Introception of the divine into the person, or to say it otherwise, the opening of the soul to the divine spark; (5) practical Introception—that is, Introception as "first imperative" of all ethics and as basic principle of our creative designs. To love, to intuit, and to act ethically and creatively are the visible results of introceptive activities of the person who thus broadens and widens their own world until it coincides with a large part of the nonpersonal, non-I world.

The moral principle in particular is described by Stern as the fulfillment (or realization) of the Self *through Introception*. In these last two words we discover all the difference to the earlier discussed principle of "self-realization." There can be no realization of the Self, at least not morally, without this qualifying addition, "through Introception." All practical imperatives with the Self in the center, such as *carpe diem* (enjoy the day), "Be true to yourself," "Seek all your possibilities, or all your potentialities," "Provide yourself with maximal utility," and the like, are but sham-imperatives saying not much more than "act as you must act," or "as you find best for yourself." In all these cases the "I" is taken as the self-sufficient and self-sustained center into which the non-I values do not enter, at least not in any essential function. For a philosopher of Introception, however, such principles cannot suffice. They mean radical subjectivism, exaltation of the "I," as the German term runs, *Verichung*, making the I the only absolute. Egotism, in one way or another, seems to be the ulterior motive.

But its opposite is just as little acceptable; namely, the renunciation of the I altogether, its wiping out as something bad and even detestable, which in Stern's terminology is the *Entichung*, occasionally also called radical objectivism. Popularly this viewpoint is known as "altruism," the effacement of the I and the complete giving over of one self to sacrifice and service. Strictly speaking it means depersonalization, the killing of the very agent by which values are created or actualized. Thus it becomes obvious that altruism in this sense is definitely a false ideal of the old individualistic school which was ignorant of the idea of person and of the intrinsic nature of all I-Thou relations. In the decline of this kind of altruism both Kunkel and Stern thoroughly agree. Altruism is no moral ideal; in fact, no value at all, because it requires the extinguishing of the self (the bad and egotistic self, to be sure, the only one known to radical individualists). "Serve!" "Sacrifice!"—why and how? It would be poor service and poor sacrifice if no personal acts would stand in its background. Radical unselfishness is just what it says: the elimination of the self, an impossible and undesirable ideal, wrongly formulated. Altruism is foreign to the nature of the self (which is always an active agent); it represents a false selflessness, and for that reason will not be defended or even advocated in this present study. Personalistic We-Philosophy has but little use for the old alternative of "egoism-altruism," for it does not really answer the very problem of how to overcome the impasse of full egocentricity. Altruism cannot give meaning or significance to the self, and the truly altruistic person has no chance of growth and enrichment. No one wins by such a type of "moral" activity because it smacks of slavish humiliation. To make absolutely clear what we are aiming at, let us distinguish between the service by a tool, a machine, or a gadget (which all are absolutely selfless) and the service by people who by serving grow and enrich themselves and their surroundings.

The solution then is neither *Verichung* (making absolute the I) nor *Entichung* (wiping out the I), neither egotism nor altruism, but Introception, the transforming of all moral acts into genuine expressions of the person by accepting into it what is outside of it. Introception then is the fusion of the objective and subjective value into one, saying freely and joyfully yes to the non-egotistic acts. William Stern dares to formulate an ethical imperative: in its briefest form it just says, "be Introceptive," and in a more elaborate form it runs about as follows: "Transform your I into a personality by incorporating the service for non-I (non-personal) values into your individual self-value," or "Build up your life in such a way that your behavior in regard to objective values becomes an integral part of your self-realization." In a certain sense the old Stoic principle of sympathy experiences a rebirth here, on the plane of a personalistic and activistic philosophy. Only by organically integrating this objective element into our own "microcosmos" will this microcosmos become an agent of the fullest value-realization, a sensitive (and creative) person, an educated heart.

Perhaps someone will object here that "Introception" is just a name but does not in itself indicate any tangible act or attitude permitting detailed description, hence this entire philosophy might appear unrealistic and vague. To this only the following chapters will give an answer. In our vision such a dynamic concept which allows the synthesis of "I" and "non-I" on a personalistic level has a very tangible meaning: it is the magic by which out of an I and a Thou grows a We, a most real "We-experience" which has its justification in a transpersonal unity. Love, intuition, empathy, sharing, togetherness, belongingness, and solidarity-feeling—all of these experiences find a common denominator in this act of "Introception," or introceiving of that which is not "I" into the Self. As I see it, William Stern has given a philosophical foundation to Kunkel's we-psychology, namely the theory of expanding consciousness.

It is not until we accept the idea of Introception as an essential activity of the person that this person's existence becomes meaningful and positive. Thus the atomism of the individualistic society is gradually overcome without turning into an unhealthy collectivism (or mass-feeling) which on its part bagatellizes the individual. Individualism without the sense for Introception is empty and ends in crisis and confusion. Introception, to the contrary, ends isolation and solitude and makes personal life meaningful. Now we can see the possibility of an unfolding of the fullest personality because it finds its chance in an ever widening Introception. Self-realization, as first discussed, seemed to us not acceptable because it lacked guidance and directives. Now, after this long detour, it assumes a different meaning. It is through the principle of Introception that self-realization receives its new character, its quality as genuine service. Would not that be a possible design for living as we seek it?

PART 1: PREPARATION

Are Humans Good by Nature?

Human nature: what is it and how shall we understand it? Answers to these questions will no doubt deeply influence our position regarding the proper design for living, and our entire outlook on life and society. Therefore a brief discussion of what might be called "philosophical anthropology" ought to find its place in this section which deals with the preparation in our search for a design for living. In fact, the preceding chapter belonged in the same context, trying to understand one aspect of human nature—namely, its social interrelatedness to the neighbor. Now we continue in a somewhat different direction, asking how to consider human nature regarding the basic ethical categories of good and evil. Is the human being basically and by nature good or bad, or perhaps neither good nor bad, or both good and bad? Obviously this is a question of prime importance and we could hardly proceed without first clearing up an issue like this. If humanity is good by nature then what is needed is just good education and environment, and the ideal society might be just "around the corner." If, however, humans are basically beasts (and, alas, many signs today suggest such a judgment) then let us discard all such pleasant hopes, leave ethics to the utopians, and try to make the best of a world which is simply not built toward higher dreams. Ethical optimism and ethical pessimism are thus facing each other, both sides with strong arguments and likewise with their blind spots. Where then should we take our stand? Not until we have analyzed the two main positions will we be able to prove that there is much truth in this presupposition or belief.

Among the many ethical schools which belong to this type we may in the main distinguish two classes, the rationalists and the environmentalists. (1) The rationalists usually follow the arguments first presented by the great Socrates. Man is a rational being, hence good. He acts badly only because he was never properly instructed as to the good, in other words virtues can be taught. More than two thousand years later the "philosophes" of the Enlightenment formulated almost the same position. "Evil is ignorance," therefore enlighten the people and they will act the right way. What a noble and (as we know) at least partly effective belief! But as modern psychology has destroyed most of the pre-suppositions of this standpoint, namely the power of reason alone to change humanity and the teachability of virtues through enlightenment, we may leave the issue at this point and turn our attention to the other school of ethical idealism.

(2) The environmental schools are obviously much closer to our own understanding and enjoy greatest popularity today. Pestalozzi's words quoted above belong, as a matter of fact, to this class also. As I see it, we may subdivide it into two major schools, the archaistic and the futuristic schools, into those who see the natural goodness of humanity as something of the past, a Paradise Lost, so to speak, to be recovered only by a return to that earlier innocence; and into those who in contradiction expect the more perfect state sometime in the future when the evil conditions of the present will have been eliminated. The utopian strain in both visions is quite apparent. This world of ours is not good, therefore it should be changed, either by way of "going back" to the *Urstand*, the sinless natural state in the beginning, or by way of preparing a better future, a more perfectly organized society where the destructive tendencies of humanity would gradually whither away.

(a) The utopian-archaistic school goes back to Hesiod (800 BC) who let the world begin with a golden age, and then saw its decadence and deterioration going on and on. The most outstanding moral teachers of this school are three: Rousseau, Thoreau, and Tolstoy. To these men, civilization is the bad boy, the corrupting agent which has spoiled man's natural inclination toward goodness and cooperation (and one would think they were right). Rousseau's fight for a return to nature is well-known; history calls it the beginning of Romanticism, another term for mild utopian thinking. And yet, when we realize the truly wicked conditions of upper French society during the Old Regime we feel almost compelled to agree with Rousseau that society must be blamed and not humanity. But how could such corruption have ever taken place, since the human being in its natural state is supposed to have lived a life of innocence where nothing bad dwelt in its heart? Could Thoreau's retreat at Walden pond restore such innocence? Thoreau's book has delighted generations but has not prompted many to imitate the author's experiment. Moreover, after two years the idyll came to an end and civilization marched on, good or bad or both. And then the same idea sprang up again in far away at Yasnaya Polyana, in the mind of the great Leo Tolstoy. He too was disgusted by the corrupt aristocratic society of his time which he contrasted with the simple life of the Russian peasant, the *muzhik*. We shall learn more about this in a later chapter. Tolstoy himself tried to live in the way of the peasants, and in numerous works he advocated it as the solution for all social ills. But again, one must admit that obviously something was wrong with this idea as the simple life did not do much to improve morals and did not lead man back to the *Urstand*, the conditions prior to the Fall. The shepherd idyll of Rousseau and the peasant idyll of Tolstoy are definitely utopian as they misinterpret basic human nature.

Perhaps we should close this discussion by an illustration of what men of this type actually dream about. I am thinking here of the story *Ivan the Fool*, one of the lesser known but most delightful and precious folk tales of Tolstoy. Ivan was a simple peasant boy who could not be spoiled by any means. The chief-devil himself came up from hell to try all sorts of tricks and temptations on him, but in vain. Ivan was not taken in by them. For instance the devil made Ivan immensely rich with gold pieces everywhere around him. But to no avail. Ivan remained the pure fool in spite of all. Finally the devil gave up, shooting down into the abyss never to come again, thus leaving the world without temptations and without evil (this story is somewhat reminiscent of the story of Parsifal who likewise was considered a pure fool and therefore capable of redeeming the Holy Grail). The story is one of the finest that Tolstoy ever wrote, revealing perhaps his most fervent dream as to how people should and could be. But, alas, it reveals also the author's unrealistic idea of humanity, namely that the simple life of the country people can resist the "march of civilization" and overcome the temptations of the old Serpent. Who would not wish it to be this way? But hard experience has taught us otherwise.

(b) The utopian-futuristic school reverses this picture, seeing humanity emerging from a poor past and moving on to a society of perfection, call it "utopia" or "socialism" of some sort. Humans are basically good, but present day society prevents them from living up to this very nature. Hence society has to be remade, the environment has to be changed, and the golden age, the age of true freedom, will then be ushered in.

We may be brief on this topic. What these thinkers have to say about society as it actually appears is, in many regards, correct. Their "educated heart" made them see the ills and flaws of contemporary society. Who would not be familiar with all the evils entailed by unrestricted capitalism and laissez-faire greed and mutual distrust, wage slavery and slums, and many more such features? The misery of the underprivileged and their sullen existence has been described and lamented a thousand times; likewise the good-natured disposition of the ordinary person who just waits for its fuller development. And yet, the utopian strain is unmistakable here. In fact, Karl Marx classified his forerunners just by this quality as "utopian socialists," men like Robert Owen (with his New Harmony experiment in Indiana) and Charles Fourier (with experiments of his followers in Massachusetts), and all the rest. But what about Marx himself, who prophesized the emergence of humankind "from the realm of necessity (capitalism) into the realm of freedom (socialism)"?[13] He saw the misery of the working class in England, attributed it to the callousness of the entrepreneurs, and he envisioned a new day, free from greed and hatred, people cooperating with each other and free from any sort of economic slavery. That will become a happy society where all causes for evil acts will have vanished, and all will freely accept their mutual responsibilities in the common enterprise. In view of our more recent experiences should we not classify also this "scientific" socialism as utopian?

Finally we have to meet the Social Reformers, also representatives of the environmental school, less openly utopian as they are less radical, thinkers of high idealistic intentions but basically believing in exactly the same pattern. Human beings are good, provided they can enjoy a favorable environment. We owe much, indeed, to these humanitarian pioneers, and I do not want to take away from their unquestionable merits. Where would we be today without their great and selfless efforts? There is only one slight doubt in my mind whether the philosophy from which they started quite corresponds to actual conditions. A simple objection is at hand: people brought up and living under most favorable conditions are by no means free from evil urges and destructive tendencies. Education works certainly for restraint, and the mores of society provide a veneer of decent living. Joy and happiness reduce temptations to indulge in urges which slumber in the dark of the subconsciousness. But environment alone does not make people good or better. There will always be a flow of kind-heartedness among people, low and high, but goodness in the sense of moral value, the pursuit of a design for living as we are searching for, a mind directed by the highest endeavor which could stand the test of calamity and adverse situations, in short true goodness, has comparatively little to do with environmental conditions. For it is, rightly envisioned, a spiritual affair.

If the environmental school is right, then we will observe demonstrable moral progress and ethics will become a technical problem. No doubt, a modern hygienic school building is a far cry from the little red-brick schoolhouse of yore. Would we claim, however, that the students then and now are so much different in knowledge and education?

---

13. See Marx, *Capital*, Vol 3, part VII, ch. 48.—Ed.

There is much truth in the optimist's position regarding the natural goodness of humanity, or rather the potential for goodness, as I would prefer to say. But it is only half the truth. The "uncritical" idealist takes the basic fact of evil and the disruptive tendencies in humanity too lightly, or neglects them altogether in a high-flung vision. For the uncritical idealist, faith in the victory of goodness is so strong that there remains little room for an understanding of the working of the dark forces of the human soul. Moreover, the uncritical idealist contends that considerations of that kind would paralyze all those activities which serve humankind in one way or another and would thus deprive us of some of the finest achievements we glory in.

What of the assertion that human nature is evil? This is the reverse of the position just described. Here evil tendencies are taken with their full weight as something naturally given and incapable of being changed or wiped out. The human being is basically a beast or brute. This position I would call ethical pessimism. No doubt it has a realistic strain (just as the other ones had a utopian leaning), but it is a *bad realism* since it takes lightly or even denies altogether the goodness of humanity. It sees nothing but the dark side of human life. Of course such an attitude, actually as widely spread as the former one, will have serious consequences for the wisdom of living. Moral advancement is here denied or at least doubted and the advice is given: make your bed in this world as comfortable as you can, but be warned.

Representatives of this line of thought are innumerable; we will not try to classify them. Just a few of the better known and more influential thinkers might be mentioned here. Let our array begin with a great name: Machiavelli, author of the renowned essay, *The Prince* (1513). Books and books have been written, blaming, praising, and explaining him. He still stands out as the paradigm of all immoralism. If men were good, the argument runs, they would not need his advice and his rules of conduct. But unfortunately, they are not good, therefore they have to learn how to act from the great masters of political cunning, above all from Cesare Borgia, the tyrant. One has called this attitude a "realistic psychology," and we will leave it at that. Fifteen hundred years of Christianity had passed by but now the true nature of humanity was recognized and the behavior described which corresponds to such a nature. Expediency triumphed over morality and, to be honest, it has been doing so ever since.

More than one hundred years later, Thomas Hobbes produced his famous *Leviathan* (1656), another landmark in our story. *Homo homini lupus* (man is a wolf to man); this old Roman proverb received here its rebirth and vindication.[14] In the beginning, so we learn, there existed "war of all against all," exactly the opposite of what Rousseau has surmised as the original state of man. Thus government was needed, and by virtue of a strange "social contract," an absolute monarchy was established for the prime purpose of restraining the perpetual warfare of man. What a vision! Are we still to call it "realistic" sociology and psychology? If we study Darwin and Spencer, three hundred years later, with their wealth of information unknown to Hobbes, we find in principle the same idea or outlook. Life is such that the "law of the jungle" prevails. Going on continually is the struggle for life with its corresponding result; the survival of the "fittest" (with Machiavelli, it was the prince, with Hobbes it was the monarch). Spencer worked on his sociological system between 1850 and 1880, Darwin's great work came out in 1859, and Thomas H. Huxley's famous defense of Darwinism, his lecture *Evolution and Ethics*, was delivered in 1893. This is the period which climaxed a biologistic interpretation and justification of "ethical pessimism."

At about the same time Nietzsche produced his semi-prophetic message of a "master morality" over against a contemptible slave morality (namely Christianity). The strong man or superman is bound by no moral restraint, and Cesare Borgia, the monster of the Renaissance, finds his second vindication. Man the beast (and in particular "the blond beast") who would not be reminded with a shudder of the display of this "beast" in Nazi Germany, with all its denouncing of Christian principles and their call for restraint. We might also mention Oswald Spengler who expressly declared that man is a beast of prey, only less noble than the latter, which does not know any "pangs of conscience" like man.[15]

Also the psychology of Freud deserves to be mentioned in this context—a psychology, as everyone knows, that is widely accepted today. And yet, what a gloomy picture of humanity if we look through the glasses of psychoanalysis. The human being is not a rational being, but the product of a number of urges and drives, among them in particular the libido (in its different forms) and the death instinct or urge of destruction. It cannot be denied that there is a grain of truth in this teaching, revealing dark undercurrents in the depth of the human soul almost completely overlooked

---

14. See Hobbes, *Leviathan*.—Ed.
15. Spengler, *The Decline of the West*, xxii.—Ed.

heretofore. Naturally enough, Freud and his school have little regard for teachers of moral ideas, in fact they are suspicious of the motives of such teachings. I hardly need to say more about this trend. Nothing remains but to make a decision and take a stand, open-minded, to be sure.

In conclusion I want to present a counterpart to Tolstoy's folk tale of *Ivan the Fool*, which comes from Tolstoy's great contemporary antagonist, Dostoevsky. He, too, invented a sort of fairy tale although with just the opposite sign. It is called *The Dream of a Ridiculous Man*, and is found in the *Diary of an Author* (circa 1880). It tells us the following story. A man dreams that he is dead but that he escapes the grave and is flying to a distant star which, to his surprise, looks exactly like our earth, but is inhabited by a people totally ignorant of sin. In short, it is Paradise revisited. The "ridiculous man" is at first quite enthralled by this absence of evil, hatred, and lust. But soon he gets restless and tells these people of his own former experiences. "The end of it was that I corrupted them all. I became the cause of their fall." Now they learn to lie, at first only for the fun of it, but to like it. Then comes lust, jealousy, cruelty, then ambitiousness and the idea of property. In the end laws are invented and subsequently gallows. Lastly they discover science. They forget their former state of innocence and accept (even affirm) their present state of suffering. At this point the dreamer awakes and the story ends with a few philosophical remarks. What a gloomy tale. No devil could tempt Ivan, but one single man could corrupt an entire society, by "infecting" them, as he says, with his knowledge, or, as we might better say, by his demonic nature. We wonder whether it is a real fairy tale.

And here we are: Dostoevsky versus Tolstoy, Hobbes versus Locke, and so on. Who is right? Our list of ethical pessimists is a depressing array of great names and serious thinkers who assure us that they are describing nothing but "reality" as they see it. Their success, the general acclaim of their teachings, should make us think. Perhaps they are right after all? But how? Do they not mock at ethics and those who propose it? To them, ethics have not much meaning beyond the conventional mores of society, rules of a game, to make life bearable. Beyond that they doubt whether there is any wisdom in life, and their maxim is about like this: "Act as if everyone were your adversary." The theory of enlightened self-interest follows this pattern, too, rather closely, though camouflaging somewhat its harsh pessimism. We will call this position "bad realism." Just as the uncritical idealism took the fact of evil too lightly, so does bad realism bagatellize the fact of human goodness. To say it otherwise, the ethical pessimist or bad realist is blind to genuine goodness, apparent goodness (which he misunderstands), or the craving of the human heart toward such goodness. Good people can be corrupted, he thinks, but bad people cannot be made good. There is despair in this outlook, as no chance is seen for goodness and redemption. After all, what is goodness?

Now we move to an attempt to solve the dilemma. Good utopianism and bad realism apparently offer no satisfactory answer. The first alternative is false (neglecting the evil in humanity) while the second one is bad (minimizing the good in humanity). Where should we then look for a way out? Obviously, any compromise solution would not do it, such as: human beings are both a little good and a little bad. Or human beings are sometimes good and sometimes bad, and sometimes neither the one nor the other (humanity is a paradox). Is that closer to reality and does it solve the dilemma in which we find ourselves? American pragmatism is at the heart of the utopian type (John Dewey) while modern psychology by and large is of the type of bad realism (Freud, etc.). Many people, however, vacillate between these two positions and thus become confused and perplexed. That ethics and morality suffer under these conditions is only too natural. Let us search for the possible mistakes in all these theories which cause the dilemma. *First*, all these theories take humanity too much in a static way. The human being, they declare, is as it is and will always remain this way. Humans are good, humans are bad, or humans are now good and now bad, or more often bad than good or vice versa. I would think that such static conception of human nature misses the issue altogether, as will soon be demonstrated in detail. *Second*, nearly all these theories are strictly monistic in their essence, that is, they consider only one nature in human character and overlook altogether the inner struggle in the human mind which we all have to go through as long as we live. In fact, most of these theories presented show a naturalistic bias; even Rousseau, Thoreau, and Tolstoy, not to speak of Marx or the representatives of the environmental school. Likewise, the pessimists with their blindness to genuine goodness are most outspokenly naturalists as far as their world view is concerned. To them a term like "spirit" is taboo or just meaningless. They know little of the dynamic nature of the human being in whose mind a battle is going on, not so much between good and bad as between different levels of existence which exclude any simple monistic formula.

Let us then try to construct such a picture of human nature which would possibly solve our dilemma and lead us toward an answer usable in the search for a design for living as we understand it.

In the language of Aristotle we could speak here of an ever-ongoing movement "from potentiality to actuality." Not being but becoming is the nature of humanity. Life might be likened to a battlefield, or a pilgrimage (as Bunyan understood it). It is a great possibility rather than a settled condition. It contains the perpetual opportunity of change. If this change is for the worse, then we speak of corruption and "Fall," and if it is to a higher level, then we speak of conversion and may call this life "redeemed." Fall and redemption are poles apart, qualitatively, and have a meaning fundamentally different from the compromise formula: sometimes good, sometimes bad. In humanity can be found both god-like qualities and bestial ones. Humanity is potentially good, but is at all times under the sword of temptation; meaning that human beings want to rise upwards but may backslide at any moment. The struggle is going on as long as we live and any claim of security and possession is hypocrisy. There are victories as well as defeats. The defeats are not hopeless since a victory might still follow. A victory, on the other hand, means a gain not easily lost, a definite step upwards to a higher level.

In Paul's Epistle we read, "For ye were sometimes darkness, but now are ye light in the Lord: walk as children of light" (Eph 5:8). Symbolically this points to humanity's dual nature. In more secular language we could express it this way: two opposing forces work in people on two different levels: the natural one and the spiritual one. These levels are sets of value and value judgments, and they contain different understandings of the idea of goodness.

On the first, *the natural level*, we meet goodness in the form of gentleness, "natural kindness," and good-naturedness, but we meet evil tendencies as well, such as selfishness end even brutality. Natural kindness is, no doubt, something pleasant, but in the fire of testing it usually fails. If conflicts arise and temptations and difficulties of all sorts press upon the person, and things do not go as wished for, this kindness all too easily evaporates as it has no firm roots. Then we see the brute come to the fore and we forfeit all former claims to decency and goodness. Recent experiences with the people of Germany speak a language only too impressive. The Germans are known for their friendliness and kindness, and justly so. But then came not a "ridiculous man" as in Dostoevsky's tale, but a demonic and devilish man, and the same people performed acts of horror thought to be impossible. No rational instruction as such and no environmental improvements make human beings good, for goodness is a spiritual affair and must root deeper to deserve this name.

The ethics of this "natural level" does not pretend to satisfy the highest claims. Mores, decency, and gentleness are the values required here (we called them "minimum ethics" earlier). Santayana speaks with some pride of the "genteel tradition" once so strong in New England but now waning more and more. It did not prevent, however, the good merchants of Boston from their doubtful business of bringing "rum to Africa and slaves to America." Restraint or discipline is here called "inhibition," and is frowned upon (beyond a certain minimum). The production of higher values is named "sublimation," but it remains unexplained how the lower level may ever arrive at such sublimation as it is not cognizant of the higher level, according to the theory. In short, the natural level (in Paul's language "darkness") is the level so well described by the bad realists. Nobody will deny that there exists also a veneer of kindness and gentleness on this level, sufficient for everyday needs, but we would hesitate to call it true goodness.

Yet we know from our own experience and from the great moral teachers that there is another level, the second one, which we might call *the spiritual level*. It is the level of the higher values and of that goodness which does not evaporate in the fire of testing. It is the level of human conscience, the level of the "ought" of all ethical imperatives, the level where the brute inside is overcome by the light that derives from the divine. It is the locus of true values. On this level the individual becomes a real person, the center of value realization and value appreciation. Here we recognize self-discipline, even sacrifice. And here we meet true goodness that is the kindness of the heart which stands up in trying situations and transforms humanity and the world.

Neither utopian idealism nor bad realism answer correctly the question of human nature. In our vision it is the dynamic and dualistic viewpoint which leads us out of the dilemma and which we will call here *good realism*. It knows the grains of truth in both former positions but does not mix them up into a neutral composite. Rather, it synthesizes them under the idea of an ongoing struggle, in which human beings (divining the higher level of values) crave after that which they have not yet attained. It means the burning up of the lower forms of goodness and their change into something transformed and absolutely meaningful. Only under this assumption do changes become conversions.

Good realism believes that every person has potentially some of this higher or true goodness inside. Dostoevsky, certainly a witness to the demonic and bad, does not tire of picturing this higher goodness in even the lowest person. And he speaks from experience gained while serving time in a Siberian jail, although completely innocent. In his stirring *Memoirs of a Death's House* he describes his fellow criminals in all their dullness and, surprisingly, also their genuine goodness. The scene in which the convicts undress for their weekly bath and tactfully help the newcomer in the difficult manipulation of the chains around his ankles is simply unforgettable. It made Dostoevsky almost a new man, and it taught him a lesson that light shines even in deepest darkness.

Humanity is not "naturally" but "spiritually" good in the proper sense of the word. But this goodness is not a static quality or possession. We are continually under the temptation of falling back to pride, anger, hatred, or (at the least) to thoughtlessness and laziness of the mind (lesser evils, though evils nevertheless). At the same time, however, we are also continually driven upward by higher endeavors that we may reach that level where a meaningful design for living becomes possible.

We have learned two things in the last two chapters concerning human nature. First: the eternal interwovenness of human beings with the being and concerns of their fellow people, the quality which we may call the social nature of the "I" or person, and second: the human place between two levels or realms where any static answer is impossible and where life becomes a great challenge and a great opportunity. With such insight gained we might now proceed further on in our search for a proper design.

Chapter 3

The Ascent to the Problem

A Great Confession

Our preparatory meditations have come to an end. We have learned something about the basic preconditions for any sound solution to our problem, namely self-education, "We-Philosophy," and the recognition of the dual nature of humanity. Our ascent may now begin, climbing so to speak, to higher levels of spiritual life and to new vistas, where the harsh realities of life take on a new meaning.

What do we actually mean when speaking throughout these pages of a "design for living"? Would it not greatly simplify our task to speak rather of ethical or moral behavior instead of the somewhat involved figure of "design"? The path of ethical theories and moral wisdom is well trodden and worked out, and this word would be fine if only people would be ready to listen to these theories and to this wisdom. But this is just the theme of our concern. Apparently there is a very definite distinction between "ethics" and "design," the former being rational, theoretical, and impersonal, a system of "oughts" to be accepted and followed after having been demonstrated; while the latter has something to do with life in its actuality, its conflicts, shortcomings, preferences, and bewilderments. In the "design" question another type of reality is implied than in philosophical ethics, which makes this discussion so urgent and alive. Today it is sometimes called an "existential" question. It has to do with the problem of how to fill this earthly path of ours with some meaning and purpose in view of all that which stands against it, or to say it more succinctly: it is the problem of how to make this life a positive venture.

What is good? What is evil? Whatever answer we could propose, for somebody it would be but relative and unconvincing. Why should we choose the good rather than that which, though labelled "morally not good," is yet actually practiced and enjoyed by everybody (while the so-called "good" is condescendingly relegated to the Sunday School class)? What do we expect from life after all? Here we live. Unasked for, we came into existence—now let life take its course and make the best of it. Thus most people would say (like Nietzsche's Last Man), and they would shut their eyes from the more unpleasant and complicated aspects of human existence, somewhat like the proverbial ostrich who buries its head in the sand. Is there truly any tangible meaning in this life, and must it be looked for only in that area which is called "good"? And if so, can such high meaning truly be achieved?

Crucial questions, indeed, which defy any quick answer. It is hardly adequate to say, "I did not ask for this life, but now let us make the best of it, eat, drink, and be merry." Human life seems after all to be more than a mere play of nature, bound by its laws or perhaps by its whims. If it were just this, then why go on when life ceases to be a pleasant play? Why face untoward circumstances of all kinds and yet carry on, as people actually do, often courageously and even daringly? Contrary to popular bias, life is more than a mere biological necessity or chance. There is a deep-rooted cry in the human "heart" that asks for meaning, significance, purpose, and "design," in spite of all scientific claims to the contrary. Actually, this search for meaning is our first question, elusive as it is. Most likely it is unanswerable in a strictly rational way. And then there lurks, hidden and yet real, the one dark fact of living—that all life comes to an end at an unknown point, namely death. Biologically it is very "natural," but for the thinking and feeling person such an answer is hardly satisfactory. There is obviously something in us that reaches beyond nature. We might call it value or (still more general) "spirit." It defies scientific explanation, but it is there nevertheless. Our great question: "why carry on, why be good, why risk life for the sake of goodness?"—this cannot be answered by pointing to processes of the body. Naturalism, in its rash simplification, does not offer at all a fitting approach to so urgent and profound a concern as ours. One has to broach the subject from the inside, from the point which we have called "the educated heart," and not from an outside which knows only the necessities of the laws of nature. The business of living is either a problem of a philosophy of the spirit, or it is no problem at all. For only such a philosophy seeks the justification of the good primarily in the human thirst for meaning and design, in spite of affliction, need, and death (and in the face of them).

I would hardly know a better way of approaching this subject, the wisdom of living and the discovery of meaning where there seems to be none, than to study one of the great confessions of all ages. It is here as it has been the case before that we can learn a great deal from Leo Tolstoy, a man who honestly fought his life battle without a mentor, without any help from outside, but with a frantic determination either to discover the answer, or to end a life which presented itself so problematically. When he was about fifty-one years old, in 1879, he wrote and published a small but heavy book entitled *My Confession* which was soon suppressed by the Tsarist regime. It made its way nevertheless and today is, to us, one of the very great human documents. It was Tolstoy's first non-fiction book, the beginning of his religio-ethical activities. One need not agree altogether with Tolstoy's otherwise radical conclusions in order to profit a great deal from this honest story of an inner conflict, almost approaching the greatness of St. Augustine's similar-though-more-elaborate document. It is in Tolstoy's relentless self-analysis that we experience the depth of human conflicts and problems which forbid any cheap answer. Tolstoy knew only too well the conventional morals or, rather, mores, and lived accordingly—until he recognized their insincerity. Our ascent to the problem of a design for living could not be better started than with a study of Tolstoy's *Confession*, cursory though this study will be.

For nearly fifty years Tolstoy had lived with an enviable peace of mind. He was wealthy, educated, happily married, with a large and healthy family, he himself likewise endowed with great bodily strength and an alert mind. His success as an author was uncontested. *War and Peace* and *Anna Karenina* were read all over the world. Then slowly things changed for no visible reason. The figure of Levin in the second novel portrays partly this rising unrest in Tolstoy's mind very well. Though a master in psychology when portraying the characters of his novels, he never before was concerned with self-analysis, with the question of how to justify the kind of life he was living. To understand this crisis, one should not forget that the fact of death (or rather of dying) always loomed in the background of Tolstoy's consciousness. The conventional life, with religion and morals, accepted by Tolstoy without much thought, was now questioned. Success, pleasure, happiness—these do not answer those fundamental questions mentioned above which were now visualized by Tolstoy for the first time, when he had reached what one could call the peak of human life. Doubt crept into his mind, and a cynicism regarding accepted values became rampant. He saw the untruth of conventional morals and religion, and detected hypocrisy in his aristocratic circles, which condoned social evils but appeared very moralistic to the outside. A fanatic urge to be honest with himself made the continuation of this kind of life impossible. With the whole impetus of his character he throws himself into the search for meaning and justification of life as it is, stripped of all conventional disguise and delusion. Why should I go on living, he asks, if all life is terminated by death and no one knows what happens then? His search was relentless and rational, with the intent to accept a negative verdict rather than a cheap answer.

"My life stood still," so he reports, because he could not detect any meaning in it. Neither family life, literary success, religion (the Orthodox Church), nor art and aesthetic enjoyment could lead him out of this dilemma. Suicide, perhaps, was the only answer (and not few nihilists of that time went this way of desperation), and yet a healthy instinct kept him from committing such a foolish deed. It warned him that there might be some faults in his reasoning, in spite of all his honesty, and suggested that he might have missed some points not yet scrutinized.

Thus he started his inquiry toward an answer to the question, "Is there meaning in my life which would not be obliterated by the inescapable death of my existence?" First he inquired of the different sciences (it was the period when Darwinism had become prominent), but no answer could be received from people who studied extraneous facts and processes. Science tells us of laws, but not of meaning. Thus he was directed to inquire of the philosophers, who are the presumed experts in such matters of metaphysics. Naturally enough, he had to eliminate first all "ivory-tower" philosophy; only thinkers who were concerned with life itself could possibly answer his query. But, alas, he did not find much help from them either. He studied intensely; Socrates, Schopenhauer, Solomon—the "wise man" of the Old Testament (the King James Bible calls him Ecclesiastes or the Preacher)—and finally Buddha, the Indian sage. But again, all wisdom which these men taught was negative and of no avail in his search. It was clear-cut nihilism, and a rational denial of any meaning that would allow an affirmative living. Socrates does not resist his death sentence and does not try to flee; death to him is no dread. Perhaps the next life will be even better than this. Schopenhauer, the "pessimist," finds salvation only in a possible denial of the will (to exist), in a termination of all urges and drives which mean nothing but suffering. "All is vanity," says the Preacher, "what profit hath a man of all his labor which he taketh under the sun?" (It is worth reading this book of Ecclesiastes as a whole, to grasp the problems with which he and untold generations with him have struggled.) And then, Gautama Buddha, the young prince of India, who so painfully discovered that suffering is the law of life. Though the story is fairly well-known, we shall briefly mention here his three famous outings from his palace. When he left his splendid residence for the first time to drive out among the people of the city he met an old and frail man with no teeth, who looked appalling. The prince who was ignorant of old age inquired and was told that all men face the same fate and that there is no escape from it. Gautama was saddened and bewildered by this experience. Then he undertook a second trip out, much against the order of his father, who wanted to keep him away from all ugliness and darkness of life. This time he saw a sick man with swollen limbs, trembling and helpless. Again he asked and again he learned that at times everybody might be stricken with sickness, since it is a general affliction of the human race. He, too, might fall sick at any moment. This news dispelled his joy and he returned only to try a third time to experience the world. This time he sees a dead man, something heretofore unknown to him. "Is this the fate of all men?" he asked and his fear is confirmed. By now he has experienced enough to understand the principle of life. Though brought up in glamour and joy, he now knows that old age, sickness, and death contradict every pleasure-philosophy, and therefore that life is fundamentally nothing but suffering. The only way which the soon-to-awaken Buddha will teach is to forego the thirst for life, to deny the will to live, until one reaches the point where one will enter Nirvana, the complete dying away or dissolution of the individual personality. Life is an evil and one has to seek ways and means to free oneself from it, and that is (in brief) the moral of the story.

"It is no illusion," Tolstoy concludes, "all is vanity. Happy is he who is not born; death is better than life; one has to redeem oneself from it." Obviously, science and philosophy could not answer his query. On the contrary, nihilism and pessimism seem to be the inescapable answers.

Then Tolstoy took a look at life as it passed before his eyes, the life of his own circles, to be true, with which he was more familiar than with that of the lower classes. And what did he see? Ignorance (the way of the ostrich), Epicureanism, Nihilism (including suicide), or simply weakness, where man sees the hopelessness but does not draw the consequences.

He accused himself of belonging to this last mentioned group, though he admitted that somehow he had a dim notion that the "consequences" (to make an end of this life), which seemed to be so logical and rational, were yet somewhere at fault. "Life is an evil without any good sense, yet, I live . . ."

How can this be? What makes a person go on living after the recognition that both reason and praxis reveal no meaning whatsoever. *Religion*, as he knew it in the Orthodox Church of Russia, was not acceptable to him because it would require a denial of his reason or common sense. *Art*, the aesthetic value, proved to be powerless in all situations of a grave nature; he later even denounced it as leading away from the things that really matter. "The more a man loses his moral sense the more he becomes aesthetically sensitive." *Family and social* (conventional) *life* likewise are not enough to satisfy the human thirst for a meaningful existence. The prime fact of human mortality has not been conquered, and any form of escapism is inacceptable for the morally awakened one. Thus Tolstoy passed through great despair.

The faith that Tolstoy thus discovered was as yet unformulated, more a condition of the heart than a creed of the intellect. It was patterned after the simple faith, meaning here trust, which the working people of Russia, the toilers of the soil, and the craftsmen, so decidedly showed when watched at close quarters. Though their life is hard, full of privations and poor in the joys of ease, though they are downtrodden and exposed to many afflictions, they are yet of good cheer, kind-hearted and willing to help each other. Tolstoy tells us of his discovery of (and later intimate contact with) the sages and saints of this social stratum, how they seem to know the meaning of this life, never consider such foolish thoughts as suicide (with which nihilists in all countries like to play around), and live by a great inner certitude that theirs is the true faith. But what kind of faith after all? It is an existential faith, we might say, not a doctrinal one. They know themselves to be in God's hand, and well guided as long as they stay in this trust. Privations and hardships are no counter-arguments because they do not demand and expect a gift of amenities from life. Life is a task to be fulfilled with a pure and trusting heart, with love for the neighbor and thanks to the Creator for what is allotted to each person. "Faith," Tolstoy learned from those people, and we learn from him, "is the knowledge of the meaning of life by virtue of which we do not destroy our life but carry on living," victoriously, as I would like to add. It is a confidence or trust, and defies any conceptual formulation. It is "the reason of the heart," to use Pascal's well-chosen term.

I think that Tolstoy is quite correct in his emphasis of the non-rational, non-conceptual character of this faith (which alone answers the question of meaning). No rational theory is able to answer in a final way questions of value and meaning. Reason is good for any strictly scientific activity, including philosophy, but the value of life and its design can be grasped only in this other way which Tolstoy rightly calls faith, and whose nature can best be characterized by the timely word "existential." It means a spiritual reality in our mind.

Meaning of Life and Meaning in Life

The study of Tolstoy's *Confession* has not been without profit. We have come to face, in a most personal fashion, the human concern for *meaning*. All further wrestling of Tolstoy centered on the clarification of this fundamental idea; and we do not go wrong to say that the same holds true also for all the other great men we have chosen as our models: Schweitzer, Kagawa, Gandhi, and so on. Meaning is the concern of humanity, meaning of life and in life. Make a person's life meaningless and they cannot carry on by any means. In Russia, a country always full of contradictions, they invented particular tortures for their convicts. They had them do meaningless things such as building a brick wall and then, when finished, tearing it down again; or pouring water from one bucket into another one, and then back into the first one, and so on. After a while someone in a situation like that tends to become desperate and finally becomes confused. Sisyphus of Greek mythology suffered similar penalties and pains. Human beings can stand much privation, torture even, and spite; but we cannot stand in any way a life completely emptied of meaning. It would mean madness. Old people, retired and without any duties, often experience similar troubles—though the giving of meaning is an internal affair and quite independent from external conditions. Meaning, I would say, is a person's great opportunity, and we are fooled if we run after the goddess Fortuna, money or sex or power, or merely after fun, and never learn to make the moment significant. Tolstoy once told of an old monk whom he visited. He had been paralyzed for twenty years and hardly capable of moving his head. But there was sunshine in his mind and much smile in his eyes so that everybody who visited the saintly man left strengthened and assured that life is something positive, even if reduced as much as in this case. Who could not multiply such examples?

There were the inmates of German concentration camps. Everything seemed to be lost, hopeless despair crept into the hearts of the many; life was extinguished even though the body continued somehow to exist. Yet there is no body without mind, and this mind is extinguished only if we lose "faith" (in the above sense). More than one story is told about men and women in these camps who kept high in morals and did not surrender spiritually, being aware that no matter how gloomy the situation may be, it is in the last analysis, not the situation but the individual, who makes it either significant or empty. Enough—it should be clear by now that meaning depends exclusively on an inner attitude and derives from the riches of man's heart. Meaning is of such nature that it can be realized at any place, time or situation. Generally speaking, it belongs to what E. Stanley Jones so aptly called "victorious living."[1]

We should keep in mind that life is neither good nor bad, but an opportunity. We can do something with it in whatever situation, for human beings are more than passive sufferers of fate or onlookers of destiny. There is no way of shirking responsibilities and letting others make things meaningful or not. Life is definitely a challenge, leaving it up to us to make the "best" out of our existence and to give it the most positive contents possible; in short, to make it rich. Truly enough, there are always some people who throw it away lightly, out of despair or boredom or plain confusion. Russian Nihilists and Roman Stoics made it even a virtue and a matter of pride. Modern Cynics likewise praise such an act and call it great. But the error in all these cases is apparent. In fact, it is more than error: it is sin and offense, a basic denial of life and its latent possibilities which the denier just cannot see. Denial of life is inner bankruptcy, a refusal of trust and a blindness to life's real issues and chances. For life is, as we said, a challenge rather than a ready content, and such a challenge requires our intelligent response. Neither optimism (a shallow philosophy) nor pessimism (a false philosophy) correspond to reality, which is actually neutral. The alternative is overcome by the activity of the human mind and heart, which shapes the situation and is even responsible for it. Faith, thus defined, means the vision that life is an opportunity to live meaningfully at whatever point at which the individual might stand. Human temporality—life's termination at an unknown point—seems to be no valid counter argument, for meaning, significance, or design, as it is something timeless and ever present or possible.

---

1. See Jones, *Victorious Living*.—Ed.

We would do well to distinguish at this point the related and yet different terms *meaning* and *purpose*. They are usually taken as interchangeable; philosophers even use the Greek term *teleology* for their common characterization. It is not quite appropriate to do so. Purpose presupposes an end or aim to be reached, hence if the movement toward it is cut short, say by early death, it never becomes realized. A work of some kind might thus become thwarted and the great purpose, unfulfilled, looks almost tragic in its fragmentary realization. Meaning, on the other hand, has a different connotation. There is no end or aim to be reached in time, because there is an ever present possibility of making the moment rich and significant, filled with the value of kindness or valor, with victory over vexations, or with the new faith in life's worthwhileness. It means reaching a different and new level beyond the determinants of nature or society, a great sort of one's finest and most sovereign freedom. Such meaning, then, is independent of time, and death is not a counterargument to it. Let the light of your heart shine, and you have done your share. Meaning, so conceived, is like the underlying theme in a great piece of music, say a sonata by Beethoven. It is there in every measure and yet not recognizable until the last beat has been heard. Who would call Schubert's *Unfinished Symphony* thwarted or a failure only because it remained incomplete? When can life ever be called complete? Meaning, we might say, is like a *Leitmotif*, it runs through the entire life and requires nothing but a sensitive ear to grasp it and a determined mind to realize it. Meaning is a creative element in our existence, though never separable and to be cultivated in itself. It is life's idea, personalistic, unique, and yet communicable by every turn of our doing and non-doing. This concept is decidedly the spiritual element of our existence. Biologically, we live under the necessity of nature, but spiritually, however, we are free unto the filling of our human existence with a meaningful contents, big or small, strong or weak, but always positive and active. The human being is never a victim, though not always a victor.

Human beings have a genuine thirst for meaning. Without meaning, the specter of Nihilism lurks in each corner (today's French Existentialisms might serve as an example). Meaning is the very content of all values, if they are only genuine. It is at this point, therefore, when talking of a life filled with meaning, that the ethical problem arises. More will be said about it in the next section.

Meaning has several connotations: (a) it might indicate, for instance, the function of the part in the whole. If it is only a whole one can recognize this function even in a torso, a fragment. Look at the unfinished Sculptures of Michelangelo and one can grasp the master's intentions even though the shapes are but hinted at. This first connotation is particularly pertinent in history. We speak of the meaning of Caesar within the whole of Roman history, but we are not yet quite sure of the meaning of our own times within Western civilization as this is still an ongoing process, open to creative response.

(b) Meaning might also indicate the "idea" or "formula" of a person's life. Thus, it represents the thing that matters most in this particular life. Everyone feels joyous when one day, one is lucky enough to discover such a formula in one's own existence. When Albert Schweitzer discovered his great principle of "reverence for life" while wistfully lounging on an African steamer which worked its way carefully through a herd of huge hippopotamuses, he rejoiced. Now he knew what he had been striving for all his life, now he had found "his formula," expressing the most profound personal meaning of his existence. Here we can easily distinguish between genuineness and illusion, or worse: hypocrisy. The hypocrite wants only to appear as such and such, but whom does he delude?

(c) Meaning is also contained in every value as it becomes realized, or in other words, realized values are bearers of meaning. In particular, meaning has to do with the acceptance of responsibility of some kind. Selfishness and egocentrism forfeit the possibility of filling life with such meaningfulness. An amoral life, playing around in one fashion or another, will fail both in meaning and value, even though society might not notice it at first. Here again Tolstoy's little masterpiece, *The Death of Ivan Ilyitch*, might serve as an instructive lesson. Selfishness, in the last analysis, is fooling one self, trusting in things which but feign meaning, yet never will create life-giving values. True meaning, which is also true value, is to be found only in what could best be called "dedicated work," work for its own sake, whatever it may be.

Nothing is more dangerous than cheap smugness and contentment. It is one of the big snares of the easy life, with gadgets and all the rest. Smugness means shirking the issues, forgetting life's tensions and dilemmas and taking lightly what actually challenges one's best potentialities. There exists always the possibility of forfeiture, missing one's personal opportunity, spiritually speaking. The repeatedly mentioned concept of self-realization shows here all its ambiguity. It might and can mean something highly meaningful (if formulated as in the earlier chapter on We-Philosophy), but it might as well just mean self-centeredness, and then miss altogether the quality of value realization or meaning. That pleasure (the old hedonistic principle) likewise is lacking of meaning and hardly needs any further commentary.

Meaning is the sustaining principle in our life. It is true that it does not lend itself easily to ordinary discursive thought. The naturalistic thinker, psychologist, biologist, will hardly show interest for such a principle. For it implies a particular, though most vital, philosophy of value which is foreign to the extraneous viewpoint that approaches our own self as if it were just an interesting piece of nature, studied in laboratories. Meaning is always "firsthand experience" (what the Germans call *Erlebnis*) and not a rational idea. I have not defined this principle but only tried to describe it. In fact it defies any sharp logical definition like all great principles of life. To fill this life with meaning is our real task and responsibility, and to neglect it may be called a crime against life, or rather a great sin. Of course this task is not an easy one and requires much determination and trust. That, however, is only natural since the value of life always stands in a direct ratio to the price we are willing to pay.

Ethics and Design for Living

This book is supposed to be an essay on the art of living, something which otherwise is called *Ethics* (if scholarly presented) or *Morals* (if stated as practical wisdom). But thus far we have explained nowhere what "ethics" actually means to us and how those principles which were discussed in earlier chapters might fit into an ethical theory of general validity. Actually, the book has been not too emphatic thus far on rational theories, fine and even compelling as they otherwise might be, because all theories remain necessarily aloof from real life. Our orientation, however, is not theoretical but existential, which means that we are interested in values only inasmuch as they become actualized in the life of a person and thus assume meaning for this person. Life's processes and concerns are understood neither as purely theoretical nor as purely practical. Necessarily they contain an element of "ought," since values are involved which condition our very existence; in this regard our approach has to be "meta-empirical." On the other hand we are facing living people with their strivings and foibles, and in this regard an element of practical psychology comes into our approach and determines it, too. Let us remember that we belong to two worlds, the world of the natural (with its urges, appetites, etc.), and the world of meaning and value which would best be called the "spiritual" world. We have always to keep this duality in mind in order to understand that we find ourselves everywhere in a situation of tension and conflict. Perfectionism remains a distant ideal of legendary saints. All philosophical ethics shows a certain aloofness to life proper, which makes its teachings find but seldom compliance with everyday practice. On the other hand, moral teachings sound fine and are connected with our practical behavior, but they tell us little about motivation and struggle and possible pitfalls. They classify life too much into good and evil, do's and don'ts. We listen, and then, in most cases, go our way without being prompted to the new experiment.

These meditations then lead us to attack the subject of the right art of living from a new angle; namely, that of our thirst for a meaningful life, for something that enriches life and makes it more worthwhile and lastingly satisfactory. Now that we have studied the famous "cage" of Tolstoy's inner struggle we might better appreciate our eternal wrestling toward meaning and its realization. And that is exactly the subject of "Ethics" rightly understood. To us, *Ethics studies the ways in which it is possible for the individual person to actualize those values which make life meaningful*. Or still briefer: *Ethics states the way along which the individual can actualize the meaning of their life*, (assuming that life is built unto meaning, allowing its actualization, imperfect though it might be).

"Ethics of Design" and "Ethics of Law" (the more customary form of ethical teachings) are poles apart. The latter is definitely rational, while the former usually takes recourse to the human conscience which defies further analysis. Right and wrong, good and evil, these are the main issues of rational ethics and moral philosophy. Human conduct should be "right", and we should do "good" regardless of the situation involved. But concepts are one thing, and our existential being, the value-orientation of our life in its totality, is another. Too often we judge only single acts or deeds in their isolation and emphasize external conduct as it "ought" to be. The development of life as a whole, on the other hand, with its inner attitudes and design, finds very little attention, and the often-desperate struggle toward its fulfillment is still less considered in traditional ethics. But just this should actually be of most vital interest, as it touches our entire being and yearning and determines our victories and defeats.

It must, however, be admitted that there is a totalitarian claim in such a "design." It runs through all of life, existentially (that is concretely), and not only in an abstract fashion, as an "ought" which we always remember, yet only too often avoid. Good or evil, right or wrong are terms of traditional ethics or morals, while "design for living" requires a different vocabulary. Life according to such "design" is more or less meaningful, superficial or profound, genuine or confused (hypocritical, feigning, posing), a failure or a victory (even in tragedy). Ethics and Design show the difference between doing and being. Hence our concern in an earlier chapter for self-control and self-education, that we finally might become what we strive to be. If I only do "acts" and am not the personality thus represented, then can an act, thus requested and performed, really be deemed good, or valuable, or meaningful? The justification of the good which I ought to do (and actually may do) is its quality of meaningfulness or significance, both for my own personal life, and also, by virtue of our social interrelatedness, for the social group which participates. "Love, and do what you want"[2]—this great word of St. Augustine beautifully represents the principle here discussed. This is "design," and it applies to being rather than to doing.

Every person has their own peculiar potentialities and no general prescription is possible. Thus our principles have to stay flexible. Be true to yourself, your best self, and you will know what is required from you. Or shall I better say: and you will know what makes life meaningful for you in a maximal way? No ethics of law can ever help you find your genuine "design", though it might be practical in the conventional sense. Likewise "self-realization", if not supplemented, cannot guide the individual either because it lacks the existential emphasis on meaning.

Ethics, we said, tells us something of the way along which we can realize our truest meaning. Could this possibly imply acts of a criminal, a mad dictator, a great embezzler, or the like? Hitler perhaps could have claimed such strange justification (confused as he actually was). It is already obvious here, and will become still clearer later on, that no such misinterpretation is possible. We definitely stated that meaning and any form of egocentrism are absolutely contradictory. The great evildoer might claim to fulfill just his deepest meaning—but it is, if not downright hypocrisy, then self-delusion. Evil-doing is always self-centered, and as such fooling, forfeiting meaning. Have you ever seen the criminal happy and satisfied? He is rather haunted, stepping deeper and deeper into the vicious circle of not only hurting others, but above all destroying himself. Hence, there is no danger of misinterpreting the formulation of this chapter, the theme of this

---

2. Augustine, *Confessions*.—Ed.

book. What we call the spiritual life, the actualizations of values, cannot be fully demonstrated by reason; and yet everybody can distinguish between what is genuinely meaningful and what only pretends or claims to have such quality.

There is a very simple criterion to find out whether someone is honest in their value-attitudes or not. We need only to be mindful that everybody is willing to sacrifice certain goods in favor of those things that matter most to them. The test then consists of just this: watch what a person is ready to give up and for what ends they are doing it. It is also a way to test oneself. Look at your own behavior and you will soon discover that you actually forego many things in order to gain others or to achieve something else. You might sacrifice your time, your sleep, your work, for something which is not of any immediate utility—and you might ask yourself: Why am I doing this? Moreover, you or anybody else might give up a job, comfortable living, health, and under certain circumstances even life—in favor of something valued higher than these goods. And this something is the thing that matters most to you or to the one whom you watch. Remember only that every giving is in itself indicative of the implied intention, and every renunciation a symbol that reveals the state of mind of the one who renounces. It might be worth pondering this question: Have I (or has my friend) ever been willing to give up something, or have we been only talking of such acts? Remember that the "amoral" person, described in Chapter 1, is not willing to do so (and he is a person of otherwise good intention) and he was not even aware of a need for it. It is here that self-education might set in. But one final word has to be added to make this test unequivocal. The things which we forgo must also be forgotten and the sacrifice which we take upon us must be done without regret—otherwise it is no sacrifice, no genuine giving. If you either feel sorry for the act or boast of it, then it loses its character as a criterion or symbol. These then seem to be the simple and very evident rules of spiritual life, hardly to be challenged by anyone not unfamiliar with such life.

We might best conclude this chapter by condensing its sum into another antithetic formula. The Ethics outlined in these pages distinguishes itself from conventional or traditional forms of moral teaching by its radical or totalitarian claim. I do not intend to appear here as a fanatic, but there are good reasons for contraposing a *Maximum Ethics* to the usual *Minimum Ethics*. These reasons root deeply in the seriousness of the business of living. An example will make it clear. The *Golden Rule*, or for that matter the *Decalogue*, represents, in my view, a type of minimum ethics. And so does *decency*. It is a necessary requirement, no doubt, to safeguard an orderly and pleasant living together, somewhat comparable to the rules of a game. But nobody would claim that these principles or rules are life-giving, providing meaning to human existence, justifying the truly good which stands in the center of all ethics. On the contrary, the Sermon on the Mount, purposely exaggerating in its demands, proclaims to achieve just this: giving direction and meaning to life in its totality, representing a maximum ethics; a "design," in the purest sense of the word, "for living." It is not the purpose of this short paragraph to dwell any longer on this topic which will concern us more as we proceed, but in this distinction between minimum and maximum ethics I see a very relevant point in our description of what is meant by design for living. If it shall be a design, a pattern, a theme (as in music), then it must be valued for life in its entirety, not only for selected parts—between which are left large loopholes of "adiaphora," neutral things in matters of conduct.

But how shall we or can we ever become saints, "perfect as our Father in Heaven is perfect"?[3] No such thought is intended here. More than ever we have to be mindful that all ethical endeavor begins with a dim groping into a yet untrodden direction; a groping, to be sure, into a richer, more meaningful and more substantial life. It means the abandonment (or at least an attempt in this direction) of the egocentric orientation of life. Meaning is attained only through hard work, by self-conquest and sacrifice, but our best endeavor leads easily to conflict and might end even in the calamity of defeat. That is the human situation that one has to face. It deserves a chapter by itself, and to it we now turn.

---

3. Matt 5:48—Ed.

Chapter 4

The Human Situation

The Principle of Greatest Resistance

A well-known play by Oscar Wilde has the title, intended to be facetious, "The Importance of Being Earnest," Earnest spelled with a capital letter, that is. I think we could fittingly borrow this phrase, only spelling the last word with a lower case, thus changing its meaning from something funny into something most serious and most appropriate for a study like the present one.

 The importance of being earnest—that is, of taking life as it is given to us for a certain span of time most seriously (which does by no means preclude laughter and joy)—this aptly introduces this chapter concerning the human situation as it actually exists. It is neither a psychological chapter (as the one on We-Psychology), nor one about idealistic abstractions. A design for living has no meaning in a vacuum of what should be done ideally; that is, the unreality of theoretical ethics. If design is to have any meaning then let us face the human situation in its full concreteness. The business of right living is essentially the realization (or better, actualization) of values by which life becomes meaningful and worth being lived. But just this value-realization is the hardest assignment of all, because we are like reeds in the wind and always under the sway of many an opposing urge. Hence the importance of being earnest, and also our inquiry into the preconditions which enable or prevent value-realizations or allow but an asymptotic approach, a failure which is yet none, that is which makes us start over and over again.

THE HUMAN SITUATION

The expression "the human situation" is a typically existentialist term indicating that every "ought" is empty if not visualized under the aspect of its possible realization in life. This human situation, which implies failures and victories, loyalties and dedications, joy and depression, is the very locus where the design for living unfolds. Somehow we carry in us this design as an immanent theme, even though we might not always focus on it in our consciousness. Yet it is there and makes us struggle along. It is the "other force" which fights the drives and urges of our non-spiritual nature. Twice we shall study the subject of the human situation: first while ascending to our goal, studying the hardships but also the possibilities and thrills of the ascent; and then again, studying the pitfalls and confusions encountered on our descent, warning signs that the struggle for realization of values never ends.

Here, at our first encounter with the human situation, we shall take up only a few salient topics: first, our possible choice between a path of lesser and greater resistance, a subject hardly ever discussed in treatises on ethics though most significant for it. And then second, the general topic of conflict in human nature. It is a characteristic of life to be ambiguous, saying yes and no at the same time. In the end it leads either to tragedy and failure, or more rarely (yet all the more admired), to victory and triumph. It implies the great joy and serenity which always goes along so well with a pattern of life that starts with absolute seriousness.

By nature we are rather lazy and inclined to complacency. We have discussed this issue in one of the earlier chapters. Particularly in those troubled days of ours we are reminded time and again "to have fun." Gadgets never made life easy (our "push-button civilization"), and we have developed a certain condescending attitude for all austerity, British and otherwise. True, we value hard work more than contemplative wisdom (which in return is more highly valued by people of the Orient) but we draw limits even in such work. As for moral endeavor, no standard exists as to the amount of exertion or relaxation. "Hedonistic" tendencies prevail in our conventional ethics, as the vision is usually oriented toward a life in its natural boundlessness rather than in its spiritual sublimity. And yet we do appreciate the great works of the masters. We admire an Albert Schweitzer who overcomes the adversities of Equatorial Africa to establish a hospital for the natives, or Toyohiko Kagawa who fights in the slums of Tokyo to bring about a change of mind of its dwellers, though he himself attracts trachoma while witnessing to his faith. We also admire the man Michelangelo who for four long years painted the ceilings of the Sistine Chapel while lying on top of a high scaffold on a mattress, despairing and revolting, and yet finishing his masterpiece. There are numerous examples of people who "did not take it easy," who cared, who minded, who were not satisfied with a shrug of their shoulders. But it shall not be denied that they were and are in the minority.

We then have a free choice between two ways which may fittingly be called the *path of least resistance* and the *path of greatest resistance*. As for the first, we are immediately reminded that a "principle of least resistance" (formulated by Maupertuis in the eighteenth century) is fundamental in physics, claiming that bodies left by themselves will follow this principle without exception. It is, so to speak, the natural thing and thus always and everywhere expected. Only by conscious effort can we break this principle and we will do it more as an exception than as a rule. Left to ourselves and not particularly prompted to the opposite, we will always seek the "path of least resistance," saving not only physical energy but also will power and exertion, and with it we will experience ease and a certain naturalness. Do not all of us like short cuts? Maybe it is not exactly the "path of virtue," but such is life.

On the other hand, do not people climb the Matterhorn or, for that matter, any mountain? Why should they exert great efforts in sport and work? It is more than muscular exercise or ambition and rivalry that motivates them. It is the feeling of conquest, of overcoming the gravity of wingless life, the great feeling of achieving what man only can achieve. Skyscrapers and suspension bridges, dams and tunnels—there is nothing natural in them, for they all mean tremendous efforts, purposefully performed along the line of greatest resistance. To be true, the purpose here is utility—that is an essentially non-moral or morally neutral principle. But we also know very well acts of such kind which are clearly recognizable as having moral value. The doctor and nurse of the infection ward or in an epidemic area are just one well-known example. Likewise, the one who enters a burning house to save a child is not too rare an event.

And so on. It dawns on us that we need not talk of "path of virtue" to grasp the truth that a higher life, the life of value and meaning, in fact any spiritual achievement, can never be gained along a path of least resistance. The proverbial poet who starves in his unheated attic room to finish his work is but another case to prove that the principle is true in any and every field of value realization. Human existence represents a raw material not quite prepared for such high aims. Matter resists its molding and has to be prepared. All great things are won only by effort, struggle, and conquest; defeat or discouragement cannot be avoided. That is incidentally one of the reasons why great ones are so rare.

Ours is a dynamic view of life. We cannot gain a final satisfaction; the actualization of our deeper meaning, our basic values without effort, endeavor, and strain. Design for living presupposes our willingness to try to walk along the path of greatest resistance, for we have to put spiritual contents into a material (our life) not prepared for it, though not unfitting either to become molded to this end. This idea of choice between least and greatest resistance in our conscious life is implied in all voluntaristic ethics (ones which recognize decisions as their first principle), though the term "greatest resistance" does not mean necessarily the effort of will-power only. A certain intellectual resoluteness, a setting of the mind, a grand vision, a thirst for the divine, a high moral spirit; they all will provide the energies to hold on and to proceed on the steep incline that leads to final realization. It is possible only by accepting a maximum principle which pervades life as a whole.

Walking the path of greatest resistance is about the same as accepting the idea of a disciplined life. Everyone, even if one knows very little about spiritual achievements, is nevertheless familiar with the necessity of inner discipline if some sort of higher plane is to be reached. Religious as well as secular teachings stress it, and it is understood as the noblest preparation to the ascent if only it is earnestly intended. Whatever the particular teaching on disciplined life may be, it always presupposes a certain dualistic world view, an antithesis between "flesh and spirit" as with St. Paul, between "duty and inclination" as with Kant. It means that a something in us has to discipline the other something in us. And we want to do so because we have a vision, an idea, a purpose, which cannot become realized without some sort of self-conquest and subduing the opposing tendencies.

The oldest form of such disciplined life is asceticism. It is present in the old religions of the East and is likewise a most prominent practice in our West. Since the earliest times of Christianity the ideal of ascetic life played a significant role in the Catholic Church. Monasticism, requesting a life of chastity and poverty, depriving existence not only of many amenities of life but demanding an exacting rule of daily practice, is too well-known as to need much discussion. This is not the place to argue the merits or demerits of this age-old system of discipline. It might suffice to say that it is beyond doubt more conducive to spiritual ascent than the rushed life of modern urban civilization. At this point it represents an object lesson of free choice for the harder path. Let us be mindful that every sacrifice is at the same time a symbol for our deepest aims. Those who give up so much must surely also gain much. I am certain that many among us are in some hidden way pursuing similar practices without heralding them. As was said before: in spiritual life there are no shortcuts, and real values cannot be bought cheaply. "We have to undergo many hardships and tribulations to enter into the Kingdom of God" (Acts 14:22, unknown translation).

Monastic asceticism is usually connected with Catholicism; but Protestantism is not less familiar with a similar principle. In fact Weber once described the new way of life within the Reformed Churches as "ascetic Protestantism." Its most conspicuous example is of course Calvin and his Geneva, and later on Anglo-Saxon Puritanism. It is a familiar pattern, not always very attractive but certainly not lacking a certain consistency and greatness. Again, people gladly chose a path of greater resistance because the values thus gained then justified the conquest of "natural" humanity. That misdirection and perversion might thwart any higher achievement is true here as well as anywhere else and must not detract us. Disciplined life within Protestation still prevails today among the stricter groups and sects, such as old type Quakers, Mennonites, Amish, Brethren, and so on, and it is cherished and highly thought of in their midst. To all of them it represents an educational technique that helps condition the mind to concentrate upon things "not of this world." There can be no love of God or, for that matter, no love of the other without inner discipline and self-restraint, that is, without foregoing the path of least resistance. Finally, in a very secularized form, we meet a similar pattern in British "austerity" of the post-war period, a last inheritance of Puritan ancestry. The British (or at least many among them) pride themselves in it. It means to them dignity and, to a certain extent, genuine moral excellence, that is, real values.

What is true with regard to religious teaching is true also with regard to philosophy, although in less popular terms. We cannot discuss the subject of living along the line of greatest resistance without referring to Immanuel Kant and his monumental ethical teachings. Kant's moral philosophy has a very rigid character, as is well-known, and it represents a maximum ethics as outspoken as it can be. His basic antithesis is the one between duty and inclination, *Pflicht* and *Neigung*. He is fully aware that people often act very nicely out of inclination and propensity, motivated by some emotion and achieving some good. But according to Kant's formulation this act has no real "moral" value. Such a value can be attributed only to the good will which acts according to an immanent moral law. Nothing done out of mere inclination can be termed good. Duty, on the other hand, the principle of rational prompting of the will, alone qualifies an act as morally valuable. In the last analysis it means self-conquest, "the prompting to an end, even though without any inclination" (*Nötigung zu einem ungern genommenen Zwecke*). What we do we should do, without exception, out of a consciousness of duty, out of respect for this general and yet self-given law. Our struggle will never cease between our inclinations (praiseworthy though they may be) and the immutable precepts of reason which constitute duty. Personally I cannot agree with Kant's sternness and extreme voluntarism. But it has greatness and strength and represents, within philosophy, the most outstanding example of an ethics "of the greatest resistance." Supposedly someone does not want to do certain acts. And yet performs them "for duty's sake," overcoming personal weakness and excuses. This person is doing so because they still value more highly this regard for the law to which they would want everybody to submit. Hence no exception can be conceded.

Kant's spirit will appear foreign to many of us. And yet it is not a mere theory of ethical conduct. The praxis of rigid duty-performance will certainly command respect everywhere, even though it contains in it the possibility of abuse if wrongly interpreted and directed. But that holds true for almost every principle and cannot decrease the grandeur of this German moral philosophy. The strongest argument against it is its rigidly conceived idea of self-conquest. I perform the act, but I do so against my inclination, so to speak, by way of an inner jolt. Thus the act lacks grace and makes the doer look as sour as a Puritan—which, in a sense, Kant was himself. Every sacrifice, we said earlier, is of value only if done without regret, graciously if not downright cheerfully. This was, however, not the style of the sage of Konigsberg.

It was a man of a different nature who once ventured to say, when asking the highest performance from his disciples: "My yoke is easy." And yet he was right. The path of greatest resistance can and will become easy if it is trodden in the right spirit. But that is a question of levels, and cannot be taken up at this place. Suffice to say that "greatest resistance" does not imply a sullen resoluteness. To the contrary, rightly conceived it is a triumph and is filled with grace.

Yet, it remains true: it is not natural human inclination. The path of least resistance is mostly preferred, or the "amoral" life of Mr. Average. A certain utilitarian or, on a different plane, aesthetic attitude will easily fool us about the real situation. Kierkegaard was right when he so emphatically contraposed the aesthetic and the religious "stage of life" (while the ethical stage to him has only a transitory significance).[1] There is a certain ease in allowing ourselves to be deluded regarding the things of last value, and aestheticism indicates just this attitude of ease. It means a kind of playfulness that nowhere takes life too seriously. A certain haziness with regard to the deeper issues of life prevails, and that permits the good feeling that all is well in our house. No intentional evil will be allowed, for the average person is fortunately of good nature. What is wrong is rather a certain thoughtlessness, a lack of awareness or concern, maybe even a callousness toward moral issues of life. How many slaveholders felt quite at ease with the situation as it was? And the same holds true for any such situation: for the German who, himself no Nazi, allowed Nazism, as for the industrial boss who cares little for the weal of his workingmen though he might spend sums for charity. The Levite and the Pharisee in the parable of the Good Samaritan represent the classical case of such otherwise decent people who were just not thoughtful and sensitive enough to do the thing which ought to have been done.

Thoughtlessness, unconcern, and the like means also a case of the principle of "least resistance." There might be some easy excuses: "that I did not know lay omission, that I thought I was doing my best, and that my intentions were not evil." To this we might answer with the statement of our introductory chapter: the educated heart. This awareness and sensitivity, the education of the heart, must become a goal of ethical striving—otherwise all talking about morals becomes relative and eventually collapses. What we do not want to see we just do not see (it is the famous blind spot); I might even use Freudian language for that—the result remains always the same: a *blunted conscience*.

Perhaps the most profound word in this connection was said by Léon Bloy, the *Pilgrim to the Absolute* (as Risa Maritain, his biographer, calls this contemporary French Catholic *homo religiosus*). Here is what he had to say concerning this weakness of which is usually taken so lightly. "The worst evil is not committing crimes but failing to do the good one could do. It is the sin of omission which is nothing other than non-love. The sin of

---

1. Kierkegaard, *Stages on Life's Way*.—Ed.

action can be forgiven, but Jesus did not pay for the sin of omission which concerns the Holy Spirit."

This sin of omission is part of the human situation, of man's weakness and his preference for the easier way. As long as we do not recognize it and resolve to awaken ourselves, we bar our way toward an educated heart.

Conflicts, Tragedies, and Victories

Before going on in our analysis of the human situation (preliminary to the final word on design for living), we might stop for a short while to turn our attention to a more theoretical excursus, helpful in the present context. It has to do with a rather simple distinction between *intrinsic* and *instrumental* values. The matter is quite evident: an instrumental value is one which is no end in itself, providing no final satisfaction, carrying no last meaning but being necessary nevertheless in the process of life. All utility values are of such kind. Only in an indirect way can they also provide a certain amount of self-contained satisfaction—for instance, if viewed from a recreational angle. All economic values, connected with money, indispensable though they are, might be classified under instrumental values. And so are the values connected with our biological functions, eating, drinking and the like; necessary, to be sure, and yet no final value in themselves. This becomes more obvious when we turn to an appreciation of the "intrinsic" values, distinguished from the former by their self-contained and final character. They do not serve any other ends, but are ends in themselves. In fact, every use to other ends always smacks of a degradation and near offense (such as if a man would have someone play fine music just so that he could fall asleep; there were times when musicians were not treated better than lackeys of a noble estate.) The distinction between intrinsic and instrumental values pertains to philosophies of an idealistic or religious character, since they alone admit dualisms or dichotomies. It is the price for penetrating into the secret of value phenomena, which otherwise remains completely outside the functions of the natural world, and would defy any reasonable interpretation. We are, our philosophers say, members of two realms, the realm of necessity ("nature") and the realm of freedom ("value"). It seems as if these two realms were incommensurable.

Plato might be a welcome guide at this place. From him all later thinkers borrowed a basic formulation of intrinsic values, of which he knew only three, the True, the Beautiful, and (on top) the Good. The True represents the value of all knowledge, in science and philosophy, the enjoyment of logical insight, of intellectual achievement. It is an end in itself which requires no further justification. This kind of value has nothing to do with practical application of knowledge. It is the joy of pure reason, or with the Greeks, of pure *theoria*, the beholding or vision of that which is not further reducible. The Beautiful, the aesthetic value, is the secret of all art and its appeal; it is the dispassionate enjoyment of "pure" form and its expression, freed from any direct urge or interest. Here, as in the value of truth, the little adjective "pure" indicates the non-instrumental nature of such a value. Beyond the True and the Beautiful we meet the last of Plato's top values, the Good, with its double connotation of the moral good and of the supreme good in itself, that which comprises in itself all other values. It too implies the purity of purpose and the non-instrumentality of the absolute goodness. These three values then, are intrinsic; that is, self-contained and needing no further justification or interpretation. They are absolutely meaningful and thus absolutely satisfying. They are expressions of the spiritual nature of life, or, to say it in a more Platonic fashion, the projection of the Absolute into the human existence. It is true that they are connected with certain interests, as the pyschologistic theories of value claim, but no interest explains the fact of values as such. Moreover, the term "interest" is easily misleading if understood as egocentric interest (as all utilitarian values are of such type). The enjoyment of art was expressly defined as "disinterested," which means unconnected with any act of willing, and it seems advisable to keep the two approaches to value neatly apart—that is, the psychological and the "idealistic."

However, idealism has its limitations, and it is not our intention to suggest at this place a Platonic philosophy of value. One realm was visualized by Plato but indirectly and indistinctly, as it was foreign to Greek philosophy: that is the realm of higher religion. Whether we speak of the God of Abraham, Isaac, and Jacob, or of the Heavenly Father of Christ, it opens to us a reality quite different from anything known to the philosophers. To this realm man turns in devotion and meditation, and as far as possible also in obedience and discipleship. The value connected with it reaches definitely beyond that of "The Good" in Plato's system; a recent scholar (Rudolf Otto) suggested for it the term "The Holy."[2] It is as genuine a value as any, although it becomes known only to those who earnestly strive after it and open their hearts to it. The well-known word with which St. Augustine begins his *Confessions*, "My heart is restless until it rests in

2. Otto, *The Idea of the Holy*.—Ed.

Thee, my God,"[3] reflects this situation very graphically. The just-mentioned restriction, however, that values become meaningful only to those who turn to them and concentrate upon them, holds true for every intrinsic value. Without proper appreciation there exists neither the True, nor the Beautiful, nor the Good.

A special character of every intrinsic value is its quality of finality, and that, of course, applies also to the value of the Holy. The heart, which rests in God, no longer asks "what for?" or "what afterwards?" It rests, and does so in sublime joy. Another quality of intrinsic values, namely their purity, applies likewise to the Holy, and very much so. Pure devotion and pure dedication are no doubt the highest form of value realization achievable in human life. Saintliness in all its forms is the phenomenon which results from such an endeavor.

Conceived of in this way, our distinction between intrinsic and instrumental values cannot be easily confused. An instrumental value cannot be mistaken for an intrinsic one and vice versa, theoretically at least. But in life, or, as we would prefer to say, in the human situation, things are different. Theory or not, values are usually mixed up and badly confounded. It is here where conflicts and tragedies come into our focus.

Of a possible misuse of intrinsic values for instrumental purposes, we have already given an example (music as a sleeping medicine). The commercialization of art today, even of charity, not to speak of science (which lost most of its pure character), points clearly enough to such possibilities. Often enough this is done with full awareness and in the open, hence without illusion or hypocrisy. As one contemporary thinker boasted, "We have lost much in our scientific age, but this one thing we may pride ourselves, and that is honesty." I am not so sure about this either. In a world in which values are so badly misinterpreted and confused, even this supposed honesty is not often much more than a resigned cynicism.

Yet the greater danger, in our view, is the opposite misuse—namely the elevation of certain instrumental values to intrinsic ones, their being transformed into last and absolute values. Money, for instance, is a highly needed good, connected with an instrumental value. Yet make money a supreme value and life is drained of all its creative possibilities. The miser who hoards his earnings (of which he is only a steward) and thus concentrates upon this imaginary value of riches, fools himself and forfeits the very possibilities of his life. Who is happier—the Poverello from Assisi, or

---

3. Augustine, *Confessions*, I, 1.—Ed.

Shylock the money lender? And who enriched life more for himself and for all with whom he came into contact? Need I repeat the story of the "robber barons" of industry and commerce? Some ended by suicide, some in jail, and most of their wealth came to naught sooner or later. A self which never transcends the limits of egocentrism eventually becomes so empty that all the pleasures of the world cannot prevent its collapse.

A similar misconception is the modern veneration of technology, the auto, the gadget, the mechanical way, and in a sense also the atom bomb. We made idols out of instruments, and thus we shall reap our reward. Technology is a good thing, no doubt, if used in the proper spirit. But it is never an end in itself, a last justification of life, a meaning which gives humanity the full dignity of personality. The confusion of the terms instrumental and intrinsic in a generally confused age leads to tragic consequences of which our urban civilization but abounds. To forestall misunderstanding it should be emphasized that I do not propose Gandhian or Tolstoyan or, for that matter, Thoreauan primitivism. Let us use and develop what human inventiveness has produced, but let us make distinctions and let the values stay in their proper place—the tool in the tool room, and God in our hearts.

Ethics deals with intrinsic values only; the purer the dedication to the good, the more satisfying the realization of the value. And pure is that which is less tainted by self-interest, egocentrism, and neglect of the "we." Beware that no instrumental value enters this sanctuary save for instrumental purpose. Else a cynic hedonism will emerge which sees no other chance in life than the enjoyment of the pleasant. Where that ends, some form of destruction or nihilism will set in. The confusion between intrinsic and instrumental values is a real snare and should not be taken lightly. At times everybody falls victim to it, and it becomes hard to disentangle this knot once it has gotten rigid.

Closely connected with it goes a similar temptation, under circumstances that are nearly inescapable. Max Weber once called it the "routinization of the charisma." It applies particularly to the field of religion. What was first a gift of grace and a true calling, for instance to priesthood, easily becomes, in the passage of time, a task of routine, an office, a form rather than a content. But the value rests in the contents and not in the performance. Routinization is the end of creativity. Whether it applies to the doing of good or the production of so-called art or to the study of the laws of nature or society—routinization fools us as being occupied with values where there are none. It is a hard requirement to be new every day in that "business of living," but there is no escape from it. Routine is also a sort of technique, a habitual performance, and as such becomes instrumental rather than intrinsic. Who could say that they never fell victim to it? And if routine becomes time honored, we call it perhaps a dignifying tradition (which it possibly is) and connect a new value to it: the value of tradition. It has the after-glow of a creative past, of a substance which once was very much alive and now exists only by virtue of inheritance. There can be something great in it, but only if re-quickened and newly experienced as reality that is as an intrinsic value. Else tradition is like a graven monument: we admire it, but live in another world.

Such are the pitfalls of life in its struggle toward value and meaning. Hypocrisy and illusion, cynicism and routine are lurking at every step unless we remain alert and sensitive, building up a life meaningful in its main line. They are the problems of the educated heart. Beware of complacency. It proves that this theoretical excursus has been not too theoretical after all, although it started out this way. Its application is now made rather easy. The human situation, we might say by now, is almost always a "situation in conflict" as far as value-realization is concerned. It involves a spiritual struggle, a *Geisteskampf*, whose outcome the individual never can know prior to life's end. All life is a struggle between conflicting forces, those which pull down like heaviness and natural inclinations, and those which lift up and elevate, flying to the heights of divine vision or *theoria* (as Aristotle loves to call it). But even if the decision for the highest dedication has once been made—even then—pitfalls and confusion, routinization and failure, not infrequently even despair, dryness of the spirit and doubt, will have to be met. That is what I call the conflict situation of life. It must not discourage us, however.

We all live with some fetters, acquired in early childhood. They represent our weak spots, our foibles and handicaps. "Living victoriously" then would mean to conquer them. Let us study how this may happen. The Apostle Paul once most profoundly exclaimed in self-accusation, "The good I would I do not, but the evil which I would not that I do" (Rom 7:19; also 7:15). It is a great word which every alert person will have experienced more than once in their life. We all do not do the good which we want to do and do, on the other hand, that which we consciously never intended to do.

> *Video meliora proboque*
> *Deteriora sequor*
> "I see the better and approve of it

Yet, I follow the worse."[4]

Thus also laments Ovid, the Roman poet, nearly identical with what St. Paul had to say. Tolstoy, whose aunt was a lady-in-waiting at the Tsarist court, once wrote to him on this subject in 1887, stating: "If in my life I do nothing but evil and do not improve a bit, that is if I do not begin to do at least a little bit less evil, then I lie in saying that I want to do the good." With this he wants rightly to say that the cry of St. Paul or of Ovid or of anyone must never become an excuse, a subterfuge for lessening our efforts, pleasant and easy as such an argument would ever be. In our present context this theme is suggested only to demonstrate the basic nature of the human situation of conflict (within our heart) and the need for incessant alertness. It is not an easy assignment, to be certain.

Conflicts of this kind do not permit medium solutions, at least not as a rule. They issue forth usually either into a tragedy, or, more rarely, into victory. At this place we need be but brief in discussing these two endings. A tragedy always happens when no way seems to open, when the vicious circle of tension drives the individual into ever-growing conflicts and ever-fewer possible solutions, the very best intentions presupposed, of course. The old Greeks knew a great deal about such tragic situations, and they explained them by the tension between *hybris* and *nemesis*, wanton pride or overbearing on the side of man (who knows no better), and retributive destiny on the side of our world-order which does not permit any breaking of its rules. Shakespeare, two millennia later, discovered the tragic conflicts in the human mind proper, taking no recourse to any metaphysical or providential interpretation. He is yet true enough in his portrayal of human struggle and its frustration. Passion plays a great role in it but not the only role. Think of Hamlet, the most tragic story of all. We recognize these plays as tragic because there is no evil intention in these heroes who just could not in all nobleness find the right way out—should I say, the moral solution?

Tragedy is no religious category; it indicates our entanglement with earthly passions and interests which prevent the disentanglement on a next higher plane. On the religious level, the Cross looms clearly, the passion, martyrdom—something which must be called victory rather than defeat. It is a rare event and most people are even in their religious struggle not free enough or strong enough to reach the next plane. Tolstoy's final years

---

4. Ovid, *Metamorphoses*, VII, 20–21.

of life might be suggested here as a most impressive example of a quasi-tragic ending of an otherwise great and noble life. The details are fairly well-known. Following his great conversion when he was about fifty years old, an incessant conflict arose between him and his wife in which nearly the entire family sided with the Countess. Thirty years of great bitterness ensued (1880–1910). It was not all Tolstoy's fault, in fact the memoirs of Sophy Tolstoy reveal her as certainly not too high-minded. But that is not the subject of our discussion; all earnest value realization will meet resistance and one could almost add that this is good. "It is only by hardship and troubles that one can enter the Kingdom of God" (Acts 14:22). Tolstoy, great in his vision but bewildered when approaching realization, was not without his inner faults and shortcomings (of which he was aware all too well, thin-skinned as he was by heart). He wavered, while Sophy knew that she wanted to stay in the way of old. The situation became ever more unbearable, as the autobiographic drama "The Light Shineth Into the Darkness" gives impressive witness. Tolstoy played with the idea of going away, but he carried on at his home until two months after his eighty-second birthday, when the conflict had come near to a breaking point. He saw no solution and in a sudden fit of indignation decided to leave like a thief, deep in the night. The next morning, when the Countess learned the facts, she attempted suicide only to be saved in the last moment by Tolstoy's trusted secretary. In the meantime the old man had become a lost pilgrim without a goal. Three weeks later he died in a small room of a railroad stationmaster who had taken the sick man in. He died with the illusion of having truly fled the world of Russia's aristocratic society. Unfortunately, it did not quite appear this way to outsiders who watched this tragic ending of a really great man.

Not all spiritual struggle needs to end this way. The other solution is possible too: victory, triumph, even in defeat. Previously we suggested that seriousness in life's dealings does not imply pessimism or a sour temper (so well-known from Puritan conduct). To the contrary, there can and will be a superior serenity in the one who has mastered life's adversaries, even should they have to give up all wellbeing, freedom, and life itself. The story of martyrs of the early Christian era as well as of the unbelievably cruel sixteenth century give ample proof of this contention. We read of many an Anabaptist, for instance, who went to the stake "with shining eyes and a smiling mouth," as the *Chronicle* reports.[5] Victory in conflict means the

---

5. *The Chronicle of the Hutterian Brethren.*—Ed.

affirmation that life and life's work has meaning, permits value realization, makes possible overcoming one's own weakness and natural un-readiness for higher ends—and all that even when externally, defeat seems inevitable. Only through defeat and despair can real triumph become possible.

As an example I think at this time not only of those men and women who were mentioned more than once in this treatise, such as Schweitzer and Kagawa, but also of Muriel Lester (her eyes always beaming with joy and affirmation) and Elizabeth Brandström (the Swedish angel of Siberia during World War I) and all the others in this noble array. Now I propose to have a look at a great man of music and inner resignation, Ludwig van Beethoven. Like Michelangelo, who was mentioned earlier, he was the genuine artist to whom life meant creation through suffering. At a rather early age he became deaf, and, though sociable by nature, he had to retire into his inner self. He loved with great intensity but it was of no consequence as far as response went: his nephew, for whom he cared so much, was a good-for-nothing, and of the "immortally beloved" we do not even know exactly who she was. And yet, a great light shone in his heart. He was not religious in the Christian sense; for this he was too much a child of the age of the French Revolution. But it was another piety which triumphed in his mind, a piety of a world of meaning and affirmation, a cosmos of freedom and joy. For years he carried in his mind the wonderful words of Schiller's "Ode to Joy." He wanted to set them into music but could not see clearly how to make it a worthy climax of all his art. He wrote it first as a Choral Fantasy but felt that it was not yet the fullest expression of what he had visualized. Finally it flashed in his mind that this Ode to Joy should become the conclusion of a great symphony, even though a choral piece was never before used in such a context. Thus the Ninth Symphony was composed. In its last movement, all of a sudden, after much fugal excitement and agitation in the orchestra, the instruments stop for one measure as if anticipating something unexpected. And then a human voice calls: "o friends, no more these sounds continue. Let us raise a song of sympathy, of gladness. O joy let us praise thee. Praise her, praise." These words Beethoven himself drew up as introduction to the hymn proper.

> Praise to Joy the God descended
> Daughter of Elysium.
> Ray of mirth and rapture blended
> Goddess to thy shrine we come.
> By thy magic is united

What stern custom parted wide
All mankind are brothers plighted
Where thy gentle wings abide . . .
(*Adagio ma non tropo ma divoto,*
Not too slow but devout)
O ye millions I embrace ye,
Here is a joyful kiss for all,
Brothers, o'er yon starry sphere
Sure there dwells a loving father.
O ye millions kneel before him.
World dost feel thy maker near?
Seek him o'er yon starry sphere,
O'er the stars enthroned, adore him.

The work is gigantic and culminates in a final *prestissimo* of near superhuman uplift. It was Beethoven's great credo in spite of all his predicament. "All mankind are brothers plighted . . . praise to Joy!"

Is that not the most overwhelming victory, the true conquest of self and its limitation, the most enraptured affirmation of this world's indwelling meaningfulness and of its only source? "O'er yon starry sphere, sure, there dwells a loving father . . . Adore him." Optimism, pessimism, they are but passing viewpoints, nothing final. For this world is neither the best nor the worst one. It is but an opportunity for us to perform the good and to overcome the temptation of the bad. Here our greatest freedom and chance are at stake. I cannot close this chapter better than with the words of a friend of mine, a Methodist minister, who once concluded his sermon with these words: "No all-out victory can ever be achieved without an all-in victory."

Part 2

Design for Living

At long last we have arrived at the very theme of this book: the attempt to give a positive answer to the question of a design for living. Has this question any reasonable meaning? What does design for living mean after all? And is there such a design discoverable beyond the customary relativistic approach? These are difficult questions, to be sure. No one can expect general agreement in matters of that kind. But it is our hope that if the kind reader has endured up to this point, that reader will now be willing to follow us up the last step of our ascent that we may gain the wider view in this realm of the spirit like the mountain climber on the summit of the mountain.

Let us briefly summarize our presuppositions or findings in our endeavor. Above all, it appears as if we were "created unto meaning," that is, all orientations in life beyond functional activities are directed toward a meaningful, intentional value realization. We might fail, we might be dull or blinded toward such concerns, but somewhere, somehow we will return to this spiritual urge as we have pointed out earlier. Human beings become mentally deranged if their lives are deprived altogether of such kind of activities. No fun or play can fool the individual in the long run. Meaning is what constitutes us as spiritual beings, as real. But meaning is nothing that can be rationally presented to us like a geometric proposition. It is something highly personal and elusive, irrational, yet nonetheless real. It is part of our existence. "Design" then means the pattern which enables the individual to approximate his life's meaning. Design is not ethics (prescriptions for acts of conduct). It is like a pattern rather the permanent theme that runs through life, more conditioning its general form of existence than its doings in each particular case. We might err, sin, fall, betray ourselves, but the pattern still remains in our personal existence (and then acts as conscience and reminder). Design is thus always a maximum ethics for the individual, no dictation from outside, but absolutistic and total from the inside. We might flee such claims and live beside ourselves like Peer Gynt, or we might become rigid and doctrinarian in this regard like Ibsen's Brand, and again fail. Yet the design remains unshaken. It is our great passion, the one to which we long to devote, and even to sacrifice, everything. As I said earlier, it is the test, to observe the things we are willing to forego and to sacrifice, and to register for what purpose we are doing so. Thus it seems that design has meaning to the one who recognizes "the importance of being earnest" (to borrow the phrase from Oscar Wilde again) in the building up of one's life.

A very different question, however, is a positive description of such a design. Is not every person different, and are we not to allow the widest margin for creative answers? It almost seems as if we had reached the limit of our description, leaving the rest to the imaginative work of the individual. Still certain general lines seem to stand out, having the character of universal human traits, or rather traits of spiritual life. These we are now out to discover. For this we have to remember another finding of an earlier chapter, the We-Philosophy, as something most essential in all value-realization. It excludes both extreme individualism (egocentrism) and collectivism (when a person becomes lost in the mass, as so often happens today). No matter which value is to be actualized, we cannot do it properly, creatively, genuinely, without sharing, without having in our mind also the neighbor, the fellow person. Truth and beauty and likewise the good and the holy are to be shared or they are not at all. Joy and suffering lose meaning and become like a bitter taste if restricted to the single ego; and above all they lose their creative quality, their centrally human nature. Be alone, the single one, or be part of a crowd, and you are not, your existence has vanished. Life is always a dialogue, a communication with the other, the Thou, the friend. That is essential to it just as much as the search for meaning.

Combine both the We-Philosophy and the tendency toward a meaningful pattern of life, and then all conventionalism, all self-interest, and all hedonistic relativism, will collapse and will give way to new answers, exalted and not easily gained though they are. I suggest to attack this task step by step, mindful that certain tasks or attitudes are still within the scope of what can be required while there exist also most lofty qualities that reach beyond that which can be demanded, beyond any "ought." Theirs then is the realm of grace. As I see it, four steps can be distinguished in such a "design for living," briefly described as regard, concern, service, and love.

Chapter 5

Regard, Concern, Service, and Love

It is the claim of this book that each of these ideas reach beyond individual preferences, that they are generally human designs applying and appealing to any and every individual, now and forever, East and West—in short, there is something absolute and inherent in them. They are of a spiritual nature; that is, they have the quality of meaningfulness, and they are of a social nature in as much as they have meaning only with regard to the fellow person. They are neither individualistic nor collectivistic but presuppose the "dialogue between I and Thou" indicated above. They are ethics and yet go beyond it. Only persons open to the divine will discover their savor and find satisfaction without self-education and self-conquest (the path of greatest resistance). Without divine influence, these steps will remain dark and prompt little more than feeble lip service. They outline the mountain path along which we may gain an educated heart.

"Regard" means to take the other person fully as a person. In a democratic society this should appear as a self-evident axiom. But in practice, it is not so simple and democracy is often enough misinterpreted as a right rather than an obligation. Thus far I hope we all agree.

For the next step we are urged to perform again what William Stern once called "Introception," that is, the taking into our own mind the affairs, interests, worries, joys and sufferings of our fellow person. Such acts of sympathy and silent participation we call "concern." It implies not so much doing, but it affirms our interrelatedness, our belonging together. Within limits we are our brother's keepers, too. Concern, it appears, falls still within the scope of that which can be required of everybody. Only the amoral person might not quite understand why thoughtlessness is wrong in itself.

A third step is urged: "service," the actual doing with the qualification of general usefulness. "*Ich dien*" is the noble motto of the Prince of Wales and is found inscribed on his coat of arms. Is service still something to be required? Is it really an "ought"? It seems so as we look around and find it in nearly all ethical teachings, although it is not always easily carried through and often shirked. "I serve" is the motto also of the Boy and Girl Scouts, of the "Society of Friends," and—strictly speaking—of all Christians, as far as they are awakened and honest in their faith. Service can well be considered a real design for living, giving meaning, making us creative (all genuine creation is in itself service), satisfying in itself and affirming the philosophy of the "we." Service is more than the Golden Rule because the latter implies by its terms no genuine mutuality as its yardstick. Service is a value only if done in the right spirit, cheerfully, gladly. A person who "serves" while grumbling forfeits the quality of value; the act loses meaning and with it satisfaction. Service presupposes the two earlier steps: regard for the fellow human being as a person, and concern for this fellow person and their affairs by an inner participation. In service these steps now become activated into a doing.

There remains only one more, the hardest step—"love." It is the crowning of all endeavor to fill life with value and meaning and to be interrelated with our fellow people. Love—*agape* in the Greek New Testament—is no longer a subject of general requirement. One cannot say you ought to love, because love cannot be commanded. Love is a gift of grace, it reaches beyond ethics and is the most perfect, most sublime, human and yet more than human, design for living. *Amor et fac quod vis* (love and do what you want), this dictum by St. Augustine is actually no longer a prescription. It hints at a state of mind, at a form of existence where the individual growth is the richer the more they love, the more the other one becomes part of the self. Love is definitely no topic of ethics or moral philosophy, for it is the working of the divine in the human. Love, it appears, is universal and evident to everybody, even though "everybody" might not accept it, yea even oppose it. In its sublimity it cannot be further surpassed—our summit is reached. Though love is the core of Jesus's teaching, two thousand years of Christianity have not produced many disciples and teachers of his principles. In fact it was claimed an impossible ideal, a paradox, and thus it was removed from our conscious ethical horizon. It has to be rediscovered in every generation, and in times of confusion like ours, its reformulation seems doubly needed. Lip service alone is not enough. If our strength fails, let us acknowledge our shortcoming, but let us not erase the ideal as the very beacon light of our existence. Thus regard, concern, service, and love present themselves to us as the answer to our search. They imply a readiness to share and a sense for responsibility. We might not conclude this summary better than with a quotation from a great American who was at the same time also a great man in a general sense. Thomas Jefferson once wrote these memorable words to a friend:

> I am ready to say to every human being;
> "Thou art my brother," and to offer
> him the hand of concord and amity.[1]

If a person can genuinely do so then they have grasped the right vision and life will become the scene of the noblest achievement.

Regard

There should be no need, theoretically, to elaborate at great length on our first point since it might be assumed that both Christianity and Enlightened Humanism (this secularized form of Christianity) have made it a point beyond doubt that the human being is a person with dignity and certain inalienable rights, a being endowed by the creator with a mind capable of choosing between good and evil, right and wrong. In short, the principle of "regard" should be something self-evident. And it should be particularly so in any moral philosophy which rests on a personalistic foundation (like the present one). It belongs to the tremendous spiritual revolution which came with the rise of Christianity and its entrance into the pagan world of the Greeks and Romans, that from now on the human being became a value in itself, or an "end in himself" (as the rationalists expressed it), something worthy in any case, no matter how low the particular individual might have fallen. Slavery, for instance, was from now on (morally at least) no longer thinkable, and likewise all other forms of bondage and degradation. To the old Greeks the concept of "person" was not known in the sense used by us, thus "regard" does not figure in their moral philosophy. Only in some later

---

1. *Thomas Jefferson on Democracy*, 151. Friedmann notes in the manuscript: "1819; to Brazer. New York Public Library, msc. V, 142."—Ed.

Stoic thinking do we meet the idea of the participation of all human beings in the universal *logos* and with it their standing under a general "natural law." It made the humanitarian principle of equality of all men at least not altogether foreign to the Ancient and prepared the soil for the assimilation of the new Christian moral philosophy. The concept of an innate absolute worth within every person without exception grew and was propagated by the church and later by the several churches. In the days of rationalism it became reformulated but retained its basic character. The emancipation of the Jews toward the later part of the 16th century, and the gradual abolition of slavery in the Western World during the 19th century are just two characteristic examples in this case.

The classical philosophical formulation of the principle that man is an end in himself and nothing else, we owe to Immanuel Kant, the greatest moral philosopher of this age of reason. In his *Foundation of the Metaphysics of Morals* (1785), he presents all rational arguments possible for its unequivocal demonstration. "Act in such a way," he at one place formulates his famous Categorical Imperative, "as to use humanity both in your own person and in the person of every other, always at the same time as an end in itself and never simply as a means to an end."[2] To appreciate this great principle one must not forget that Kant is definitely on the side of the dualists who make a clear distinction between reason and nature. The human as a biological being stands under the law of necessity and is therefore different from man as a rational being, who knows freedom. This rational being then has dignity and worth, is an end in itself, and hence requires regard. To be sure, Kant does not expressly draw this conclusion from his own principle as the examples which he presents prove (prohibition of suicide, borrowing money without intention to pay back, etc.). With him, not the principle of regard for the person, but that of "reverence for the moral law," ranks paramount. His approach is idealistic, not personalistic, rational and theoretical, not existential and concrete. One of his strongest arguments runs about as follows: "Men can compel me to perform certain actions directed toward certain ends; they cannot, however, make me adopt any such end as my own." It is the argument of basic inner human freedom, taught first by Socrates and later by the Stoics, but it has little to do with regard, though it implies the understanding that what is not possible in my case will likewise be impossible with anybody else. Appealing as Kant's formula is, it appears still inadequate unless supplemented by a principle of social

2. Kant, *Groundwork of the Metaphysics of Morals*.—Ed.

interrelatedness which requires mutual obligations. From Kant's starting point, the self-regard of the individual due to their inner dignity does not engender by itself regard of other individuals as well, at least not as an inescapable postulate. Thus is the limitation of a rational and idealistic ethics centered on the autonomous individual. The experience upon which all We-Philosophy rests, the organic I-Thou relationship, the interwovenness of the individual (with all their freedom) into the greater whole of society, is basically of an irrational nature. Nevertheless, Kant's Categorical Imperative in the formulation of the above contains a great vision and carries in it the possibility of development toward a philosophy of mutual regard between persons. Perhaps it could be said that this was done by Kant's great contemporary, Thomas Jefferson, a man nearer to the exigencies of life than the philosopher of Konigsberg. Nine years prior to Kant's "Formulations," the great *Declaration of Independence* confirmed, at least in a preliminary form, this principle of regard, namely as a demand, a right, and as the foundation of a great commonwealth in the making.

It was Jefferson who assured the world that such principles are self-evident; that is, without need for further argument. And we agree with him. But such is life that theory and praxis seldom coincide. The Founding Fathers of 1776 all agreed with the philosophy of the *Declaration*; and yet, it still took nearly ninety years until slavery was legally abolished. The self-evident principle was just not overwhelming enough to conquer the dominant self-interests of wide circles. Thus we observe many times lip service given to a thought theoretically accepted and yet practically denied. Regard is a principle which still today has to be taught and stressed with devotion, it is to be fought for and if need be to be suffered for. Humankind in general, we should remember, does not like the path of greatest resistance after all. To regard my colored fellow man as an equal, to take Jew and Gentile basically as partners in the common concern of living, to do away with the discriminations of the distaff side of humankind, these are things by no means as self-evident as rationalists assumed. If any one of us comes in contact with persons in dependent positions, with a servant, a maid, a handyman, any inferior, do we always, or at least in most cases, show these persons all the regard which is due them? The term "bossism" is too well-known in America as to preclude any such forgetfulness of the principle of regard. In countries of truly democratic spirit regard should be a thought so plain as not to require any further elaboration. For it belongs to the essence of democracy. But alas, more words still seem to be needed to make this principle live. Without its practical realization, no further step toward our remaining principles of concern, service and love would be possible. For how could we be concerned about any fellow person, how could we serve them (not to speak of loving them) if we have no regard for them? It is the presupposition of our next step and a very important one indeed.

A small book of recent times has emphasized anew this principle by putting it into the very center of moral philosophy. Victor Gollancz, its author, a well-known London publisher, gave the book the very appropriate title, *Our Threatened Values* (1943).[3] In this book he develops the idea that "respect for personality" is the key to all moral life. A person might be as unpleasant as possible, and may even be my "arch-enemy" (if there exists such a one), still I must not refuse to respect him, or else I no longer could regard him as a human being. This very vivid plea for "respect for personality" is strong and impressive and I do wholeheartedly agree with the author's thesis that to forget this basic respect means to threaten our finest moral values. It is the situation of our day. There is, however, one point that I would take exception to. It pertains to the question of whether "respect for personality" is already the last and final principle of moral life to be asked of everyone, or whether further developments beyond it are thinkable. It is the thesis of the present book that regard is but step number one in our vision of a meaningful design for living. It is by regard for my fellow person, by respecting their dignity, that I live up to the rudiments of a We-Philosophy. Only by means of such regard (which knows no exception!) do I help in creating a real community of human beings which is different from their merely atomistic coexistence. The Golden Rule might here be well brought into play. Since I myself expect such regard from others I have also to show it to them. What would the regard be worth which I receive, the smile and kindness, maybe even the flattery and homage, if the other were no person-with-dignity but only a slave, an inferior being without the status of personhood. It would be a show and illusion, and we could not carry on living in this way.

The philosophy of superman, of the elite, of the right of the stronger, is definitely opposed to such a Christian-Humanistic concept. Nietzsche, for instance, derides any such inclination. The strong one has priority and it means "slave morals" to deny it. Only an elite, the "blond beast" as he occasionally chooses to call it, has a claim to dignity and regard, while the inferiors (whatever they be) do not count any further. A very graphic

---

3. Gollancz, *Our Threatened Values*.—Ed.

illustration of such a denial of the basic human claim for regard may be found in Dostoevsky's great novel, *Crime and Punishment*, a work from which much can be learned. Raskolnikov plays with the idea of being a superman, an individual of elite qualities and therefore beyond the moral law. "All is permissible" is his motto, as it was the slogan of the Russian Nihilists in their heyday. He knows an old and wretched woman, a pawn broker, without goodness in her heart—a being, as Raskolnikov claims, only detrimental to society. And now he wants to prove to himself his moral sovereignty as superman; he plans to kill her. To him this is no crime, maybe even something favorable (as many owe money to this woman); in any case, to do away with her is like killing an insect, nothing else. It should prove that he is not bound by a general morality or rules of bourgeois decency. The strong can always do what they deem fit. Thus the old woman is slain, while the murderer remains unknown. What follows is the very core of the novel. Human beings cannot just break fundamental laws of human existence. Raskolnikov in the long run was to learn this great lesson. He cannot stand his deed any longer, in spite of all rationalization, and eventually surrenders to the police.

What was said of this diabolic philosophy of the superman, the great "single one," the denial of regard for human beings in general, holds true also for all collectivistic philosophies, the very opposite to the first named philosophy. Marxism in its Russian interpretation gives us an unfortunate illustration of this thesis. There the single one, big or small, does not count at all because only the people as a whole, the masses, figure in this theory. It is not the individual with their infinite worth but only the collective, the whole that matters, forgetting that there cannot be a real whole if the members have no value-function. Human beings are not ants, and to disregard this simple commonplace bears evil consequences, as everybody knows. Spiritual truths are just realities which do not permit any violation, and boomerang-like, the violation comes back to the perpetrator, bringing to naught what seemingly was so carefully thought out. Radical individualism (singularism) as well as radical collectivism, are both blind to the basic I-Thou relation of a true We-Philosophy, and are evil in intent even though they might have appealing arguments. Disregard for our fellow person, our neighbor, our brother, means disregard for a spiritual truth, the infinite worth of the human person. And it is obvious that such an attitude means the destruction and privation of the joy which goes along with right and meaningful living.

But not only have these two radical philosophies missed the fundamental law of human existence. Well-intended paternalism and condescending benevolence are evils, too, though not obvious in the same way. Fundamentally, paternalism means treatment of those who are under one's sway like infants—friendly and benevolent actions, perhaps, but depriving the individuals of their dignity and self-decision, their autonomy. Paternalism is a great temptation for everyone in power. Enlightened despots followed the maxim: "Everything for the people, nothing by the people" (because people are dull and do not know what is advantageous for them). The Restoration period after Napoleon saw a Holy Alliance of unhappy memory where potentates vouched to treat their "subjects" as a good Christian father would treat his family. A look in the pages of history will suffice to unmask this hypocritical misuse of power. And who would not think of Rudyard Kipling's famous dictum, "The White Man's burden of the little brown brother"? It meant actually the shameful denial of dignity and regard for the "colonial people" of India. Unfortunately many Christian missionaries in Asia followed exactly the same illusion. Their motto was to lead the children—kindly to be sure, but not to permit them ever to grow up. The missionary remained always the "white Sahib." And what about the Negro slaves in Dixieland? Was it not the same story? Paternalism means, basically, refusal to regard the fellow person as possessing dignity and the potentiality of autonomous decision. But that alone makes one a full person, a value center, and means the giving up of all immaturity of infancy and childhood.

The principle of regard does not allow room for any exceptions. Even the criminal, the murderer, must be looked at as person and not only as fiend. Read Dostoevsky's *Memoirs from a Death House* to understand this fundamental truth. Just briefly let us discuss here several cases where misunderstanding or misuses are possible; that is where the temptation to camouflage power as (condescending) benevolence comes up. Slavery was mentioned more than once. In Ancient Times, a slave was looked upon as a tool, an implement, having lost his soul when becoming a slave. Aristotle, for instance, developed such a viewpoint without the least reluctance. The secret of personality, of divinely endowed freedom to choose and to decide for the good (or likewise for the bad), was not yet discovered. But in modern times one wonders how such disregard was ever possible and even defended by some ministers. A remainder of this older viewpoint still lingers on in some circles. A glance at South Africa, for instance, and its shameful racial policy of today should serve as a warning. Read Allan Paton's gripping novel, *Cry, The Beloved Country*. But, by and large, we have come to recognize the wrong of slavery in any form and the distortion of the human image by bondship. It was achieved by men of great vision and courage, by a William Wilberforce, a William L. Garrison, and many more. The great revolutionary forces of a genuine Christian spirit were working through these men. We recognize this today and accept the verdict of history.

With regard to criminals, something was already mentioned. The horrible dungeons of past periods, the torturing and the refusal of regard to treat the criminals as human beings, as fellow people who went astray; all that, we hope, has gone for good. Experiences of recent times, such as the methods in Hitler's Germany, prove that we still have to fight this old fight. But let us also recognize the improvements that were achieved. Prison reforms are a reality, and governments today believe not only in protecting society but also in the idea of reforming the law-breaker. Once he finds regard or respect, the criminal might try to prove worthy of it, and this—in a happy circle—promotes further regard, and so on. But here again, we would never have arrived at this point without the incessant fight of great Christian personalities who staked all their own well-being in this struggle. Their names are little known, but their work persists. John Howard (1726–1790) is perhaps the best known of them, but Elizabeth Fry (1780–1845), the English Quaker, and Mathilde Wrede (1864–1929), the Finnish baroness, are not less outstanding and memorable in their work. The fight is going on, but the vision points at least in the right direction. It is, as always, the path of greater resistance.

Another case where regard or disregard is at stake is the situation of the working man or the factory hand, mainly since the days of the Industrial Revolution. Whosoever reads of the conditions in the earlier days of the nineteenth century will be downright shocked about this lack of even the most primitive regard of human rights by the early entrepreneurs and their managers. The picture of semi-naked women, drawing carts in coal mines while partly crawling on feet and hands, looks almost too horrible to be true. Small children, taken from foundling homes and worked to death, were a common sight. These days are over in Europe and America (though not in other areas), but even today there are many regions with still the lowest standards of working conditions. I myself have seen factories processing lead material which mock any description. Early deaths, and all the misery connected with such surroundings, speak a strong language of disregard of the basic human maxim, "to use men always as an end in themselves and never simply as a means to an end" (Kant). Whatever improvements we know today are the results of a long and hard struggle, and labor leaders must be credited for it, even though it is true that not all of them were moved by purely ethical motives. Some managers thought that a benevolent paternalism could help much and avoid the well-known fight with the unions. It appears that this too is an illusion. No one can stand mere benevolence and condescension in the long run, for it is a concomitant to freedom that one really wants to shoulder one's own responsibility.

The place of women in society is another subject pertaining to this discussion though less evident for Americans of today who experience complete emancipation and equality of the two sexes. Reference to the nineteenth amendment of 1920 might help reconstruct a condition of but recent past. Until about the turn of the last century the woman was always regarded as in some way inferior, and unfit to manage her own affairs. Read Ibsen's *A Doll's House* to imagine the tremendous revolution which has come with the emancipation of women soon after 1900.

Today we are talking of the emancipation of the child. At long last, children too receive a certain regard and are taken as full people even though they are not yet fully developed. Child government in schools, a certain regardful tone of parents or teachers when talking to children, the abolishment of all parental absolutism—what a change within the last twenty or thirty years!

Finally, one brief thought should also be devoted to people whose capacity to be real persons might be put into question: the mentally ill. Have they not lost all or most personalistic qualities, all or most qualities of human beings? This was the opinion in the days of old Bedlam (St. Mary's of Bethlehem) in London which became proverbial for its barbaric treatment of these poor lunatics. True, these times are over too, since we have learned that the benighted ones are still human beings capable, though somewhat reduced, of experiencing sympathy and regard. When during the last World War conscientious objectors were used in mental institutions as attendants, a remarkable experience was gained. While the professional attendants were wont to a rough and unconcerned treatment of these poorest, the young non-professionals, usually stemming from a religious background, practiced a new form of treating their wards. The response of the ill ones was surprising. They felt kindness, patience, even love—in any case regard—and reacted accordingly. Improvements were observed, more quiet and orderly behavior was achieved, in short the living proof was presented that regard is a fundamental principle of human existence. It is not all, to be true, but it is the starting point.

In drawing the sum of all these observations, we might also say that it is perhaps here and here only where one could possibly speak of a real progress or advancement in the field of ethics and moral behavior. Slowly we have learned to show a certain regard to our fellow people, no matter who they are and how they are. Slavery and serfdom have been condemned everywhere as inhuman and no longer permissible; criminals and insane persons receiving a more decent treatment than at any time before, and that holds true also for prisoners of war. Women and children have likewise gained the recognition they have ever been entitled to. But in spite of all this progress, much remains still to be done. There is no reason to pride ourselves on what has been achieved; rather we should be mindful that regard still remains the "ought" after which we have to strive continually, lest we fall back to former barbarism. It was one of the sad degradations that in Hitler's Germany things could happen which were thought impossible even a short while before. It meant the outright denial of everything belonging to the great Christian and humanistic heritage, a violation of all Western tradition. In the last analysis, there cannot be something truly human which is not also truly divine. If, in the field of man's activities, the truly divine is abandoned, there will remain nothing "purely human" either, for this is the law of our existence. We are mindful here again of Victor Gollancz's well-chosen phrase concerning our "threatened values." If we refuse, as he says, "respect for personality," even to our adversaries, then we forfeit the chance of making our life meaningful. Whatever we refuse our fellow person we refuse, in the last analysis, ourselves. No "single one," no despot, no boss, no thoughtless overlord, reaches genuine satisfaction and happiness, as much as he might indulge in ostentatious enjoyments all his life. Only a philosophy which gives full dignity and worth to every human being corresponds to the nature of our existence. And from here it follows almost inescapably that the proper way of living together in mutual regard becomes a maxim which no one may neglect without harm to their self. Regard for the other (that is, taking them fully as an end in themselves) is then the very first insight of our search for moral guidance, or, in other words, the first step in a meaningful design for living.

PART 2: DESIGN FOR LIVING

Concern

The first step engenders the second, and it proves a real blessing that in things spiritual a creative emergence of something still nearer to the divine meaning is possible and even urged onward. It is a joy to be enabled to go on and produce in our mind more than we anticipated. This more is now the principle of concern—a principle almost unknown in literature until recently, although we could have learned it from the great religious traditions of our world. Concern transcends traditional philosophy and philosophical ethics, and belongs already to another level which I would be inclined to call the religious one, rightly understood.

What does concern mean at this place? Perhaps I am permitted to relate a little experience of my own through which I learned what it means to be concerned. It is a rather insignificant incident, and yet—to me it was a great lesson. For a while, in 1939, I lived in England in the home of a very kind elderly lady. We both drove to visit a German Jewish girl who had just arrived as a refugee from the continent, being now employed as a house maid in an English country home. Understandably she was rather unhappy in her situation. About two weeks later the elderly lady asked me whether I had some news from this girl. When I answered in the negative, she said to me, "I think she would need to be looked after." That to me meant concern. It is an apprehensive interest in and a care for another person, motivated by—and here I stop. What actually does motivate such interest and care? What made this kind lady in England remind me that the girl really needed to be looked after? The lady did not know the girl at all and had no contacts with her fate whatsoever. Was it Christian love, *agape*? Hardly. Was it regard? Likewise no. It was a kind of general sympathy, a compassion or feeling-with, an inner participation, and maybe even an unmediated identification ("if I were in her place . . ."). And we remember again the happy term which William Stern uses in his value philosophy: *Introception*, taking the other person's interest into one's own mind. Such Introception is by no means easy or an everyday event, but it is a very high ranking moral activity of the mind. No doubt it would have been more comfortable just to forget the case (as I had done) and to enjoy the pleasant things around us. To go and look up those who are in need and worry, to share in their predicament, to be a friend where friends are missing—is that not the path of greater resistance but also of greater reward and satisfaction?

Concern, then, comes very near the concept of "Introception." It means taking the other person's experiences, joys and worries, interests and anxieties, into our own system, making them our own joys and worries, interests and anxieties. Concern is doing exactly this, only with a stronger emphasis upon the worries and anxieties of our fellow people with the centering of Introception upon the more unfortunate experiences of life. Thus, concern is more than mere regard but less than active service; it is the conditioning of the mind preliminary to any service. Concern is born out of a desire to share and to participate with the experiences of others. In this way it is similar to and yet different from the feeling of sympathy which rarely prompts any subsequent action. It implies a certain solicitude which usually goes along with a tender care, and it means taking the other's predicament seriously and as if happening to one self. Concern will lead to an urge to alleviate the bad conditions of others, although in itself it is not yet the same as service or love, but rather a certain, almost oppressive, state of the mind. It is possible to make it a general "ought": "Be concerned!" Awake to humankind's plight, develop in yourself this sensitivity which we have called an educated heart! Yes, it is still within the limit of what can be required, though it presupposes the vision of a higher plane. No doubt, concern is a noble attitude, the unmediated identification and suffering with the fellow man. But once achieved, it spells satisfaction and meaningfulness for our own existence.

In his *Alternative to Futility* (1943), Elton Trueblood, the Quaker, makes a very remarkable proposal fitting into the present context.[4] He recognizes the crucial time we live in and feels the need for the crystallization of a "redemptive Society" which could bring forth the spiritual forces needed to lift this world of ours upon a plane above futility, redeeming it, so to speak, from its nearly hopeless plight. People everywhere who accept the same essential goal and the same principles leading to it, might thus be bound together in a horizontal (though invisible) fellowship. Nameless in practice, it would in reality be an "Order of the Concerned." It means being concerned with the predicament of modern man and subsequently with the discovery of an alternative to futility. The minimum conditions to become a member of this imaginary and yet most real "order" are the following: commitment, witness, fellowship, vocation, and discipline. The bond of union, however, is their common concern. It is not the place here to elaborate on this idea whose spirit is very close to that of the present book. To us it was primarily to serve as an illustration of the significance of concern for the life on a spiritual plane. Trueblood does not suggest particular actions, but

---

4. Trueblood, *Alternative to Futility*.—Ed.

a particular mind as his solution, and this mind he characterizes rightly as concern.

The opposite of concern is thoughtlessness, a state of mind unburdened by any introceptive activity. It can be a happy naiveté, an easygoing self-centeredness, an ignorance of the bonds which tie us essentially to our fellow people, of which we are not conscious at all. It is this amoral type of living which fills perhaps the greater part of our lives. Most likely we need periods of such being unburdened, but it is not possible to justify a life totally unconcerned and egocentric. We have to awaken from this sleep, and have to become aware that as much as we expect our neighbors to participate in our own affairs we have also to reciprocate, that is to open our mind and heart to their worries and concerns. Only thus we widen ourselves and make life a real adventure of the spirit.

But concern is more than a mere application of the Golden Rule. What characterizes the concerned person is rather that the concerned person does not wait until the cry of the afflicted one or until a request for help lands on his desk. It is rather that the concerned one looks after the situations which need to be "looked after" before anybody even dreams of asking for one's sharing or comfort. Those who are concerned with the conditions of people in calamities, in sickness, shame, jail, or on the open road, go and offer themselves, while the afflicted ones did not even suspect that people exist who care. That is the redemptive quality of concern and the character of a path of greatest resistance. In our next chapter we will meet people who were concerned and then went out and served. Not everybody, however, finds the great strength to go their way to its final culmination. But to develop the quality of being thin-skinned enough to experience concern for all the downtrodden and those in misery and despair, that is an "ought" which definitely belongs to a design for living worthy of such a name. My elderly English friend was right: people need to be looked after.

Service

Regard, concern, and service are three steps of a very consistent sequence: regard recognizes in every human being the dignity of a person; concern then takes this person's interests and worries into one's own mind; and service finally is the doing of something in the interest of this person. Service, it becomes apparent, is an action that issues forth from concern, although the latter is in itself not yet the prompting force or motive, as we have described in the previous chapter. The motive of service is just the desire to serve, and as such represents a new step in our design. Service is definitely not the same as altruism and has nothing to do with it. Service is based on a "feeling-with," an identification with the other which excludes the unhealthy "ideal" of altruism. Contrary to a socially interpreted Darwinism (which knows only the survival of the fittest by way of a relentless struggle for life), human life is, rather, based on the principle of mutual aid and service. Are not most people glad, even happy, to be of service to someone else or to some super-personal task? Is it not more natural to the unspoiled one to be of some avail than to fight the neighbor tooth and nail? The good American custom of barn raising could serve as an object lesson for cooperation and service, though it is not quite a full representation of what is meant by service in the present context. It demonstrates only the reality of the we-feelings and our social interrelatedness. And it illustrates that service not only can be a joy, but actually is joy.

Service is the principle taught to Boy and Girl Scouts, and it is likewise the principle in all YMCA and YWCA work. It becomes redemptive on the international scale of the American Friends Service Committee, the Mennonite Central Committee and the Brethren Service Committee; organizations that are concerned with the suffering of people everywhere in the world, sending out relief teams and single workers wherever they might be needed. "To the hungry, God appears in the form of bread"—this great word of Mahatma Gandhi has become only too true in these recent years of unimagined suffering, Someone had to offer this bread. And it is no surprise that concern and service become manifest within the three leading peace churches of our world who are intent toward such reconstruction to redeem the evils of all strife and warfare.

Assuming the We-Philosophy, the most meaningful and therefore satisfactory attitudes and acts of all are of the nature of service. Service becomes the source of a new and hitherto unknown joy. Service not only serves the needy ones, but it also serves the one who offers this service—if it is offered in the right spirit. Service is redeeming; that is, lifting upon a higher plane the one who commits themselves to such a form of life.

One of the finest literary expressions of the truth may be found in Tolstoy's short story *Master and Man*, a real gem of world literature, which everyone should become familiar with. Vassili Andreitch Brekhunov is a wealthy merchant, self-centered, unmindful of others, very conceited, but happy in his wealth and life's success. In the midst of a bitter cold winter he decides to go on a trip to cash in some claims. He is accompanied by good old Nikita, the servant who takes care of the sledge and horse, a meek and humble Russian peasant who has never known anything better than to be a servant of a big man and master. And so they start; night soon sets in, but greed makes the merchant want to push on. Perhaps they yet can reach their destination. Twice they stop at places, twice they carry on (foolishly, however) in view of an oncoming blizzard, snowdrifts, and invisible roads. Thus by the middle of the night they are completely lost; Nikita is resigned, but Vassili, his master, is gripped by a real panic. The situation becomes more and more weird, but Vassili is still filled with thoughts of the money he will soon cash in. He does not think of the servant. "It would be nothing to him to die. What can his life matter to him?" he ponders, warmly wrapped in his fur coat while poor Nikita has not much protection but a thin blanket. He unties Brownie, the horse, and tries to ride away; perhaps he can find a shelter easier this way, until at early dawn he would continue to get his claims. They travel for the next half hour—or is it more, or less? He does not know, for it is ghastly enough, a snowy desert at night; at the howling of a wolf, Brownie stumbles and throws him off. Exhausted he finds himself suddenly back at the sledge. Nikita is slowly freezing to death inside the sleigh, hardly reacting to his master's call. And here a remarkable change takes place in Vassili's mind.

All at once he is thinking not of his money but of Nikita, the "unimportant" servant. He unhooks his belt, opens his fur coat, and lies down upon Nikita to warm him up and to protect him from freezing. "There you are," he says, contentedly talking to himself, "Just lie still and grow warm, and we . . ." Here it is, the little pronoun "we," so foreign heretofore to Vassili. He swallows a lump in his throat. He has lost one mitten, the poor horse is shivering and likewise near the point of passing out, but Vassili experiences a new upsurge of life which he has found in saving Nikita's life. He does not feel his numbed hand and he does not feel any longer the terror of this weird night. The joy of being of some use for Nikita, of service for somebody other than his own person, gives him such a satisfaction that he forgets all the rest, and above all he forgets himself. He is Nikita and Nikita is he, and his life is no longer within himself but within Nikita. "Nikita is alive!" he cries to himself in triumph, "and therefore so also am I." That is to him now the greatest thing of all, and he knows it. He learns this lesson while his body becomes more and more numb. When peasants dig up the sledge next morning, Vassili was no more, but Nikita recovers after a while.

REGARD, CONCERN, SERVICE, AND LOVE

It goes without saying that Tolstoy wanted to tell us more than a moralistic story here. It is a philosophy, or rather a religious faith, which expresses itself in what this story might bring home to the reader. Service, rightly offered, has a redemptive power. It lifts the individual's self, his "I," upon another plane where it meets the Thou, in order to join together into the We. That is the redemptive element in all service which goes beyond the alleviation of need and the administration of relief of some sort! It is the new experience of a true we-feeling: the giver and receiver become one, and it is hard to make out which of these two is graced more. This is the turn on the amoral blindness of Mr. Average to the awakened sensitivity of the educated heart. And to serve (not only to help in cases of extremity) is yet so easy, and so much called for.

Service is not necessarily an overt act. It can also be nothing but an attitude, a cry, an openness of the mind for the other's need, worry, or despair. Sometimes it is service just to listen to somebody's story, and properly listening means pushing one's own ego far into the background. A word of cheer and trust, an expression of confidence, is sometimes as much as and more than material help. There is need for service at every corner of our daily life, and the opportunities are without end. And yet, beware of a false and somewhat hysterical selflessness (altruism) which never has redemptive power. It must be always a We, never an isolated Thou (as little as an isolated I).

Not all so-called service will be service in this design for living sense. There are Red Cross officials or relief workers who do much good and yet cannot claim such higher meaning of their work. Or doctors, nurses, teachers, ministers—all who are in a serving position. Do they all actually serve? Do they redeem the situation, enrich it by lending a hand to the needy brother? In an earlier chapter we discussed the different pitfalls which endanger our way of value realization. One was paternalism, that certain condescending attitude of the more fortunate one, when he comes into contact with the weaker one. Very often alms are given in this way, thus losing all essential meaning. You might travel thousands of miles to administer to the needy but if you then look down paternalistically upon the "wretched" Indian or Chinaman, or whoever it might be, forgetting the basic principle of regard, all the service was in vain as far as its personal value is concerned. The hungry might take your bread and at the same time despise you for his humiliation. To quote the great Catholic saint, Vincent de Paul, "Only by loving them will they forgive us that we give them bread."

Service is essentially a confession that we are being bound together into a "we" that cannot be dissolved. "All mankind are brothers plighted where thy gentle wings abide." And the gentle wing might be the joy of this sublime discovery. Service is a practical way to this discovery, but it must be genuine service, not only some sort of doing without the right mind and understanding.

How often do we say without giving much thought to it, "I do not care" or "it is not my business, I do not put my nose in it," and similar phrases? And yet, in a proper sense, we have to care, we have to be concerned, and we have to be "our brother's keeper" (which, however, does not mean that we are our brother's warden). We should always keep in mind the consequence of a We-Philosophy, namely that we are mutually responsible for one another. That holds true not only for our physical well-being but also for our spiritual conditions, our inner strength and convictions, our faith in humankind, and beyond that, our faith in God. One thoughtless word might destroy much, and so could a bad example that we set. To be my brother's keeper means just this: to be engaged in a common enterprise of I and Thou, to be co-responsible for what we achieve or fail together. To be concerned and, subsequently, to serve is the function of just the one side of this common enterprise, that part which is up to me. The other person might not approve of my attitude at first, might not appreciate it, and might even refuse my service. In the long run, however, service (if offered in the right sense) will always be understood and welcomed. I (or we) all need the helping hand in our endeavor to reach higher and more meaningful planes. Service, thus conceived, has definitely a redeeming power in it.

Service is the last step on our ascent which still can be required—that is, which implies to a certain extent an "ought," because it is within the reach of everybody to be of use and help, to give from our riches to those who have less (and I do not mean primarily in a material sense). Service means definitely the end of rough and tough selfishness and self-centeredness. It means a giving which, as Jesus said, is more blessed than receiving (Acts 20:35). This might be a good rule of thumb for every day: Whatever you do, do it with pure motives, not for egocentric purposes (to gain influence or advantage, or any sort of glory), not out of mere conventionality, not for the sole motive of pleasure, but out of an objective purpose, whatever it be. Remember, for instance, Madame Curie. Hers was pure research, finding the truth and nothing else. But by committing herself to such a task, she became a model of moral greatness, as well as an example of selfless devotion and true service.

Opposite to service would be the much-heralded enlightened self-interest, struggle for life in the Darwinistic sense (the law of the jungle), practiced so much in business and politics, or any form of amoral activities (the playboy, the aesthetic attitude, art for art's sake, and so on). At times we all do so and nobody can claim to be free from it. Perhaps it is even good at certain times, since we have, so to speak, also a corner in our heart which bids for self-assertion. But keep this corner under control, for there are always imps at hand which like to confuse the issues, calling black white and white black. Think only what was said above about the confusion between instrumental values and intrinsic values, or think of the confusion between doing and genuine giving. Not every activity, not every charity even, can qualify as service, and there are many opportunities for hypocrisy of some kind. Thus, the above rule of thumb seems to be preferable to any kind of relativistic liberalism. We judge this or that as a harmless excursion into the amoral and here we think we can no longer find our way back.

Thus service is and should be a guiding principle in our design for living. It can be strived for, developed, and learned, until it becomes almost our second nature. In this it differs from love, which is a blessing and a grace beyond the power of our good intention. "Thou must love" makes little sense taken as an imperative, but "serve!" is still a possible call to all people; the call to find oneself by giving oneself. Service has the power to make people free because it meets our spiritual calling and exigency, giving us a self-consciousness beyond any egotistic means. It binds giver and receiver together in a joyous togetherness, even in calamity. It is a deeply human activity.

Do we need to relate here the thousand and one experiences along this line? There exist work camps in many places of need (in Europe and the Near East) and there are children's homes all over the country and beyond, where service becomes a genuine maxim. And in every single case satisfaction and joy are experienced on both sides because the right relationship between people has been achieved, where otherwise the law of the jungle might have had its sway. Only a few single personalities might be mentioned here to illustrate our point. As a rule they are people with much compassion since only through it they will discover the weak spot where help is needed.

There is, for instance, Henry Dunant, the man who almost single-handedly brought into existence the International Red Cross after having witnessed the almost indescribably acute suffering of the wounded on the battlefield of Solferino (1859). As a man of some means and a citizen of neutral Geneva, he came to the battlefield first as a mere onlooker and observer. But contrary to others he left with such a feeling of horror and compassion, and his mind did not find rest until something was done that such suffering should never happen again. In 1862, he published his *A Memory of Solferino* as private print, circulating it among people of influence. The final result was the Geneva Convention of 1864, upon which all future Red Cross activities rested. An immeasurable service was thus done to mankind in creating a service agency for the victims of war and other calamities, but the man who had sacrificed all his fortunes to this end disappeared into oblivion until he was found again, now of old age, to receive at least a small share of humankind's gratitude.

There is also Jane Addams, the woman who almost without intention became the mother of the numberless strays and waifs of Halstead Street, Chicago. Out of pity and compassion she collected them, first to occupy them, then also to give them meals, and finally to create a real center to belong to. It is Hull House of Chicago, model of similar settlements in many cities of today. In London it is called Kingsley Hall and its noble originator was Muriel Lester, a woman who deserved our highest esteem and admiration. She too began, against her family's advice, unplanned and driven only by compassion and an urge to serve, to make manifest the love in her heart for the downtrodden ones of London's East End. Kingsley Hall became also a great center of spiritual and religious revival, and when Mahatma Gandhi came to London in 1930 to the great Round Table Conference, he lived in Kingsley Hall, amidst those lowly ones who would understand him better than those of higher social standing. Miss Lester was a woman of deepest Christian devotion and commitment. Wherever she came to bring her message of peace, service and faith, response was not failing. She made it convincing, that sharing is a blessing and serving a grace. Only through faith in God's love and forgiveness can we gain the strength to fulfill that service which means a giving of a new trust to humankind.

Miss Addams was a free thinker; Miss Lester was a profound Protestant Christian, while Father Flanagan (d. 1918) was a devout Catholic. His Boys Town, near Omaha, Nebraska, is too well-known as to need much introduction. Here he collected (since 1917) juvenile delinquents as well as other wayward youth, believing that no inescapable fate makes these youngsters deviate from the right way. "There are no bad boys," was his guiding belief. Here he gave them a chance, the great opportunity of self-government combined with a loving counselor-ship. This great experiment in love and service soon became world-known and its founder went both to Japan and Europe to establish similar organizations.

Need we more to prove that service has a redeeming power? Of course, it is always service coupled with compassion and with love—for only great lovers will also achieve great service. Many more such names could be listed here. But for just this last named reason we shall better postpone their discussion until we have turned our attention to the last and greatest step in a design for living; that is, love, or *agape*. It definitely transcends the mere service motive, and opens a new plane, to the description of which we now turn.

Love

To speak of love is too sacred an affair to do lightly and without the right orientation of the mind. Here we touch the divine in that quality which is still within reach of us when on the highest plane of humanity. It is our deepest belief that humanity is created in the image of God, and that means that in our blessed moments we may grasp a glance at that which is above us, because it is of like nature. In love, the spiritual world opens itself fully to us, and when rightly understood, we find in love that which is absolutely meaningful and final. In love we fulfill ourselves as far as our power may go, but even in its highest forms it should always be understood as merely a reflection of what we dimly imagine to be the divine center. For that reason, a meditation on love goes beyond the scope of a practical philosophy of how to design one's life. And yet, how could we design it if the highest vision should be missed? No doubt, love lies beyond good and evil, and beyond what traditionally is called "ethics." Still, it is its culmination and its supersession, and must not be absent when the great issues of life are discussed. Love is a rare gift. If we leaf through the pages of history, we do not meet many people who manifest this unique force. For that reason, many a thinker thought it an impractical ideal, something which everyone would praise but hardly ever try to realize. I cannot agree with them. Love is a reality of great power and great appeal, and though perfect love was achieved possibly only once, it is yet the lofty goal which moved so many to great endeavors and achievements. The philosophers are in many cases at odds with the idea of love (think, for instance, of Kant) because it does not fit into their rational system. But it is yet a reality which the heart will always understand, once it has become sufficiently sensitive. Regard, concern, and service; would these steps not remain incomplete without love, the binding force which ties us together and to God? It is love that gives right meaning and right direction to the three preliminary steps which thus receive their final place in spiritual life.

It is hard, perhaps even impossible, to analyze love in a rational fashion. But it can be revealed by demonstration—that is, by professing it and witnessing to it. But before we enter such a study of its traits and of the ways of its realization in life, let us first learn a few pertinent testimonies that we may grasp its essence and its working in a more immediate fashion.

The master text on love is, of course, the Sermon on the Mount (Matt 5–7) which should be familiar to everyone who longs to progress in the realm of the spirit. "Love your enemies, bless them that curse you, do good to them that hate you and pray for them which despitefully use you and persecute you" (Matt 5:44). Similar words we read everywhere in the New Testament and in Christian literature: "I was naked and ye clothed me, I was sick and ye visited me, I was in prison and ye came unto me." (Matt 25:35–45); "If thine enemy hunger, feed him, if he thirst, give him drink, for in so doing thou shalt heap coals of fire on his head. Be not overcome of evil, but overcome evil with good," (Rom 12:20–21, Prov 25: 21–22); "If a man say, I love God, and hateth his brother, he is a liar. For he that loveth not his brother whom he has seen, how can he love God whom he has not seen?" (1 John 4:20–21); *Amor et fac quod vis* (Love and do what you want!) St. Augustine[5]; "The evil is the material of love. God reveals himself to us as the conquest of this evil, that is in love" (Tolstoy).

"We know that God is love, and that love will conquer everything. But if we try to apply love and it fails, then we say slightingly, 'Love is not efficient in this case,' as if God could ever stop being operative in us. It is only because we do not believe enough in love that we fail to do the works of love" (Tolstoy). "One should try less to do good than to be good, try less to shine than to be pure. Man's soul is like a vessel of glass . . . the cleaner it is, the better will the light of truth shine through it" (Tolstoy). If a single individual achieves the highest kind of love, it will be sufficient to neutralize the hatred of millions" (Mahatma Gandhi).

---

5. Augustine, *Confessions.*—Ed.

"I made the same experience time and again that good provokes the good, just as the evil engenders nothing but evil. If the evil finds no echo, then it loses its strength and dwindles down for lack of supply. I know of not a single case where this law had failed . . . In all jails in South Africa, which I became acquainted with, the wardens first showed great unfriendliness toward us. But after a while they invariably changed their behavior because I never retaliated in their way." (Gandhi, *Memories from South Africa*)

Kagawa writes that "Love's victories are never cheaply won. Christ conquered only through the Cross."[6]

Love then is the divine force in us, more operative in some than in others, but present and known to everybody, even the hardest criminal (as Dostoevsky so convincingly has shown us). There is definitely a paradox in the working of love; its strength is greatest when it appears to be weakest. Read Paul as a witness to it: "When I am weak then I am strong" (2 Cor 12:10); "The weakness of God is stronger than man" (1 Cor 1:25); "My strength is made perfect in weakness" (2 Cor 12:9); and "out of weakness we were made strong" (Heb 11:34). The strength of love is (contrary to that of service) not a strength of willpower, but of spiritual uplift—hence, the "secret of the Cross," as Kagawa described it in his *Meditation of the Cross*. Love actually means this invisible lifting-up to a higher plane of the one who is exposed to love's working; that is, its redemptive strength, its wondrous process which differs from everything else known in human experience. Love makes free and sovereign, though at the same time it makes most humble and far away from any boasting. It makes man conscious of a concrete meaning of life.

"What is hell?" asked Father Zossima in Dostoevsky's *Brothers Karamazov*: "I maintain that it is the suffering of being unable to love." That is, in the briefest form, the truth about life and meaning of life. He who cannot love cannot experience joy, satisfaction, and a free spirit—hence life becomes to him just this hell. Genuine love transfigures the world, the person of the lover as well as those who are infected by his love. This idea of transfiguration of man seems to be particularly familiar to Orthodox Christianity. The works of Nicolai Berdayev, for instance, abound in meditations on this point. Love is always creative because it is the manifestation of the divine in life. It creates life where there is none, awakens where there is sleep, finds a way out where despair sees but an impasse. Love discovers

---

6. Kagawa, *Love, the Law of Life*.—Ed.

a hidden suffering in the brother's heart, love knows about this heart and finds a direct contact to it. Love makes us open-minded for that which is positive with our neighbor and at the same time sensitive for that which needs support and understanding.

The more someone loves, the more they grow in it and become able to give. It is just the opposite from any material giving; there, the more you give the less you will have to spend. In love, the more you give, the richer you yourself become for such spending. If you have one child you will give him all your love; if you have five, ten, even a hundred children under your care, will they not get exactly the same love as the single child received before? Love grows with loving.

Love is infectious, or more correctly, contagious; that is its most victorious trait. Tolstoy is very insistent on this point and the deepest argument of his faith is that in the long run love will triumph. "Nothing else is needed," he writes in his *Diary*, "but to surround men with love and kindness. It is the strongest means to prepare the Kingdom of God." And Gandhi quotes just this thought in his extraordinary essay *Neither Saint nor Politician*: "Somewhere Tolstoy says that not more is needed but to forgive our nearest neighbor to calm down this world without much further ado. For, inasmuch as we stop fighting our neighbor, the circles of union thus established in the right fashion would grow more and more, until it finally covers the entire world." This sounds utopian, and is utopian if taken in such simplicity; but it is also a great faith and the affirmation that love alone will eventually redeem this world of man. Gandhi, Schweitzer, Kagawa, Quakers, Mennonites, Brethren—they all believed and believe in this self-propagating force of love if rightly offered. It is like the ripples on the surface of water when a stone is thrown in—they spread into ever-widening circles.

Love is something very different from friendliness, kindness, good-heartedness, well-wishing, and the like. Such attitudes lack the power of transfiguration, and quite often express an inner weakness rather than strength and spirituality. It is against them primarily that Nietzsche thundered his anathema. There are many people who are good-natured and well-disposed, but it is quite obvious that such a disposition is something fundamentally different from genuine love, and that it derives from a different psychological level. The same holds true with regard to pity and general sympathy, which likewise are often mistaken as expressions of love, although they lack the active element of the latter. In all these cases we meet one of those confusions which obscure an understanding rather than clarify it. Basically we may say that love, the *agape* of the New Testament, is nothing primarily emotional or sentimental as those above named qualities, but rather a rare flowering of human spirituality. Pascal called it "the reason of the heart." There is nothing negative in it as in pity, which in most cases derives from a pessimistic viewpoint (Buddha, Schopenhauer). Likewise it should be stressed that love is not necessarily always sweet. In fact, it might often contain an element of austerity and even harshness. But it always has the strength of redemption and the tendency toward helping, uplifting, and transfiguring.

Another instance of antithesis is the distinction between love and law. It is in the nature of law that it always points to a commandment; which requires obedience without further regard of personal references. There is an ethics of law which even prides itself of its impersonal character, of this independence from any purpose or intention. The Ten Commandments of the Old Testament might serve as a good example, and following them the six hundred-odd laws that Judaism developed in the course of its history. Who would not know the Apostle Paul's passionate disclaim of this Law in favor of both grace and love? (Theologically, he stressed more the antithesis of the Law and grace, but ethically it is the antithesis of the Law and love.) And then again St. Augustine, whose bold dictum, "Love, and do what you want"[7] has been quoted by us more than once. It again implies an outspoken disdain of any legalistic point of view in matters of right living. Nearer to our time is Kant's great ethics of duty: it is not strictly an ethics of law since "nothing can be called good in all the world but a good [i.e. rational—Friedmann's interpellation] will." Duty, as he conceives it, is a condition of this will, hence a purpose rather than a law. But then, why should we obey the call to duty? To this Kant answers: out of reverence for the law, the one law that transcends the subjective limitation of the individual. It is a universal law, although it is not commanded by any objective lawgiver but by the moral personality itself, by the rational nature of humanity which autonomously sets first the law and then obeys it, regardless of any inclination to the contrary. It becomes quite obvious that such an ethics of duty has little appreciation for "pathological" love (as Kant writes) which is beyond the reach of all rational imperative, valid for all and applicable without exception. There is no need for further argument; within its purpose duty is a great principle and capable of a real invigoration of moral life.

---

7. Augustine, *Confessions*.—Ed.

But there is no basis for comparison with what is here understood as love, for love is no longer a philosophical concept to be defined by reason. It is rather the manifestation of a spiritual reality belonging not to the realm of philosophy, but to that of faith.

Because of its anti-legalistic nature, love is also not a "commandment" in the strict sense of the word, although the term is used twice in the Johannine writings (John 13:31, 1 John 1:21). The disciple could understand this new teaching as a commandment of his master, indicating something like this: "If you want to be my disciples, that is, if you want to enter the Kingdom of God, then you must never end in loving your brother whoever he be." In this way it might be called a commandment. But in all other ways it is far from anything being commanded. It is rather something being commended, being pointed at, and lived before as an example. Love cannot be realized by a mere effort of one's will, although it can be developed as much as it can be stunted.

Catholic teachings are rather outspoken and clear on this question of ethical requirements, distinguishing between a maximum and a minimum ethics. The Decalogue (the law) is binding for all (and possible for all), while the superior demands of the Sermon on the Mount are considered only as "Evangelical Counsels." They have meaning only if freely accepted and recognized as the principle of one's own higher calling, something to be rediscovered time and again while on the steep ascent to a higher plane. Yes, the demands which we read throughout the Gospels are counsels or instructions for the one who is to commit their life to the service of the kingdom of God. They will have to be learned and then, as far as possible, assimilated. They do not necessarily mean monastic vows, since there are many walks of life which lead to this highest goal. But they all have one and the same guide post, and that is love in its most sublime meaning.

It would be a grave misunderstanding to take this love as something impractical and unrealistic. Just the opposite of it holds true, as the glorious array of great people of love vividly proves. Love is very well applicable in life, as suggested by the detailed counsels of the Gospels.

> "I was hungry, and ye gave me meat, I was thirsty and ye gave me drink, I was a stranger and ye took me in, I was naked and ye clothed me, I was sick and ye visited me, I was in prison and ye came unto me." And when thereupon the righteous ones asked "when did we do so?" the King of the parable answered, "Inasmuch as ye have done it unto one of the least of these my brothers, ye have done it unto me." (Matt 25:35–40)

All Christian philanthropy (in its widest sense) stems from teachings like these. Unfortunately, the story of this philanthropy has never been written and the whole field of the working of love has been badly neglected. Even our vocabulary is inadequate in this regard. "Philanthropy" and "charity" can very well be administered without exerting particular forces of love, and the giving of alms can become even embarrassing and the opposite of what love stands for. There are hospitals and homes for the indigent, orphanages, and all kinds of charitable organizations, but in most cases they can claim no major merit in the line of our subject. Social work and social welfare have something to do with that feeling of co-responsibility which was discussed in an earlier context and which is rarely refused by society at large, but it has next to nothing to do with the works of love enjoined in the teachings of Jesus. It is not the action proper which matters but the spirit behind it and the dedication of man to his task. As we said earlier: love is always creative. It ferrets out those who need it most, and in so doing it means cheer and affirmation in spite of all the misery encountered.

We have already met some of those who might be quoted here: Kagawa and Schweitzer, Muriel Lester and Father Flanagan, then the three great names in prison reform: John Howard, Elizabeth Fry, and Mathilde Wrede. Too easily do we forget that what we enjoy today in human advancement is due to a few who pioneered against a world of indifference and even hatred. It is amazing how little-known these persons are. In most cases they remain anonymous, for they shy away from all publicity and are loath of public praise unless absolutely needed for their work. They distrust all fame, for "charity vaunteth not itself, is not puffed up, and seeketh not her own" (1 Cor 13:4-5). They are never self-centered but dedicated to a work worthy of the effort, and usually not undertaken without the prompting of the forces of love. Their story is usually simple and lacking dramatic tensions, but it is a story of heroism in which everything is staked. They conquer in the way that love always conquers: without much noise. There is a sparkle of the divine operative in them, but people pass by without becoming aware of it.

A very noble example of such a worker of love is Elsa Brandström, the "Swedish angel" of World War I. Her name is nearly forgotten today as is her work, save in the heart of those to whom she had meant life and not death. Her book, *Among Prisoners of War in Russia and Siberia*, is a document of a great soul though presented with much humility and unpretentiousness.[8] How this daughter of a wealthy Swedish merchant, who on

---

8. See Brandström, *Among Prisoners of War*.—Ed.

many trips through tsarist Russia had learned to know the land, its people and their language, soon after the outbreak of the first World War felt urged to look after the prisoners of war: Germans and Austrians, Hungarians and Czechs, Poles, Yugoslavs and all the rest, pitifully barracked somewhere in the wide plains of Russia and Siberia. That is certainly a story of grandeur, a manifestation of the power of love. Singlehandedly, she worked near-miracles, a woman among a barbarized soldiery. This was particularly true during those terrible years after 1917, when revolution and civil War had disrupted even the last bit of orderliness and care. A typhoid epidemic raged while Bolsheviks and counter-revolutionaries fought a relentless war. Nobody cared whatsoever for the hundreds of thousands of prisoners of war who were thus caught in the midst of an indescribable misery. How in this situation Miss Brandström worked and saved the lives of many, must be read in the book itself, which contains her memoirs. It will then become plain why she is still gratefully remembered today by those who survived, and considered to have been an angel sent by God himself. Only concern could make her go to Siberia and worry about those for whom nobody else worried, only service could yield such practical results, and only great love could risk and achieve so much.

Here is another story, perhaps a little better known, and yet still in need of greater attention. It is the life of Pastor Bodelschwing (1834–1910), the father to the epileptics and other afflicted ones, the friend of the tramps on the highways and the lost children of the great cities and the founder of the home of Bethel near Bielefeld, Germany. In him love becomes truly redemptive, particularly in the face of this eerie disease also called "falling sickness." These poor afflicted ones did not need a doctor (who could not help them anyway), but the guide to a faith that could open to them opportunities which would never be destroyed. How devotion, love, dedication, and unbelievable patience brought light to these sick people is a story too involved to be condensed into a few lines. But how inventive the good pastor was. He built new homes for all the needy whom he nursed and brought back to new life and confidence. They became a great family in the end. Whatever he touched became a symbol of working love, and no one was wretched enough as not to find a loving look by the man who believed in life's forces when all hope seemed to have vanished. Like Job, he was stricken himself when four tender children of his were taken from this life by a pernicious disease within a few weeks. His faith kept him upright in this bitter visitation and his work did not permit a letdown in the long run.

He had regard for everyone, the tramps and the alcoholics alike, and thus started them on their way back to rehabilitation. Doors opened wherever he knocked. With his sensitive heart he saw clearly the plight of the farmhands in Northern Germany who could never acquire even the smallest lot to settle on. Thus he initiated a movement to make it possible for these landless workers to eventually own a home, and he lived long enough to see the success of this enterprise. A life so richly graced finds fulfillment and realization only in unlimited giving. With creative imagination he found ever new ways out, and most of his undertakings still carry on as a living proof of the forces that stood behind them.

Thus our story could go on. Big and small names equally deserve our attention that we may learn from them the great lesson: that love is practical, that love is real, that love is redemptive. Love is connected with concern, but it is not the same. To prevent misunderstandings, it might be helpful to distinguish the two Greek words that are both translated as love: *eros* and *agape*. Scholarly books were written on this subject but we do not suggest to dwell too long on the issue. *Eros* is that driving force in us which is just on the edge between body and mind, although Plato ennobled the term to make it mean the upsurge of the mind toward the invisible world of ideas. It means a passion, the only driving force known to the Greeks. *Agape*, to the contrary, is a word of later derivation. It applies to the idea of love of the New Testament which the King James Bible translates with charity. It lacks the quality of passion and assumes an exclusively spiritual character, a force not describable by psychology and yet real. It is suggested that this term *agape* became more generally used to signify that love which is capable of conquering evil and of redeeming the world. It is, as we said at the beginning, a reflection of a divine quality of God's love. And since love is of a strictly personalistic nature, it follows with inescapable consequence that God, too, can only be thought of as a person.

Thus to us *agape* is something very different from philanthropic humanitarianism, without diminishing the latter's merits. To us *agape* culminates our vision of a design for living—though, in a sense, it goes beyond any conscious effort toward such a design. It is *the absolute meaningful*, hence it is always affirmative and "long suffering." It demonstrates that life is at first neither good nor evil but is the great opportunity for the realization of that which has intrinsic value. There are many such possibilities, but I am inclined to agree with the Apostle Paul that "if I have no charity, it profiteth me nothing."

PART 2: DESIGN FOR LIVING

Last Conclusions

Our search for a design for living has almost come to its end and certain conclusions have been reached. Thus it seems only proper to stop for a brief review of the things that we have encountered on our ascent and have recognized as significant for the shaping of the right pattern of life. From there we might venture to last conclusions pertaining to the art and meaning of living.

Our first attention would belong to the question: do we discuss in this book *a* design for living or *the* design? It is a question of great importance and whatever the answer it will find skeptics and opponents. If I say "a" design the reader might say well, as a personal confession I respect it, but it has hardly any bearing for me. If I say "the" design (with a certain absolute claim) then the reader might say that it is overbearing to assume such a prophetic attitude. You should be aware of the motley nature of humanity and of the fact that we cannot know absolutes. If a person can reach even a minimum of agreement, they should be happy. Relativism, as everyone knows, is the keyword of our time and any step beyond it will provoke attacks from many corners.

This then is our problem and it seems somewhat late to answer it now that we have nearly finished our journey. Of course, I am aware of our manifold nature and of our sovereign freedom to choose our pattern of meaningful living. In fact I have been saying this all the while in so many words. And yet, I cannot help believing that there is a basic pattern applicable for all, something absolute, which nobody can disregard *if* they take life seriously. I definitely believe in a certain dualistic worldview in which body and mind, nature and sprit, law and freedom are unreducible opposites. In such a worldview alone the term "spiritual life" assumes meaningfulness. And this in its part enables us to approach intelligently the subject of value and value realization. Of course, there are many other ways of coping with the value problem—for instance, the psychological interpretation of values as expressions of human interest. Very well, but then no distinction between instrumental and intrinsic values is possible, ethics and all so-called "higher life" become relative, and any call toward an effort along a line of greater resistance becomes somewhat uncertain, if not downright questionable. Any monistic (i.e. naturalistic) approach to ethics, so popular nowadays, ends where our book began in a hedonistic or self centered practical philosophy. No further argument will be presented here given that a major section of the book was devoted to a demonstration of what "design for living is not."

I think it has become plain by now that deep in our heart is rooted a dim longing for making one's life purposeful, following a certain design, which provides lasting satisfaction and which enriches personal as well as social life. These were, so to speak, our presuppositions and the justification for the entire venture to elaborate on the theme of "design." We cannot close our eyes and forget about it. Calamities are at hand at every corner, and the experiences of young Buddha (old age, disease, death) are too convincing as to brush them aside with the simple advice: eat, drink, and be merry.

Yes, I believe that once we accept these basic insights and the problems of value realization, search for "the" design for living is justified: a search for a pattern of inner attitudes which is the common possession of humankind in its nobler endeavor. We claimed that the main topic of our book is the education of the heart, in a similar way as it would be the topic of a book on science to educate the mind. The "educated heart" is the term which points toward a more sensitive understanding of the great issues of human living: those which deal exclusively with one self (meaning, work, self-realization, suffering, and above all death) and those which are determined by our living together in society, in fellowship and mutual sharing. These issues are general and valid for all, no matter how different individuals otherwise may be.

What was presented earlier as "We-Philosophy" applies likewise to everybody; no one can exempt themselves from its principles. The basic truth, that the mature mind overcomes the egocentric limitation and learns not only to regard the fellow person, but also in some ways to share with them, is too plain and self-evident as to need further defense. Every violation of it means at the same time a violation of the order of life as we know it. Like a boomerang, every lack of concern and every disregard of our fellow human will come back to us as a forfeiture of our life's greatest chance. No mature and self-controlled mind will refuse to share with others in the good things of life as well as in calamities. In fact, an original urge drives us time and again to seek places where accepting responsibility, sharing, and participating are the needs of the hour. Thus again we contend that this "We-Philosophy" has a certain absolute claim and must find its proper place in "the" design for living, diversified though our human nature is.

This is also the case for the belief in a meaning in life. Tolstoy's *Confession* gives us here a helpful lesson. "Faith," we learned, "is the understanding of the meaning of life by virtue of which man does not annihilate himself but lives." It means that we can live in the right way only if we know or dimly grasp a positive (non-instrumental, non-egocentric) meaning of our doings. This meaning is understood not by way of discursive thinking (like affairs of science and philosophy) but by an intuitive process which may best be called faith, though it is different from any creedal faith. Naturally this meaning is different with every person. You might be a simple ditch digger or an artist of Michelangelo's greatness, it does not matter: meaning must be present in every life and can be attained in every walk of life. It presupposes only a pure approach and dedication to one's work and an interpretation of it as service. Not every service needs to be of a practical, philanthropic nature. What matters is only this: *whatever you do, it ought to assume the character of giving.* (We might add that there is still plenty of space left in our lives for personal enjoyment, pleasure and fun, and perhaps even a little bit of foolish self-assertion. Of course, the most abiding self-assertion will be gained only in those activities which do not pertain to this parenthetical remark.)

Thus let us take the sum. We look at the human being in the first place as a person, a value center, a creative being, a being with dignity and freedom. We claim that life cannot be lived without meaning, but we claim also that we are fooled as long as we are seeking this meaning in merely egocentric self-interested activities. We omit at this place all considerations discussed in the two chapters on "The Human Situation" where fallacies, pitfalls, and other complications are studied. At this point we consider life as an opportunity for planning, trusting that it will be possible to realize the plan or design, to a certain extent at least. There are values of which can be realized and that implies that we can do something meaningful which at the same time is deeply satisfactory. Combine then this insight with the basic principles of a "We-Philosopy" and the conclusion is evident: there must exist a design for living which is valid and acceptable for all, generally speaking. To deny it and then to indulge in some sort of skepticism is a dangerous thing, for the evil forces in this world are always on the alert and will take advantage of it. In this field there exists no neutral ground.

By now it should become apparent that it makes sense to speak of "the" design for living, or a pattern drawn up for humanity in general, which yet allows a thousandfold varieties in its actual realization. Regard, concern, and service are then the ethical attitudes and acts which in a general way describe what is needed for a life thus conceived. No matter what we do and for what goal we are striving (beyond the purely egocentric one) it will have to be done in conformity to this pattern. There is no neutral ground, as we said before, and pushing "the things that matter most" in the background shows but a lack of understanding of life's intrinsic task. Whatever we do, we are bound by an immanent "ought" to do it without offending the claim for regard for our fellows men. This is not "a" pattern, it is "the" number one pattern of a life which yearns for an achievement on a higher plane.

Consistently this first insight leads to a second one. Not only have we to show regard, but also a certain concern for the predicaments and ills of our fellow people. Any serious neglect of this principle will make that higher achievement precarious, if not impossible. What creative work could be done and what satisfaction could be achieved while we try to live as if in a dreamland, like Buddha before he decided to go out from his palace and see life? The thin-skinned and sensitive person, the one with an educated heart, will no longer dream away in self-conceit (as Vassily Brekhunoff was dreaming of his success on that terrible night). He will know that whatever may be done, alertness is needed so as not to violate basic principles of life: regard for the dignity of my brother, and concern for his plight, mute though he might be in bearing it.

And then step three: service. Who would oppose it by disclaiming it as merely a subjective formula? Should not life as a whole have this character of service and dedication? Whenever we have overcome the egocentrism of subjective life (if we were able to overcome it) and have reached an objective attitude to our tasks, then the work becomes superpersonal, a service, and in all higher forms of work, even a dedication. It means purity of motives, an objective approach, and the awareness of our ties to all humankind.

Thus, up to this point, we actually make the claim to have delineated a few significant principles of the design for living which are adequate to and asked for by our nature as citizens of two realms, the realm of necessity and that of freedom (which is the same as the realm of the spirit). The theoretical basis to such a vision is the "We-Philosophy" and its correlated principle of Introception. If we conform to those principles, we increase the forces of the good in the world and stall the progress of the evil.

But the very climax lies still beyond, where the terms good and evil lose their meaning. Love does not know enemies, hence it knows no limits in its functioning. That is the secret of Christ's teachings on the Mount: it is beyond any "ought," perhaps even beyond any conscious design, although we read that love was called a new "commandment." Actually this love was a new revelation, a new opening, to manifest the spiritual life at its glorious culmination. Love is God himself, as the apostle John once said. Love cannot be requested but only demonstrated. Whosoever feels able will follow this way, and it will be a blessing through the ages. The great beacon lights of love, however, are rare as is everything that is precious.

One quality is more or less common to all these steps and that is the human capacity to *share*. It is a noble attitude. Have you ever watched children to whom you offered some candies? Some grab and eat as fast as they can; other take and let the fellow child or even the giver first nibble before they eat themselves. They enjoy sharing and it comes natural to them. And then all laugh and there is perfect joy and happiness. Regard, concern, service, and love: do these steps not imply sharing, a joyful participation, even where there is only sorrow and hardship to be shared? It is the secret that makes living together such an uplifting experience, and fighting each other (according to the law of the jungle) such an ugly and depressing affair.

Once again, we are not talking here of utopian dreams, although we described a path of greater resistance. Regard, concern, service, and love are realities and their actualization has meant a great advancement of humankind and its standards of life. Still it is an endless assignment and does not allow any smugness or sleepiness. Rather, it requires strength and commitment to prevent any reverse and the sneaking in of the forces of hell. Our present day existence supplies only too many examples in this line as to allow any doubt. Thus we could call this design for living the outcome of a vision which is at the same time concrete and yet ideal, and its basis is less a philosophy than a faith.

There are two more points to be discussed before we may close this final meditation. One has to do with a most urgent issue of all life: the dread of death. It is a well-known inner condition and there are not many who are completely free from it. The good advice to "eat, drink, and be merry, for tomorrow you might be dead" is not as good, after all, as its advocates make us believe. Liquor does not drown this fear and *eros* does not banish dread. People with little substance of their own are more subjected to this kind of anxiety and dread than those who know somewhat the purpose of their life. Psychologists and psychiatrists try their best, assuming that the dread of death is just an unhealthy complex to be dissolved by the methods they know. Unfortunately one cannot deal with death and its certainty in such a fashion. In this field, the psychiatrist is no expert, or rather he is in the same boat, subjected to the same dread and as helpless in the face of it as anybody else. What about philosophers; should we perhaps ask them? They have fine systems and everything has its proper place in them. Unfortunately death is no topic for philosophers and it mocks their systems and concepts. We do not know what death is and we only know that in this world death is real; life is terminated and nobody knows when and how. This helplessness and uncertainty makes many people dread these thoughts and be almost haunted by them. We want to live and live fully (whatever that means), and we are afraid of any termination which will cut short our great opportunities and the only form of existence concretely known.

But strangely enough, not everybody feels this way, and there are some who are not afraid at all and need no liquor or *eros* to overcome what never can be overcome this way. Now then, are they blind, unmindful, or dull, that they cannot see and know what everybody sees and knows? I do not think so. The answer is rather that all depends on the inner riches of a person. The one who knows what they are living for, who actually brings the spiritual world of values to a realization, who through service or love grasps something of the absolute and makes it concrete—in short, a person who lives from the substance of being, and not from illusions and self-deceptions (and liquor or *eros* are of this kind); they have no fear of death. As Tolstoy, who himself went through much anxiety of that kind, has to say: "The dread of death stands in an inverse ratio to the value of life. For a life completely dedicated and pure this dread would be nonexistent." It is here that the idea of meaning gains its tremendous significance. Meaning is not exactly the same as purpose; the latter has usually a time dimension needed for its fulfillment, while meaning is the ever-present theme and motive of all doing. If I want to build a house, I need time, and I shall devote all lay activities toward this end. If I want to serve however, or if I feel strong enough to love. I need no particular time; it is like the melody that runs through life as a whole. If I think that my life has a special purpose, it would be tragic to be called away before this purpose is achieved. If I have grasped, however, the main theme of my life then the fact that this life has but a limited and unknown span will no longer matter. I shall do whatever I am able to do and as long as it is allowed to me. What matters is the *present moment* with its chance to fill it with value and meaning, not the future, reachable or not. This is the glorious overcoming of the human lot of finitude. It is implied in the idea of a design for living that can be realized at any moment, supposing that we are awake and find strength to do what we ought to do, or to be as we ought to be. For a life of great fullness, like those we mentioned in our models, death loses all its uncanny threat. We do not have to solve the riddle of man's mortality, but we have to overcome it. "O death where is thy sting? O grave where is thy victory?" (1 Cor 15:55).

There remains but one more and rather-brief paragraph to round up this summary with its final conclusions. After so many words one might be asked to condense all this insight into one brief formula for further meditation and practical use. Such a formula is of course no imperative, although it may look like that, and no commandment although it could be misunderstood as one. It is a formula introduced by an "if," as is the case with all principles of a spiritual nature. "If you want to reach a higher plane and if you are longing for a life that is truly worthwhile, then I might advise you to do as follows . . ." And this is the answer that comes forth from our understanding and the meditation connected with it (offered, to be sure, in greatest humbleness): *Act always so as if you were your brother's keeper*. But to make things absolutely clear, let us remember: to be one's brother's keeper does not mean to be one's brother's warden. The warden deprives a person of their freedom; the keeper, to the contrary, gives freedom by showing regard, concern, service, and if possible, love. Thus a right relationship is established between people, and life has found a new and redemptive direction.

Part 3

Troubles Ahead

Conclusion

The Human Situation

"It is so hard to believe because it is so hard to obey"; this profound dictum of Kierkegaard (in his *Diaries*)[1] may well serve as a motto to this second chapter on the Human Situation. It reflects the wisdom of a man who was more concerned with the "existential" situation than with the ideal "ought" of ethics. He was most sensitive to the tension between the vision of a high goal in all its glory (the faith) and the attempt toward its realization in life (the obedience to its call) which matters above all. For only by making the ideal concrete does it become existent, and thus meaningful to us. But just this requirement creates a specific "human" situation of frustration and despair which must not be overlooked when man is dealing with things spiritual.

The previous section contained such a vision, call, or ideal "ought," but already the warning was sounded that the human situation might make its realization most precarious. And that means more often than not a tragic dilemma for humanity. We discussed such a situation once before, preliminary to the final ascent toward our design. Now, as we have attained the wide perspective of the summit, and make ourselves ready to descend into the lowland of the practical, we become mindful again that only few and blessed individuals find the way to a pure, or nearly pure, realization of the high values of the design for living. The great majority of us will speak with Kierkegaard: "it is so hard to believe," namely in the sublime reality of the divine which alone justifies life and endows it with meaning, "because it is

---

1. Kierkegaard, *The Diary Of Soren Kierkegaard*.—Ed.

so hard to obey," namely the very call of conscience, the small still voice of the heart, the commandment of Christ, to go and do. Only by doing can we experience the truth from which all activities spring and in which all commandments originate. Faith and action belong inseparably together. But it is exceedingly hard to obey, to do what we ought to do and to abstain from what we should not do. Tolstoy, rather imperfect in practicing what he had envisioned as his calling, once wrote to his friend Engelhard (1887):

> If I know the way home to my house, but behave like a drunken man staggering from one side to the other, does that make the way wrong which I intend to go? Assist me, if I go wrong that I may return to the right way, but do not lead me further astray, sneering and saying: look, he says he is going home while he lands in a quagmire. Do you not see that I am wrestling, exerting all my strength, to extricate myself from this situation and that at least I am trying to obey the commandments of Christ.

This is a great human confession which might help us to realize that we all are in a similar situation, staggering from one side to the other while assuming that we are on our way home.

The concrete reality of life here and now finds itself always in a struggle with the ideal, the "ought," the vision. A philosophy of life must take this situation into account, understanding that people might get confused and therefore need signs of warning along the highways of life. That is what we are suggesting to do in this second chapter on the Human Situation. "Troubles ahead" sounds like "bad corner" or "dangerous hill" (which by the way might be appropriate headings too, for what we are setting out to discuss). But just as such signs will deter no one from continuing on their way, so also does the insight into the uncertainty and near hopelessness of full realization not mean defeatism or pessimism, and it should not make us stop in our highest endeavor. Mere philosophizing about human impurity or the inability toward human realization would be a poor attitude, and a mistake, to boot. For on a small scale and in accordance with the gifts endowed to us, we actually do realize our design, once we become alert to it. But our further discussion might help make us more sensitive to the pitfalls, obstacles, and mirages which we meet on our way, and which to become victim to is after all so extremely easy.

It seems appropriate to call these troubles ahead summarily "temptations." It is characteristic of temptations to feign values where there are none and to fool us into a wrong lane in the assumption that it will bring us to our destination faster. It is good to be reminded that temptation is at all times a situation (I am inclined to call it an existential one) in which every human being may find himself at any time, no matter how good his intention is or how alert his mind. Otherwise we would not be human. Hence the usefulness of a study in which this situation is viewed from as many angles as possible.

We might well begin by distinguishing between two kinds of temptation: the first one is of that kind that it can be immediately recognized as such at least within a certain cultural pattern. For instance adultery or fornication (to use Biblical terms) is certainly easily recognized as such temptation and seduction. The Bible speaks in this context of "forbidden fruits." There is no discussion at this point of the moral evaluation of a situation of this kind; it suffices that a sensitive person will be at the bottom of his heart always conscious of the precariousness of the situation and its potentiality to lead astray.

Much more dangerous, however, is a situation where such an awareness is lacking—that is, where humanity meets temptation in much more subtle forms. Then social conventions and mores may make them appear all right, even decent, which makes us still more apt to fall victim. For instance, amassing money looks perfectly legitimate; everybody either does it or wishes they could do it. And indeed, to have some savings in a society of so much uncertainty like ours is perfectly in order, even prudent. Yet who would seriously deny that amassing money is one of the real temptations of life, camouflaging the borderline between prudence and greed, concern for a minimum safety and gross materialism (with all its consequences). While society does accept certain standards with regard to sexual deviations, thus making certain temptations stand out more (though hypocritically allowing double standards for all events), the same society approves other critical situations without hesitation, setting no standards whatsoever toward their judging. There are situations that are not openly stigmatized as temptations although their qualification as such is obvious to the one who scrutinizes their functioning more closely. All temptations appeal to the "natural" person, hence might not be recognized as dangerous by anyone who knows nothing beyond the so-called "natural" conditions. But that does not make the temptation less tempting, less a pitfall or mirage.

If we want to study these strangers in ethical tracts, we cannot learn much from the textbooks of psychology or from rational treatments of moral philosophy. As temptation represents a typical existential situation, we cannot do otherwise but look for information where existential problems are foremost dealt with, namely in the Bible on almost each of its pages we meet such human or existential situations. The Bible is not a book of philosophy that is rational and abstract, but a book of life that is spiritual yet concrete (and that means existential). Its level is no longer "natural" but beyond the natural and for that reason the book shows such a sensitivity to the dangers of an un-regenerated naturalism. Temptation in it has always a certain "demonic" character; it comes from forces opposed to the light of the highest (think of the serpent in the Garden of Eden) and therefore requires much fight and exertion if victory is to be attained. Theology, for instance, considers this situation so fundamental and inescapable that it makes it its very cornerstone (original sin!). But since we are not concerned with such viewpoints at this time, we might approach our subject afresh, and to a certain extent, less theoretical.

Whichever book of the Bible we open, we meet situations which lead one astray, though often we are not aware of it. The story of the Fall is just the first one in this long record of human stumbling and yet seeking God. King Ahab and his greedy desire for Nabob's vineyard, and King David and his lustful desire for Uria's wife are some of the better-known stories of temptation and man's failing. The book of Job, scholars tell us, is not a real story but a fiction, a "philosophical drama," in which God enters into a strange bet with the Devil that a man can be put under strong temptation and yet will resist. What a tremendous plot, how these friends supply argument after argument against Job's gain, how misery heaps on misery—an assemblage of temptations unheard of thus far in the Old Testament. Yet Job resists (an Adam in reverse) and by this, to be sure, does not solve the problem of his misery theoretically, but he solves it existentially—that is, by living faith. Still more profound and leading into the utter depth of the human problem is the great story of the temptation of Jesus in the wilderness, after the event at the River Jordan. Again, it is a story of victory, and as such a true guide in any philosophy of life. "And Jesus being full of the Holy Ghost returned from the Jordan and was led by the Spirit into the Wilderness being forty days tempted of the devil. And in those days he did eat nothing." We then learn of three temptations: first to make stones into bread by some magic and thus become the very master of all. Jesus's answer was that we shall not live by bread alone (Deut 8:3). Then follows the temptation of power: "All this power will I give thee—if thou wilt worship me" (indicating that political power is, more or less, tied up with things demonic). And again Jesus answers, "Thou shalt worship the Lord thy God and him only shalt thou serve" (Deut 6:15). The third temptation deals with the miraculous: Jesus should throw himself from a high pinnacle of the temple expecting that an angel from heaven will keep and preserve him, thus insuring Jesus his supernatural authority. And again he answered with a quotation from Deuteronomy; "Thou shalt not tempt the Lord thy God" (Deut 6:16). "And when the Devil had ended all the temptations he departed from him." All three synoptic Gospels have this story (Matt 4, Mark 1, Luke 4) making it a most decisive event in the life of Jesus, and rightly so. It is true that it is a story of great intimacy—nobody was present or could know what was going on in the innermost mind of the one who was soon to start his great ministry on earth. And yet, how could a story be truer than this? Had Jesus succumbed to any one of these very understandable temptations: magic, power, the miracle—he would have been just another Adam and could not have led the way out. On the other hand, this story is more true to life than the one of Job—more human, so to speak, and less imagined, to gain power, influence, authority. Are we at all times particular in the choice of our means? It is certainly the principle of greatest resistance that is at stake here, and which makes this victory over the power of darkness deeply meaningful and so significant to every one of us human beings. Dostoevsky with his fine sense for the precariousness of all human existence—a life on the borderline between Light and Darkness, victory and fall, the divine and the demonic—gave a new significance to this story in his great *Legend of the Grand Inquisitor* (told by the cynic Ivan Karamazov to his saintly brother Alyosha). At this place we are not concerned further with the particular application implied in the speech of the Inquisitor, but the human side of any of these three temptations comes signally to the fore. In short, Dostoevsky implies that the Devil's suggestions (or whisperings) to Jesus are understandable, and to resist them is nearly superhuman, not recommendable for Mr. Average. "We have improved upon thee," cries the Grand Inquisitor. But the story ends as it has to: without argument and answer. Jesus kisses the old sinner and disappears.

Of course, the temptations in this story do not by any means exhaust the possibilities of the human situation with its ever-recurring need for decision making and the choice between the way of lesser or greater resistance. Of the many troublemakers that we meet on our journey through life, a few more, most common and most confusing at the same time, shall be discussed on the next few pages. And again it will be the Bible from which we shall learn most in discovering distinctions and receiving guidance. On top of or list we find three such troublemakers: *money*, *power* and *sex*. Moralists have difficulties pointing their way through these most baffling experiences and no easy answer is available. All three have a certain place in human doings and yet all three have their reverse, their confusing, not to say outright demonic qualities, muddling up standards and finally bringing us to fall—that is, making us miss altogether any meaningful design for living.

Only the briefest outlines of the problems implied can be presented here. Money, power, and sex each carry with them values of true character, but they likewise feign and fool us with regard to value and make us end up where we never intended to be: in the very negation of anything which has meaning. Despair and evil-doing, delusion of others and confusion of oneself, are certainly the opposite of our highest aims—namely, to make life meaningful. The design for living went completely afoul.

Money is at the same time necessary and apt to change into a great temptation. As such, the New Testament calls it Mammon (Webster's Dictionary comments: "the demon of cupidity"). "No man can serve two masters," Jesus says in the Sermon on the Mount, "Ye cannot serve God and Mammon" (Matt 6:24). The idea is that money has an instrumental value, the function of a means or tool, and as such has its proper place in life. But it easily changes its character, assuring a pseudo-intrinsic character; money for money's sake, for the sake of wealth and riches and borrowed self-assertion of the one who possesses it. And then it fools us about the values of life. Many a fairy tale deals with this human dream of becoming rich and independent and a great lord . . . until we awake from these illusions and discover the great emptiness of this "value." Andrew Carnegie in his *Gospel of Wealth* (1889)[2] wrote the great encomium of acquisitiveness; thus he made vocal what actually had become a driving force among so many people of Modern Times. And it was not even *ad majorem Dei gloriam* as material success had been looked upon in the days of Puritan Calvinism. It had now become completely secular: money for money's sake, profit for profit's sake. Is that a real design for living as the "Gospel of Wealth" tried to make us believe? Charity and generosity posterior to these motives cannot change the picture, since the great principles of regard and responsibility are certainly lacking. Possession beyond the needs of the day may be justified under the title of stewardship (the Christian interpretation of proper-

---

2. Carnegie, *Gospel of Wealth*.—Ed.

ty), but even then a correctly understood co-responsibility with our fellow people will basically influence the entire economic function of money or any related possession. The moral pathos of all projects of communal living, also of socialism (ethically understood), seems to have its root just in this awareness of the continuing character of money. Possession, wealth, and riches mean also separation, isolation, and the direct antithesis to all we-consciousness. It is not by mere whim that the great Saints (and great people besides them) lived in voluntary poverty. It made their ascent easier, less burdened with a potential temptation to turn away from the true goal of all life—the realization of genuine values.

That power is another temptation of this kind that is quite commonplace today. Political organizations cannot exist without it, and yet we know its fooling character better than we know the deceptiveness of money. Power can certainly not serve as design for living, not even when combined with "good intentions." "Power corrupts," wrote Lord Acton, "and absolute power corrupts absolutely." And he should know it—being an outstanding historian when British imperialism was at its peak. "Power is evil in itself" said Jacob Burckhardt, the historian of the Renaissance.[3] He, too, should have known it. Not much needs to be said at this place regarding the paradox of power: necessary and fooling at the same time. We have discussed it in connection with the Legend of the Grand Inquisitor; we could also have quoted some extravagant passages from Nietzsche's *Zarathustra*. Whoever has followed our train of thought thus far will need no further comment. The nonresistant attitude of certain religious groups, such as the Mennonites and Quakers, has its roots just in this understanding that man should be conscientiously alert in facing this great temptation (with its glittering outside). Whosoever has replaced the "we" for the "I" will no longer put his trust in power. But let us remember that the subtleties of this temptation are such that it can happen in almost every situation: in married life, in the classroom, in shop and office, everywhere. "Bossism" is a very expressive colloquial term which reflects this tendency to dominate and to make the I (capital letter) the last value. It violates the principle of regard and in the long run spoils any true design for living. Power and love do not go together, contrary claims notwithstanding, just as exclusiveness does not fit with inclusiveness.

To demonstrate a similar confusion for our third case of temptation, namely sex, will not be quite as simple. True, the Apostle Paul is fairly

---

3. Burckhardt, *Reflections on History*.—Ed.

clear and outspoken in this case, calling sex the "flesh" or the "lust of the flesh" which leads astray from true discipleship if left without control and restraint. Ever since Paul the controversy between asceticism and secular forms of life has been going on. Yet it is not so clear a situation and the finest minds could not find a satisfying answer to the challenge of sex. Poets were inspired by it and great lovers like Tristan and Isolde, or Abelard and Heloise, Romeo and Juliet, have always ranked high in the human imagination. Of course, their love goes beyond mere "lust of the flesh" (which alone is the concern of the Apostle Paul). Still, the practice of celibacy in the East and West indicates that an awareness of the temptation in all things sexual cannot easily be brushed aside. What can be said at this point in view of a healthy philosophy of life which recognizes humanity's double nature? Monogamous married life, solemnized by the authorities of state and church and issuing forth into a family with broadened mutual responsibilities, is certainly the answer throughout humankind. Existentially, sex still remains a paradox: uplifting one to a noble enthusiasm and admirable creativity on one hand, and dragging one down into the morass of moral depravity (perversion, prostitution, etc.) on the other hand. One becomes a real person only through a "we" experience—possible in genuine love between man and woman but man may likewise lose his person by indulging in the urges of the body to which nothing corresponds in the mind. The story of Tannhauser in the Venus mountain is a good symbolic expression of this situation. Not even the Pope in Rome could absolve him from this aberration; it was a dedicated love of a pure woman who finally brought about the salvation of this unhappy "sinner."

Sex may mean an invitation to a life along the line of least resistance, namely self-gratification. It is a misunderstanding of "human" destiny, and for that reason may result in disgust and deepest disappointment. But it can also be applied under the control of responsibility and then be fused into a great scheme of life. A Catholic author has this to say in this context: "Since the primal powers of sexual life imperil every Christian, it becomes necessary to assist him on his way to God through the sacrament of matrimony in which each part accepts responsibility for the sexual life of the other one." This is very true, though not easy in its practical application. Like money, sex should never become an end in itself (an intrinsic value), enticing though it is. The mere fact of the existence of "venal love" should make us suspicious regarding the internal paradox in this human experience. At the same time it can uplift and become enchantment as well as lowest debasement; and it is the responsible person, the ethical and spiritual quality in man, which brings about the decision. Alertness will be needed, and likewise regard for the other person, if sex shall become a boost and not a doom. Yet even then it must not be considered as an end in itself.

It might be good to summarize briefly at this place the results of our search into some phenomena of temptation. It is a twilight zone of human existence, where yes and no meet and where confusion is hard to escape. Three cases seem to stand out in particular: money, power, and sex. Money stands for acquisitiveness and possession, and greed easily perverts its natural function. The way out, by which this element may be worked into a general design for living, is the interpretation of ownership as stewardship. Likewise power stands for domination over other persons, and lust for power tends definitely toward the dark side of human life. The way out, the proper place of any such human relationship within a meaningful design for living, is cooperation. Finally, sex or the "lust of flesh" as the Bible calls this urge, erotics as modern lingo prefers, uncontrolled and unfettered leads to most deplorable consequences, barring any chances for a meaningful building up of life and personality. Its organic function within a design for life, that justifies any human endeavor, would be through the institution of marriage. In all these three cases, the principle which changes the picture and takes away the dangerous sting is co-responsibility, the moral principle implied in any genuine "We-Philosopy."

But it should be mentioned that throughout history other and more radical answers, too, have been tried time and again. If money, power, and sex are each pitfalls or snares that spoil a meaningful design for living, then why then not shun them altogether? Thus the idea of apostolic poverty and mendicancy arose to avoid the demony of possession altogether. Buddhist monks and Franciscan friars are just two examples in this line; it is obvious that their way cannot be integrated into a general design for living, and it is even doubtful whether such a way can be called a solution. It is not a conquest, a transformation of something potentially useful, but its cutting-off. Likewise, in the case of power, it too can be declined altogether in obedience to the teachings of the Sermon on the Mount. Non-violence (Gandhi) and non-resistance (Quakers, Mennonites) are two possible patterns of a life which shun power as far as possible. Again, it may be the right decision for certain persons or groups but it cannot be made a general postulate for a design for living. Thirdly, sex too, can either be transformed or shunned; in the latter case we call it asceticism and celibacy. It is a well-known pattern in many Oriental religions and it is a leading principle in Catholicism since earliest times. It has its merits, no doubt, but cannot be taught in the framework of the philosophy of this book, which tries to describe the forces of transfiguration rather than those of denial. But whichever way a person chooses in this regard, it will always be a way of greater resistance. It is the lesser resistance which makes temptation possible. One has to train oneself to such insights and practices. Kierkegaard was right: "It is hard to obey."

Of course the list of all the troubles and pitfalls has by no means been exhausted with the above discussion. We must, however, restrict ourselves to only a few more remarks. In an earlier chapter, we touched slightly upon one feature of life which may be overlooked more easily than any other one: thoughtlessness. Léon Bloy called it rightly the "sin of omission." There is no evil intention nor evil-doing involved, and yet the results are bad, and life as a whole may be spoiled because of such thoughtlessness. Benjamin Franklin's methodical self-checking was, after all, not such a bad technique. We all need it at times. Sluggishness, lack of decision, evasion of responsibilities ("I am not my brother's keeper"); all work in the same direction. It is not easy to meet the exigencies of life in a responsible, a personal fashion. We will have to say a few more words concerning escapism in the final chapter, but the mere fact that we sometimes (rather often) try to run away from ourselves and our responsibilities should give us material for thought and meditation. Many things go wrong in personal and group life, simply because man too easily shirks the higher obligation and looks for the "natural," the easy way out.

People often fall prey to many self-deceptions and false ideals, assuming a "pose" instead of a well-worked-out genuine pattern of value-realization. Often people are experts in all the sciences or in all the tricks of practical success, but are at a loss in the very center, in the art of meaningful living and the art of making responsible decisions. There is, for instance, the intricate question of the right relationship between means and ends. Most people want good ends, of course. But do we always, or at least mostly, contemplate concerning the right means? We had better meditate a little on Matt 12:27–28 (see also Mark 3:23, Luke 11:15–19) to understand better our own bewilderment, and confusion. Evil means do not produce good ends—in the long run at least. This should not be forgotten when decisions are due. Is it permissible to lie if need be? Shall I spank my child if they are disobedient? How shall I respond to name-calling and meanness? There are a hundred and one such questions, such dilemmas, and no prescriptions can be laid down like a law (and that is only to the good, for legalism kills the spirit). But that does not mean that there are no standards, no guiding posts, and no beacon lights. Sometimes the right response looks foolish, even impossible, in the short view. In the long run it is the only thing that actually matters. There is no need to repeat here the arguments of our earlier chapters, but wisdom and strength of character are needed if we do not want to miss our greatest opportunity: our own life.

The Germans call what we are discussing here *Geisteskampf*, a term not easily translated (perhaps "struggle of the mind"). If we read the *Confessions* of St. Augustine or the *Pensées* of Pascal, we learn something regarding this *Geisteskampf*; likewise the *Journals* of Kierkegaard or the *Diaries* of Tolstoy, plus all his correspondence. They are a revealing literature, documents of great human agony but in the end, spiritual victory. From them we may learn the lesson of how to conduct a life searchingly, honestly, toward the realization of what actually matters most. We are too often lost in confusion, temptation, doubt, or thoughtlessness; we confound meaningful and fictitious values. And then we wonder why life has become dry, and not at all the adventure our teachers had painted it to be.

Two more problems need to be touched upon. First, a great principle of Western culture: activity for activity's sake. It is foreign to those from the Orient who are usually more inclined to a contemplative life. But with us business seems to have an attraction in itself. Sometimes it is called the "Faustian" urge. "Let us do something! . . . not *what* you do but *that* you do is the thing that matters." Is that actually true? The story of Dr. Faust should make us think it over twice. Are we not meeting here again a temptation of a peculiar and most subtle kind? Of course, inactivity is also bad because it tries to close the mind to one's responsibilities. Still, activity as such does not necessarily mean more responsibility than its opposite. To dramatize some high-sounding purpose might be easy, and we all are familiar with such phraseology in politics or in the business world. It is of little avail. History is full of examples of this kind of super-activity. The individual as well as the country will, in the end, miss the higher calling and fail. Not the doing, but the purpose, gives meaning and design, though the carrying out of the purpose belongs to it too.

The other and last problem in this our descent from the lofty summit of the last chapter has to do with the by-no-means small danger of losing one's quality "of being a real person." H. E. Fosdick has written a fine book on this topic. Our mechanical and mass civilization leads itself all too easily to such a pitfall. We want to still be "persons," responsible beings—and yet, either we had never become such a person or unwittingly have lost such a qualification in the grinding mill of our everyday life. We have become a cog in a wheel, a dummy, a hand, a number, a card puncher, or a mass man. Is that not a temptation of almost tragic character? Look at all the faces at the rush hour, say on Times Square, New York; that depersonalization and mechanization should ever reach such dimensions should make us worry. It is an abdication of humanity in the service of some anonymous powers. Life is then no longer worth all its exertions and strain, and to talk of design for living becomes almost a mockery. No easy remedy have we to differ. Whatever was said in these pages was addressed to our fellow human beings as far as they are persons—and for that reason anxious to find their way and design. To be a person, however, means the acceptance of individual responsibility, an awareness that the welfare of humankind depends (within limits) upon our service and concern, our love and regard for the neighbor. Only in the fellowship of responsible persons can we attempt to do what alone matters in life—the realization of a meaningful design for living.

Postscript

Freedom of Will and the Issue of Escapism

"Life consists not simply in what heredity and environment do to us but in *what we make out of what they do to us.*"

—H. E. FOSDICK, *ON BEING A REAL PERSON*[1]

A study of ethics seems to be incomplete without a chapter on the problem of free will. For such is the human mind that we are always bothered by some theoretical "buts" even though we know perfectly well that practically, we do judge, and that we assign and assume responsibility for our doings and failures. Since our own approach is more existential than theoretical—for we are interested in the practical working of values and what might be behind them—there was no place thus far for this very old and yet still live topic of freedom of will versus determinism. Hence, it has to be taken up in this postscript, still a part of the whole, and yet only meaningful after all the rest has been discussed previously.

Even so, it is not our intention to indulge here in a prolonged theoretical treatise, weighing all the pros and cons and ending up on the fence. If the topic of free will has any justification within a book on practical philosophy, then it is only in the context which the heading of this chapter indicates: namely, as viewed from the angle of a possible excuse for not doing what we feel we ought to do. It is what I am inclined to call the "issue of escapism." Supposed the will is unfree, determined by heredity and environment to such a degree that the assumption of freedom of decision and will is but

---

1. Fosdick, *On Being a Real Person.*—Ed.

an illusion—what would necessarily follow from such an alleged factual statement? Apparently this: that strictly speaking, in a "scientific sense," I am not accountable at all for my doings and decisions, and that all the talk about freedom and responsibility is more or less a popular misconception. Experimental psychology definitely takes this position, and thousands of students are taught this doctrine year by year. Psychology, it is claimed, is just as much a science as physics or chemistry, and who would doubt that a falling stone has no freedom of choice whether it wants to or not. Give a person dope and he will act differently. Put identical twins into different environments, and totally different persons will grow up, and so on and so forth. The argument is only too well-known, almost trite. Mechanism, determinism, scientism—call it by any name: human beings appear as not actually responsible, and everyone talks about moral behavior appearing to be based theoretically on an "as if" basis. We act as if we were free, but the psychologist knows better and tells us that this is but a pious illusion or assumption, time-honored. Whosoever wants to talk about ethics, the claim goes, apparently has something to hide. Actually, we act as all animals do, by urges and drives, by hereditary patterns and environmental adjustments. Conventional mores are all that are left in ethics. A hedonistic motivation combined with a practical restraint (we called it "enlightened" self-interest) serve as the only consequence left. Humanity's infinite value and dignity, our longing for value-realization, and our unconditional regard for our fellow people—these things have little theoretical foundation in such a mechanistic world view. The "educated heart" is an idealistic term, we are informed, and the serious scientist would not have much use for it. Hence all the contentions and "oughts" of this present book do not make much sense, at least not in an age of scientific study of humanity. Live as well as you can, show a certain amount of decency and self-restraint (the "taboos" of society), but by and large live as healthily as you must live, and do not indulge in dangerous "inhibition" (a favorite term of psychoanalysis). Who would not be familiar with such viewpoints? In fact, we grow up with them. Responsibility loses meaning in such a frame of mind, and legal punishment for the law breaker is justified but as protection of society, without any further moralistic implication. In short, morality is more or less abolished, beyond the scope of conventional patterns or mores. C. S. Lewis called it fittingly, the "abolishment of man."[2]

2. Lewis, *The Abolition of Man*.—Ed.

This is what I bluntly call the issue of *escapism*. I challenge it all along the line of its arguments. We are sometimes unhappy to live with restraint, and occasionally long to be like an animal of prey. Then we break all bonds and experience a short (and illusory) spell of uninhibited "good time." Sometimes it is a protracted affair, a life of double morals (as in the case of "Dorian Gray" or "Dr. Jekyll and Mr. Hyde"), sometimes it is simply a life wanting altogether of standards, the normal and "healthy" egotistic life of our business civilization which is but little cognizant of that term with which we set out on the first page: *the educated heart*.

But perhaps we are at fault? After all, facts are facts, and determinism might be the truth. The old conflict between theoretical science and practical life shows up here again. If it were only a matter of theory: determinism or indeterminism, the case would be not too serious. By means of "epistemological" arguments we might be led to accept some sort of "a priori" categories such as causality. Kant, who proposed this interpretation, found himself in a painful dilemma, and solved it by saying that what might be true for "pure reason" (determinism) no longer applies to "practical reason," which penetrates way down to the very thing in itself. And here freedom is the answer. Unfortunately such theoretical dichotomy is of little avail for our purpose. Our mind would not be at rest with such a "on the one hand, on the other hand" argument. Actually we all feel at times the split, tension, antinomy, paradox (or whatever one likes to call it) in our own life. "The good I would I do not," exclaims St. Paul in a moment of deep human despair, "but the evil which I would not I do" (Rom 7:19). Is that meant as an excuse, as some sort of escapism? Surely not. The problem is urgent indeed, and does not stop at the theoretical level of learned discussion. It is the philosopher's business to say clearly where he stands and to demonstrate the limits, if there are any, to the psychologist (as the latter only too often takes the position of an opponent of the moralist).

As it happens so often with questions of such intricacy, the answer has to be looked for, not on either extreme but somewhere in the middle. Neither position is completely wrong nor completely right. Freedom is an undeniable fact of our inner experience, and no one can claim such an experience as mere illusion. I simply know myself as being able to make decisions and to be free, and all the more so if I compare my situation with those rare cases where a person might feel himself to be under duress of some sort (as for instance in, the case of a habitual drunkard). We do choose all the while (as between a red or a blue necktie), and more significantly, we do make decisions. This great ethical concept of decision might best be defined as "responsible choice," with its anticipated consequences for which we assume full responsibility, guilt or merit. Perhaps the strongest demonstration of this prime freedom of the human personality is the capacity to go along the path of greatest resistance. This the scientist does not consider in his normal-type psychology, and if it happens he is inclined to ascribe it to some "abnormal" features. And yet, we know very well, that it is within the reach of everybody to refrain from this and that, to fast or live a celibate life, or to withstand sleep in order to finish a significant work, or to pray. In short we have the freedom to decide between competing motives, and may choose the harder and less natural one. For we are persons with an immanent dignity of value preference.

At the same time we know also by immediate experience how much of our life is a product of a hundred and one conditions beyond our reach. We belong to a certain sex, male or female, which certainly determines much in our life. We belong to a certain time and civilization (say mid-century America), which again means a narrowing down of the scope of our decisions, if there are any. We are of a certain age; we belong to a certain social group, urban, rural, high, low class, and so on; and all this, we know, co-determines our lives. In short, we are far from being all our own creation. This we definitely know without consulting any psychologist who, on his part, might but add still a few more determinants. But this we ask: do these determinants really make up the total of the human personality so that no room is left for value judgments, conscience, decisions, remorse, and the like? If it were so, we would be but mechanical beings and not persons, which has been the biggest fact in all our discussion.

Perhaps the answer to this dilemma opens at this point. I am inclined to call the situation "frame determinism." Let us imagine a given picture frame: it certainly determines the size of the picture for which it is made. It determines also some other features of this picture, as for instance, whether it is to be looked at lengthwise or crosswise. And yet, within this shape and pattern there remains plenty of freedom to fill the space as the artist deems fit. I would call this freedom the "play," margin or leeway within the frame. It is the metaphor for that elusive thing called human freedom. We all are bound by this frame, be it our inheritance or environment or anything else. It does not permit any completely arbitrary decision. An American today will be different from a Chinese man today or a Greek of 500 BC, and so on. But within this framework falls the task of fulfilling our possibilities in the highest personal fashion. It means the responsible choice between several motives or possibilities. I might, perhaps, illustrate my point by another simile of great expressiveness. When we listen to or study Bach's great compositions, we always marvel at his perfect mastery of the laws of counterpoint and harmony, of the principles of the fugue or the canon, and so on. He accepted all these laws as binding and absolutely necessary. This was the frame of his work. And yet, how marvellously did he fill it with his subtle compositions. There was plenty of freedom left within these determinants; in fact, the latter enhanced the value of the composition. Modern artists sometimes complain and break through all rules in order to express their ideas—but (to us at least) that seems a greater work and a deeper expression which obeys the rules of the framework, yet transforms and transfigures this framework whereby the work becomes intelligible to all.

Motivation stands all the way against mechanical determinism (whether psychological, physiological, economical, sociological or what else). A motive is no cause, but a sort of suggestion. It is not the blind "id" of psychoanalysis but rather the rational element of our conscious life which stands up against unbridled affects. It is certainly true that all life is a struggle between the "id" (our subconsciousness) and the super-ego, the moral principle which constitutes our personality. The mere fact that such a struggle exists indicates that a certain freedom of decision is inherent in every human person. Othello kills Desdemona—not voluntarily but under a terrible affect of suspicion and jealousy, a blinding affect, which obliterates for a time the superior judgment of his moral personality. When he awakes from this unfortunate spell he becomes aware of his guilt (namely, to allow effects to blind his higher ego) and he draws the consequences.

The super-ego is our moral potentiality, and the "ought" or moral imperative would then be to live up to one's optimal potentialities in a conscious fight against all lowering tendencies of "taking it easy," forgetting responsibilities and so on. That such an imperative has meaning after all proves in itself that man is conscious of his freedom.

All claims to the opposite then cannot be classified otherwise but as escapist arguments, as justifications for one's choice of the easier way or the line of lesser resistance. Fortunately, it is not too difficult to prove this contention. In a remarkable book just in between psychology and ethics, Erich Fromm has splendidly demonstrated these escape mechanisms. He calls his book *Escape from Freedom* (1941),[3] and deals mainly with the psy-

---

3. The British edition of this book has the title, *Fear of Freedom*.

chological presuppositions upon which modern totalitarian societies rest. We often wonder what makes people give up their freedom in favor of an automatic conformity (so well symbolized in the picture of goose-stepping columns) and even go so far as to commit unbelievable savageries if so directed. Since even the worst partisan still remains a human person with inherent freedom and dignity the answer can only be one: this freedom appears to some people too hard to bear. It is, to use another word, a "dreadful freedom" (as Marjorie Grene once described the mood of the French Existentialists) which is rather denounced than used.[4] It does not concern us at this place whether this position is right or wrong; neither shall we analyze why people today are more inclined to such an act of renunciation than in earlier generations. What matters alone here is the recognition that authoritarianism and its concomitant, conformism (what the Germans called *Gleichschaltung*) and all the other forms of standardization of life root in the last analysis in such an escape from freedom; a voluntary escape, to be sure. Psychological determinism, in a sense, belongs more or less to the same category: it too becomes a justification for less effort and less acceptance of responsibility, hence a sort of scientific excuse as is befitting a scientific age. We can almost hear people say, "I cannot help being so, and there is no other way open for me," or something of that kind. And with this the case rests.

Strictly speaking, this psychology is of rather old reputation. Napoleon knew it quite well (being a dictator) when he proclaimed, "French people do not care for liberty, all they care for is glory," an insight that permitted him to marshal twenty million Frenchmen through endless years of war. More sophisticated, perhaps, is Dostoevsky's insight into the same human situation. In the great speech of the Grand Inquisitor (in the *Brothers Karamazov*) he has the old church man contend that Jesus made life too hard for men by giving them freedom and full responsibility for all their doings and designs. The church, so he claims, has improved upon that, has taken away such freedom and has made life a happy play of children as long as we are willing to obey the leadership of those who know of the prime human freedom, the authorities of the church, Again, we do not propose to discuss here the question of whether Dostoevsky's view of the church is correct or not. We wanted only to illustrate the application of the same principle which is behind all such escape mechanisms (including psychological determinism), namely a strange, voluntary self-abdication,

---

4. Grene, *Dreadful Freedom*.—Ed.

an act of freedom by which man renounces his freedom and willingly accepts "chains." Perhaps life thus becomes easier, less restrained (in view of the temptations of the so-called natural way) and less "dreadful" (in view of responsible decisions). But, so we ask, is it still a life worth living? Does it contain the possibility of a design, a meaningful realization of intrinsic values that form the possibility of becoming a real person?

The great leaders of humankind, East and West, reminded us of our greatest inherent good: to find and fulfill our personality in freedom and self-responsibility. But it is true that such freedom is a dangerous thing in view of the many pitfalls and temptations, and also in view of the possible sufferings provoked through non-conformity. But that is part and parcel of the human existence. Otherwise, talking of design for living would have very little meaning. Only by striving toward our highest potentialities, by giving ourselves to the superior task of regard, concern, service and love, do we find an answer to the question: what do we live for? We might not always do well, and our realizations might be disappointing and even vexing, but the perspective itself, however, is right, to look at our fellow people as our brothers and sisters. Somehow their concerns then become part of our own person, and by this strange process of "introspection" our freedom is no longer dreadful but joyous. The way to such a design, to be sure, is not simple and not cheap. It means above all the awakening to what the very first chapter of this book called its theme: the discovery and development of the educated heart.

Select Bibliography

Augustine of Hippo. *Confessions*. 2nd Edition. Translated by Marie Boulding. New York: New City Press, 2012.
Baldwin, James Mark, ed. *Dictionary of Philosophy and Psychology*. 3 vols. New York: MacMillan, 1901–1905.
Bentham, Jeremy, *An Introduction to the Principles of Morals and Legislation*. Edited by J. H. Burns and H. L. A. Hart. London: Athlone, 1970.
Berdayev, Nicolai. *The Russian Idea*. Translated by R. M. French. New York: Macmillan, 1948.
Brandström, Elsa. *Among Prisoners of War in Russia and Siberia*. Translated by C. Mable Rickmers. London: Hutchinson, 1929.
Buber, Martin. *Between Man and Man*. London: Routledge, 2002.
———. *I and Thou*. Translated by Walter Kaufmann. New York: Scribner's, 1970.
Burckhardt, Jacob. *Reflections on History*. Translated by Gottfried Dietze. New York: Liberty Fund, 1979.
Burkholder, J. Lawrence. "Philosophy." *Global Anabaptist Mennonite Encyclopedia Online*. 1989. http://gameo.org/index.php?title=Philosophy.
Carnegie, Andrew. *Gospel of Wealth*. London: Applewood, 1998 (original 1889).
The Chronicle of the Hutterian Brethren. Rifton, NY: Plough, 1986.
Confucius, Analects. Trans. Roger T. Ames and Henry Rosemont Jr. New York: Ballantine Books, 1999.
Emerson, Ralph Waldo. "Self-Reliance." In *Essays: First Series*. New York: Dover, 1993 (original 1841).
Finger, Thomas. *A Contemporary Anabaptist Theology: Biblical, Historical, Constructive*. Downers Grove, Illinois: InterVarsity, 2004.
Fosdick, H. E. *On Being a Real Person*. London: HarperCollins, 1943.
Freud, Sigmund. *Beyond the Pleasure Principle*. Translated by James Strachey. New York: Liveright, 1961.
Friedmann, Robert. *Leo Tolstoi. Religio*. München: Georg Müller, 1929.
———. *Mennonite Piety Through the Centuries: Its Genius and Its Literature*. Goshen, IN: Mennonite Historical Society, 1949.
———. *Hutterite Studies: Celebrating the Life and Work of an Anabaptist Scholar*. Edited by Harold S. Bender. 2nd Edition. MacGregor, Manitoba: Hutterian Brethren Book Centre, 2010 (original 1961).

SELECT BIBLIOGRAPHY

———. "Symposium." In *Harold S. Bender: Educator, Historian, Churchman*. Scottdale, PA: Herald, 1964.

———. *The Theology of Anabaptism: An Interpretation*. Studies in Anabaptist and Mennonite History Series, vol. 15. Scottdale, PA: Herald, 1973.

Fromm, Erich. *Escape from Freedom*. London: Holt, Rinehart, and Winston, 1968.

Gollancz, Victor. *Our Threatened Values*. London: Gollancz, 1943.

Grene, Marjorie. *Dreadful Freedom: A Critique of Existentialism*. Chicago: University of Chicago Press, 1948.

Gross, Leonard. "Friedmann, Robert (1891-1970)." *Global Anabaptist Mennonite Encyclopedia Online*. 1987. http://gameo.org/index.php?title=Friedmann,_Robert_(1891-1970).

Hobbes, Thomas. *Leviathan: With Selected Variants from the Latin Edition of 1668*. Edited by Edwin Curley. Indianapolis: Hackett, 1994.

James, William. *The Principles of Psychology*. 2 vols. New York: Henry Holt & Co., 1890.

Jones, E. Stanley. *Victorious Living*. Nashville: Abingdon, 2015 (original 1936).

Jones, Howard Mumford. *The Pursuit of Happiness*. Cambridge, MA: Harvard University Press, 1953.

Kagawa, Toyohiko. *Love, the Law of Life*. Translated by J. Fullerton Gressitt. London: John C. Winston Co., 1929.

Kant, Immanuel. *Groundwork of the Metaphysics of Morals*. Translated by Mary Gregor. Cambridge, MA: Cambridge University Press, 2012.

Kelemen, Erick. *Textual Editing and Criticism: An Introduction*. New York: W. W. Norton, 2009.

Kennel, Maxwell. "Mennonite Metaphysics? Exploring the Philosophical Aspects of Mennonite Theology from Pacifist Epistemology to Ontological Peace." *Mennonite Quarterly Review* 91.3 (July 2017) 403–21.

Kierkegaard, Søren. *Stages on Life's Way*. Kierkegaard's Writings, Vol. 11. Princeton, NJ: Princeton University Press, 1988.

———. *The Diary Of Soren Kierkegaard*. Edited by Peter Rohde. London: Citadel, 2000.

Klingelsmith, Sharon. "A Bibliography of the Anabaptist Mennonite Writings of Robert Friedmann." *Mennonite Quarterly Review* 48.2 (April 1974).

Kraus, C. Norman. Review of *The Theology of Anabaptism*, by Robert Friedman. *Mennonite Quarterly Review* 48.2 (April 1974) 265–6.

Kroeker, P. Travis. "Anabaptists and Existential Theology," *Conrad Grebel Review* 17.2 (Spring 1999): 69–88.

Lévy-Bruhl, Lucien. *How Natives Think*. Translated by L. A. Clare. London: Knopf, 1926 (original 1912).

Lewis, C. S. *The Abolition of Man*. London: Oxford University Press, 1943.

Lilienthal, David. *This I Do Believe: An American Credo*. New York: Harper, 1949.

Marx, Karl. *Capital*. Vol. 3. Translated by David Fernbach. New York: Penguin, 1993.

Middleton, Christopher, ed and trans. *Selected Letters of Friedrich Nietzsche*. London: Hackett, 1996.

Miller, Levi. "Leo Tolstoy and the Mennonites." *Journal of Mennonite Studies* 16 (1998) 163–80.

Nietzsche, Friedrich. *Thus Spoke Zarathustra: A Book for All and None*. Translated by Adrian Del Caro. New York: Cambridge University Press, 2006.

Otto, Rudolph. *The Idea of the Holy*. 2nd Edition. Edited and translated by John W. Harvey. London: Oxford University Press, 1958.

SELECT BIBLIOGRAPHY

Ovid, *Metamorphoses*. Translated by David Raeburn. London: Penguin, 2004.

Pascal, Blaise. *Pensées*. Edited by P. Sellier. Paris: Bords, 1991.

Ratzlaff, Vern. Review of *The Theology of Anabaptism*, by Robert Friedman. *Direction* 3.1 (April 1974) 191–92.

Roth, John D. "Pietism and the Anabaptist Soul." In *The Dilemma of Anabaptist Piety*. Edited by Stephen Longenecker. Bridgewater, VA: Penobscot, 1997.

Sartre, Jean-Paul. *No Exit and Three Other Plays*. London: Vintage, 1989.

Schiller, Friedrich von. *Wilhelm Tell*. Trans. William F. Mainland. Chicago: University of Chicago Press, 1973.

Schweitzer, Albert. *Africa Notebook*. New York: Syracuse University Press, 2002.

Smith, Adam. *The Wealth of Nations*. Edited by Campbell and Skinner. London: Oxford University Press, 1997 (original 1776).

Sorokin, Pitirim Alexandrovich. *Social and Cultural Dynamics*. 4 vols. Cincinnati: American Book Company, 1937–1941.

Spengler, Oswald. *The Decline of the West*. Edited by Arthur Helps and Helmut Werner. Translated by Charles F. Atkinson. New York: Oxford University Press, 1991 (original 1925).

Stern, William. *Person und Sache: System des kritischen Personalismus*. 3 vols. Leipzig, 1918–1923.

Thomas Jefferson on Democracy, Edited by Saul K. Padover. New York: Mentor Books, 1949 (original 1939).

Thoreau, Henry David. *On Civil Disobedience*. New York: Dover, 2014 (original 1849).

Trueblood, Elton. *Alternative to Futility*. London: Harper, 1943.

Tsanoff, Radoslav A. *Ethics*. New York: Harper, 1947.

Von Schlachta, Astrid. *From the Tyrol to North America: The Hutterite Story Through the Centuries*. Translated by Werner and Karin Packull. Kitchener, ON: Pandora Press, 2008.

———. "Robert Friedmann—Searching for the Meaning of Faith for the World." In Robert Friedmann, *Hutterite Studies: Celebrating the Life and Work of an Anabaptist Scholar*. Edited by Harold S. Bender. 2nd Edition. MacGregor, Manitoba: Hutterian Brethren Book Centre, 2010.

———. "Anabaptists and Pietists: Influences, Contacts, and Relations." In *A Companion to German Pietism, 1660–1800*. Edited by Douglas Shantz. Leiden: Brill, 2014.

www.ingramcontent.com/pod-product-compliance
Lightning Source LLC
Chambersburg PA
CBHW062042220426
43662CB00010B/1611